A TIMELESS TREASURE

100 YEARS OF FRESH AIR SOCIETY CAMP

Fresh Air Society
Max M. Fisher Building
6735 Telegraph Road, Suite 380
Bloomfield Hills, MI 48301

ISBN 0-9713529-0-9
Library of Congress Control Number 2001118644

Summary: History of the Fresh Air Society, a Detroit Jewish
camping organization, which began in 1902. The camp program
later became known as Tamarack Camps.

Type set in Baker Signet, Cochin, Coronet

Proceeds from the sale of this book
benefit the Fresh Air Society.

To everyone that has been touched by the magic of camp.

W.R.B.
To Gary, Abigail, Jacob, Emily and Bijou

L.G.B.
To David, Hannah, Sarah and Sasha

THE TAMARACK TREE

Larix laricina

Tamarack Larch
From the Native American word 'Hackmatack'

Deciduous, coniferous tree of cool, temperate
regions of the northern hemisphere

Life expectancy about 180 Years

TABLE OF CONTENTS

ACKNOWLEDGEMENTS

It was never difficult to get anyone to talk about Fresh Air Camp and Tamarack Camps, but none-the-less, I would like to thank all of those alumni who took the time to share their thoughts and pictures with me. To Laura Berman, a special thank you for your confidence and guidance. To my husband Gary, my beloved editor, more thanks than I can express for those Saturdays and Sundays and nights with the kids and reading pages of copy. To Laurie Blume, you are an incredible artisan and friend. To David Blume, thank you on behalf of both Laurie and myself for those Saturdays and Sundays and nights with the kids and reading pages of copy. Special thanks to Holly Teasdale, Leo M. Franklin Archives for her mentoring; to Heidi Christein for guidance through the Jewish Federation Historical Collection; to Marvin Berman for hours of assistance; to Howard Davis for his admiration and detailed recollections; to Michael Maddin for opening his files for our perusal; to Rick Goren for his assistance; to Elise Rowin for her editing; to Dena Raminick for her interviews; to Ellen Knoppow for all of the detailed research. Finally, thank you to the Tamarack Camps' office staff for all of your assistance and patience, and (Linda and Susie and Debbie) for the childcare. And a very special thank you to Marcia Robinson.

INTRODUCTION

"Inspire people not to be satisfied with just getting by.
Wherever we are now, we can move even further."
Irwin Shaw

This is a story about passionate people. About ingenuity, perseverance and devotion. It is the chronicle of a community treasure
that has outlived most other Detroit Jewish agencies, surviving a
Great Depression, three wars, the hippies and a recession. How?
Why? The answer is simple: because of the thousands of people who,
once touched by the magic of camp, vow to never let it fade away.

I was not a Tamarack camper. As I interviewed camp alumni,
walked through Ortonville, heard descriptions of Brighton and
Camps Agree and Kennedy, and listened to the tales of teen travel
trips, I found myself yearning to go back to my childhood so I could
give it a try. The images and memories in this book are those of the
hundreds of people who opened their doors, scrapbooks and hearts
to share the memories of a time and place they hold dear.

Describing camp is like going to the Grand Canyon, shooting
three rolls of film and finding that the pictures fail to capture the
true depth and beauty of what you just experienced. Instead, they
offer an essence of what you saw. Camp is a unique, personal journey; one of those rare life events that profoundly effects who you
become, imprinting values and memories that 10, 30 or 50 years later
remain vividly clear.

A Timeless Treasure offers the chance to glimpse into camp life over
time and meet many of the people who helped keep the campfires
burning. Part I travels through the decades while Part II peeks more
closely at a few of camp's gems. In between each chapter are photo
collages and short vignettes that take a closer look at some of the
people and places of camp.

What began with picnics on Belle Isle and evolved into Ortonville's
vast 1,500-acre mecca, Tamarack Camps has drastically changed over
these past 100 years, but amazingly, much has remained the same:
the thrill of receiving a letter from home, the warmth of a nurturing
counselor, the joy of singing day and night, the taste of independence
and the impact of learning to love your Jewish identity through
informal rituals. Generation after generation, camper after camper,
these precious memories and timeless gifts continue to enrich our
lives and our community.

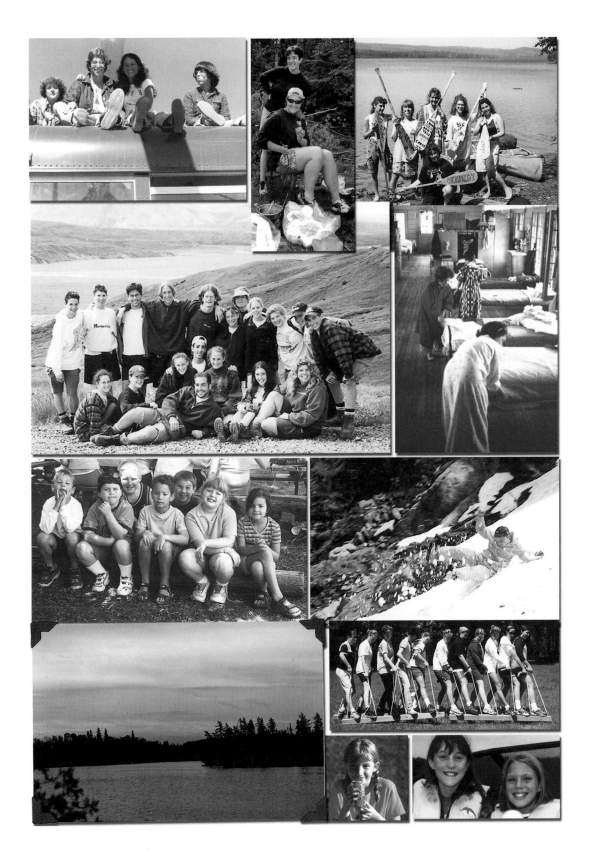

Alaska '91

MAKE NOT WAR

PEACE AND HARMONY

YOM SHALOM
יום שלום

PART I

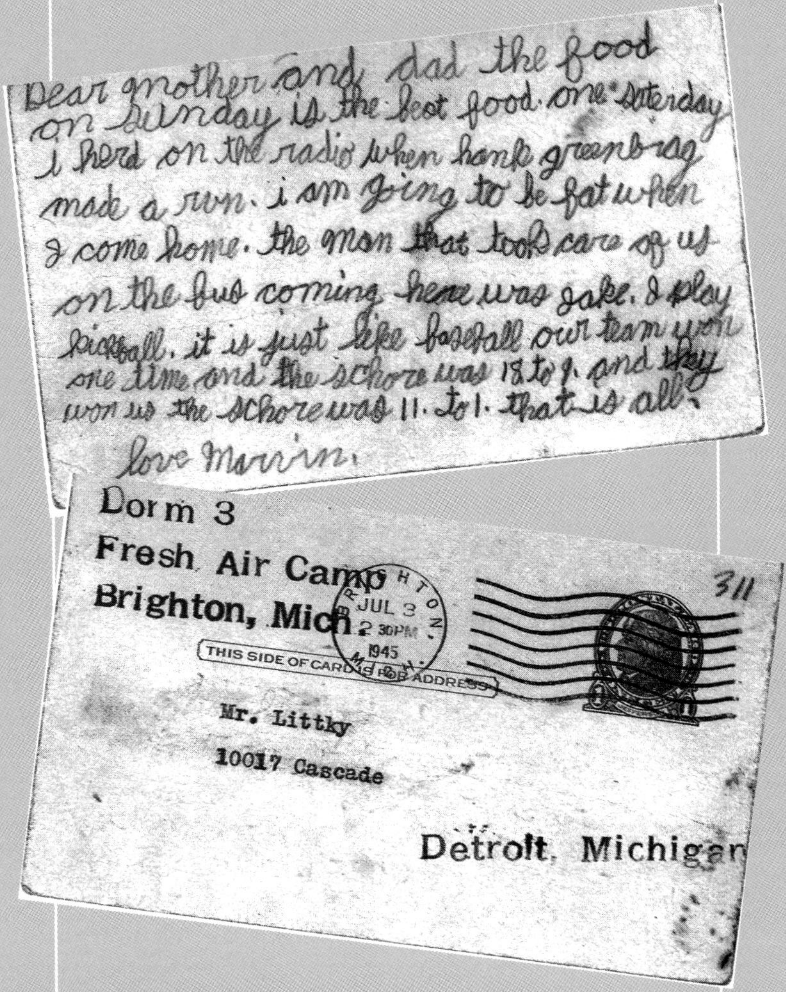

Dear mother and dad the food
on sunday is the best food one saterday
i herd on the radio when hank greenbrag
made a run. i am going to be fat when
I come home. the man that took care of us
on the bus coming here was jake. I play
kickball. it is just like baseball our team won
one time and the schore was 18 to 9 and they
won us the schore was 11. to 1. that is all.
love Marvin.

Dorm 3
Fresh. Air Camp
Brighton, Mich

THIS SIDE OF CARD IS FOR ADDRESS

HTON
JUL 3
2 30 PM
1945

311

Mr. Littky
10017 Cascade

Detroit. Michigan

THE DECADES

A VERY SIMPLE BEGINNING
1902-1920

"The one rule camp followed was that the children were there for a good time! They were in the country, away from the city, next to the water. Literally for them, it was a fresh air camp...a change of environment...into the country... something true in their lives to know and talk about."

Mr. A.J. Levin, first male counselor 1916-1919

O n a sunny, August afternoon in 1902, a group of children and their mothers clambered aboard a streetcar headed to Detroit's Belle Isle. They joined a mass of others who loved to flock to the glorious island park, to spend the afternoon strolling or bicycling along wide boulevards or taking slow, scenic drives in their new horseless carriages. Some came for the favored sport of the day, rowing, while others brought along bathing suits to enjoy a cool swim in the river. The island was a popular destination, and it is likely that this particular group of visitors probably caused a few to glance in their direction.

The children and their mothers, dressed in their freshly pressed but terribly frayed clothing, didn't come to the park to stroll, drive, row or socialize. They were newcomers to the city, mostly Russian

BELLE ISLE OUTINGS During the summers of 1902 and 1903, Blanche Hart and Ida Kopple, took "deserving children for day outings during the hot months" to Belle Isle. Arriving by streetcar, the children were treated to a hearty meal and enjoyed a leisurely afternoon on the island. These were the first outings of what became known in 1904 as the Fresh Air Society.

and Eastern European immigrants, hungry, awkward and bewildered by American ways. They came as guests of two women, Ida Kopple and Blanche Hart, to escape the city, enjoy a hearty meal and let the fresh air fill their lungs. These were the first "campers" of what would become known as the Fresh Air Society.

Hart's and Kopple's Belle Isle excursion embodied the spirit of Jewish Detroit. The two women, German-descended Reform Jews, were educated and wealthy. They lived in comfort, had the freedom to move about the city at their leisure and were passionately aware of the inequity that surrounded them. Like many other Reform Jews of the day, Hart and Kopple devoted much of their time assisting the less fortunate…newly arrived Jewish immigrants who had fled a Czar and a homeland that threatened to persecute their every move. The newcomers were deeply religious and came to this country penniless, but determined to live a life free from harassment and carve out a niche of their own.

Detroit's Cosmopolitan Metamorphosis

In 1900, Detroit was beginning its rapid metamorphosis from a rugged trading post to a cosmopolitan industrial center. The city of 285,000 was enjoying growth and a healthy fiscal prosperity. Jobs were plentiful. Detroit's diverse labor force hammered out stoves, railroad cars and equipment, wheels and pharmaceuticals. The automobile age was emerging upon the city's streets as Henry Ford and other visionaries competed to build the finest horseless carriage. It was common to see Ford and others don their racing gear, hop into their motorcars and race along Woodward and Jefferson Avenues. There were endless places to dine and shop. Hudson's, People's Outfitting and Sander's confectionary were among the most popular.[1]

Unlike other big cities of the day, Detroiters mostly lived in single-family dwellings; tenement housing was rare. The wealthiest lived in grand homes that lined Woodward Avenue. East and west of Woodward, were scattered communities, many of them largely populated by one ethnic group or another. On the lower east side of the city, surrounding the avenue known as Hastings Street, lived the Jewish community, both the rich Jews and the poor.

Early Jewish Roots

Detroit's Jewish roots can be traced back to the late 1700s, when a few traders and early settlers came to the small trading center located on the Detroit River. It wasn't a popular destination. Travel in and out was limited and uprisings with the Indians and French were frequent. But, over the next century, Detroit settled into its role as an American town, made improvements to the waterway system and built railroads. With that came industry. In addition to lumber and copper, Detroit produced marine engines, railway equipment and other mal-

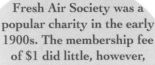

CHARITY

Fresh Air Society was a popular charity in the early 1900s. The membership fee of $1 did little, however, towards paying expenses. Blanche Hart often went to her friends in the community for financial assistance.

(photo courtesy of Leonard N. Simons, Jewish Community Archives)

leable steel products. The city grew and so did the number of Jewish residents. By 1880, 1,000 Jews called Detroit home.[2]

These early Jewish settlers were a resourceful group of entre-preneurs and civic leaders. Samuel and Simon Heav-enrich were noted clothiers and philanthropists; Mark Sloman was a fur dealer and civic leader and Magnus Butzel, also a clothier, became Vice President of the state Democratic Party in 1880. Most of the Jews who lived in Detroit during the mid and late 19th cen-tury were of German descent and belonged to the reform Temple Beth El, which was founded in 1850. Beginning in 1882, however, the demographics began to change as the first waves of Eastern European and Russian Jews began flocking to Detroit.

Between 1881 and 1914, more than two million Jews entered the United States. Over 75 percent were Russian. In Detroit, the Jewish population exceeded 10,000 by 1900 and more than 34,000 by 1914.[3] Largely Orthodox, these families came to find a religious community living a life vastly different from their own.

> "We had a large, risky looking raft that was absolutely safe...and a flat-bottomed rowboat. They (the children) would pile into the rowboat and I'd take them for a ride along the shoreline and head for the raft. While rowing I would tell stories. The boat was so flat and the water so shallow that you couldn't tip it over if you tried," said A.J. Levin, camp's first male counselor who was hired in 1916.

THE BOAT

Together, a Divided Community
Reaches Out To the Less Fortunate

Although the Jewish community lived geographically very close to each other, the community was rift with vast economic, social and religious gulfs.

The Reform Jews clearly enjoyed the "better" life. They were among Detroit's prestigious middle and upper class residents and, for the most part, were regarded in high social esteem. They lived in grand style on the city's finest residential streets, dressed in current fashion, formed their own social clubs and organizations and tended to be lax in their observance of holidays and the Sabbath. The bla-tant assimilation of the Reform and their religious lethargy infuriated the Orthodox.

The immigrant community clustered around Hastings Street. Their residential quadrant was known as the Jewish Ghetto, located east of Woodward between Brush Street and Riopelle, Watson and Monroe.[4] With no temple of their own, the first immigrants quickly formed their own houses of worship: Shaarey Zedek, Beth Jacob and B'nai Jacob. The Orthodox preferred to wear traditional garb, grow long beards and observed strict Kosher law. Their old-world, dogmatic ways were an embarrassment to the Reform community.

Huddled together in small, rented houses, the Orthodox lived on streets largely neglected by the city. They were the last to get sewers and lights and, because of the quality of life in the area, were more likely to contract a variety of illnesses. Work was easily found, but at wages insufficient to raise a family. Many chose the entrepreneurial route, setting up shops or push carts along Hastings Street, the center of Jewish commerce.

It was along Hastings Street where Reform and Orthodox came together and differences were put aside in favor of supporting one another.

Lined with dozens of small shops selling everything from kosher meat to novelties, the street was an endless procession of pedestrians, noisy motorcars, slow moving horse drawn carriages, vagrants, peddlers and playful children. With nowhere to go, the bustling street, often thick with soot from nearby manufacturing shops and factories, became their playground.

No one knows exactly what sparked the original idea of the Belle Isle outing. Maybe it was a hungry child begging for food or money, or maybe a young ruffian splashed mud on the long dress of Hart or Kopple. But it was along Hastings Street where Kopple looked past the ragged clothes and dirty faces and saw young *kinder*, hungry and eager for attention, anxious to roam and play.

Kopple approached Hart with her idea, a relatively simple notion. Per-

COOKIES
Every Sunday afternoon, a limousine carrying Eugene Sloman, his wife and a barrel of broken cookies from the National Biscuit Factory would arrive at camp. The children eagerly anticipated this weekly treat and were even more delighted when the couple would surprise them with candy, fruit or small toys.

haps, in their minds, they thought the gesture somewhat insignificant. But, they did it. They chartered a trolley car, packed a few picnic baskets and escorted a group of these young children and their mothers to Belle Isle. The idea was to give them a day in the fresh air and a healthy meal. It was an obvious success. One hundred years and more than one hundred thousand children later, the Fresh Air Society's camping program is one of America's oldest and is one of Detroit's longest running Jewish agencies.

Fresh Air Movement

Through the late 1800s, as thousands of new Jews entered the community, numerous relief agencies – both Orthodox and Reform – were formed to help those in need. Members of Temple Beth El and Shaarey Zedek were vigilant in seeing that no Jew ever went hungry or without shelter. Many of the agencies and programs initiated by the two congregations and other agencies duplicated one another. Helping the poor became competitive. In 1899, Rabbi Leo M. Franklin of Temple Beth El, helped form the United Jewish Charities – UJC (now known as the Jewish Federation of Detroit). Its purpose was to unify the community-wide relief effort and to avoid the duplication of services.

By the time Ida Kopple and Blanche Hart boarded that streetcar in 1902 both had demonstrated their devotion to helping the less fortunate. Hart had become Executive Director of the United Jewish Charities and Kopple was active with several of the Temple Beth El relief programs.

The two women launched a concept new to Detroit. Their idea, however, was not totally original. The "fresh air movement" had begun some 15 years earlier in New York as a growing number of social agencies and concerned caregivers began to organize day camps and short-term overnight programs for children from the

MEALTIME
There was always plenty of good, nutritious food at Fresh Air Camp. Children were weighed before they arrived and monitored for weight gain while there. During the meals, chaperones would stand nearby and make sure that each child ate everything on their plate.

slums and ghettos. Throughout the country, a myriad of hybrid programs were developed to improve the health and lives of poor children. The camps would expose them to sunshine and fresh air and
provide them with fresh milk and food.

The success of the first Belle Isle outing led to many others. "No
child should ever be denied a true outdoor experience," expressed
Hart. After a visit to Cleveland's Camp Wise, Hart came back determined to create a permanent camp program. In
1904, the Fresh Air Society was officially organized. It was funded by the UJC and friends.
Its mission was to "take deserving children for
day outings during the hot months" and to "fur-
nish milk and ice or food to the needy sick." The
Society's first annual report noted that some 175
children had been escorted to Belle Isle.[5] "A
few of these children had never been to our beautiful Belle Isle and
two children had never been on a street car," wrote Kopple.

PEANUT HUNT

Favorite Activity:
A bushel of peanuts would be
spread across the ground. The
kids would race to pick them up
and see who had the most.

In the summer of 1904, Hart took her experiment one step further. She paid $50 for one month's rent on what she described as a
"tumble-down" house in Kingsville, Ontario. She and fellow volunteer, Anna Solomon, rid the house of mice, dirt and dust so that a
group of 25 campers would find suitable accommodations.

Hart recalled this first overnight experience in a letter she wrote
in 1941. "We had difficulties with immigration authorities as we
were taking aliens into Canada. These were ironed out by several of
our lawyer friends. I am confident immigration authorities did not
enjoy going through dirty bundles of clothing that our guests brought
with them. Our first task when reaching camp was examining heads
(for lice) and a thorough clean-up of each one."[6]

DEPARTURE
It was a noisy,
bumpy ride to
Station 22, the
Fresh Air Camp
stop on the Detroit
Interurban streetcar
route. Chaperones
accompanied the
children as they left
the city and rode
out toward
Mt. Clemens.

The experiment was called off just two weeks later when the water supply at the house ran out. It did not matter, though. A permanent campfire had been sparked.

Camping Becomes A Staple Of Detroit Jewish Life

One summer later, a house in Roseville was rented and then later purchased by the Fresh Air Society in 1908. It accommodated 50 and those who came shared the responsibilities of cooking, cleaning and ground care. In 1912 Fresh Air moved again, this time to a more appropriate setting on Lake St. Clair, 15 miles from the city, four miles from Mt. Clemens. Located right off the interurban streetcar route, Venice Beach was a congested summer cottage area that was ideal, at the time, for the new camp concept. Hart diligently worked to raise the $10,000 needed to purchase the site and renovate the buildings that would accommodate 100 boys and 100 girls. Children were referred to Fresh Air Camp by various Jewish agencies. Only those who most needed fresh air – the poorest and often times the sickest – were accepted.

Campers and their volunteer "chaperones," usually young women or some of the children's mothers, arrived via interurban streetcar. Upon their arrival, various members of the Fresh Air Society, including Hart and Gussie Brown, the first camp administrator, greeted

VENICE BEACH
Using bathing suits provided by the Fresh Air Society, campers enjoyed their daily swim time.

Helen Rachinsky, R.N., attended to plenty of cuts, bruises and sore throats. Twice a day she doled out "cod liver oil to the puny and undernourished children, most of whom show(ed) noticeable improvement in a surprisingly short while."

them. In addition to her duties at UJC, Hart remained very involved in the administration and general program of camp. She was a frequent visitor both during the week and on weekends when she often took a dip in the water with the children. Gussie Brown handled the day-to-day operation of camp, and like Hart and her peers, had an unselfish devotion to children. She was energetic and adored by the kids, and her background in child psychology did much toward making Fresh Air Camp one of the best summer camp programs of the day.

Days at Venice Beach were very simple and regimented. Children swam, played games, were fed and rested on schedule. "We had hot cereal on alternate days,"[7] recalled a camper named Eve Dishell (Marcus), who attended camp somewhere around 1913. She recalled spending lots of time reading and coming in second place in a camp spelling bee. "We collected hair snakes in jars and watched the hairs in motion. We hiked...sang and mingled. There was a bathhouse right on the bank of the St. Clair River."

In 1916 Abraham J. Levin, "A.J.", was hired as the first head male counselor. At age 19, A.J. was paid less than $10 per month, and as he recalled, he was "glad to get it." He and

his charges slept in a large shed, while the girls slept in the more comfortable house. The inequity was irrelevant. "Their (the children's) time was well filled and never seemed to hang heavy,"[8] remembered A.J.

In 1976, A.J. Levin recalled his days at camp. "The days went from breakfast until 8:30 or 9:00 at night. The girls did 'girly' things such as embroidery, crocheting and the like, and the boys played baseball and other boy games. The one rule that camp followed was that the children were there for a good time! And, that they did have."

Not one child paid a penny to attend Fresh Air Camp in those days. They came to get out of the city and into the country. To be near the water, recalled Levin. "Literally for them, it was a fresh-air camp. A change of environment …into the country, something true in their lives to know and talk about."

A.J.
Abraham J. Levin was the very first male counselor, hired in 1916. A precise, fun-loving man, Levin carefully recorded a photographic record of the early Fresh Air days. He shared his photos and his memories in a taped interview in 1976.

I WAS Boy's RECREATIONAL DIRECTOR
AT THE CHARITY FRESH AIR CAMP ON
JEFFERSON NO. 2 MT CLEMENS MICH
ON LAKE STE CLARE
FOR THREE SUMMERS

The Fresh Air Society reached out to help urban children find a new kind of excitement, an appreciation for the out-of-doors that was nearly impossible to find within the city. Those dreams were realized many times over. One young girl exemplified their mission. Belle Freedman (Kosofsky) was born in New York in 1909. Her family of 11 lived on Montcalm Street, in the poorer section of town, crowded together in a small house with little food and clothing, but plenty of spirit.

In 1999, a fiesty 90-year-old Belle described herself as a happy, eager camper. It is easy to imagine her as just that. Although

Camper 1917

her blue eyes have dimmed with age, her once brown hair is now bright silver and her movements are slow and careful, one can picture her as a gregarious, effervescent young camper.

Smiling happily, Belle recalled standing by the Hannah Schloss Building on High Street, just west of Hastings Street, in 1917, waiting to board the interurban streetcar that would take her to Station No. 22, the Fresh Air Camp stop.

Once there she immersed herself in the campfires, writing, crafts and singing. She preferred wading in the water over swimming and holds the memories of those refreshing escapes to Lake St. Clair as heavenly.

She remembered standing around the campfire, joining hands with her fellow campers and singing, "These bones shall rise again," a playful collection of verses that recall the story of Adam and Eve. Two generations later, with photos of her grandchildren beside her, she sings and claps the song. Laughing all the while, her face glows with the joy that the Fresh Air respites brought to her life.

"Fresh Air Camp was heaven to me. We were given three meals a day. In those days, we didn't have money, so camp provided us with uniforms and flannel nightgowns. They even gave us bathing suits to wear!"

Belle Freedman (Kosofsky) eagerly awaited her summer vacations at Venice Beach, attending Fresh Air Camp for several years during the late 1910s. She is pictured here at her high school graduation. *(photos courtesy of Michael Freedman)*

Belle went to camp as long as she could, but by the time she was 12 she spent her summers helping out at home. She could have never known that years later Fresh Air Camp would again revive her spirit.

At 19, Belle married Hyman Freedman, a kosher butcher and grocer. Grossly underpaid, Hyman organized the kosher butchers into a union, a brave move that nearly cost him his life. In the 1940s, union-busting gangs attacked Hyman, leaving him with injuries, both physical and emotional, that never quite healed. Hyman died in 1959 at the age of 50. Belle, 48, was left behind with three sons – Larry, 24, and Barry and Michael, both less than 10 years old.

The younger boys barely remember their

father, but they certainly remember the years after he died. "My mother was very courageous during that period," remembered Michael, who was six when his dad passed away. After Hyman's sudden death, the comfortable life Belle once knew was gone. No savings had been left behind and the family was broke. Belle secured a loan and purchased a small house in Oak Park. She walked to Belle Drugs on the corner of 9 Mile and Coolidge and pleaded for her first job.

Working on the front counter, Belle earned enough to feed her sons. Yet, surrounded by an increasingly wealthy middle class, she knew her sons were missing out on much of what the community had to offer. Then, she recalled the experience that brightened up her childhood, Fresh Air Camp.

"She saw a great need for us to have a respite from our lives," recalled Michael, who today is Vice President of Communications at George Washington University. As if an echo, Michael described his own camp experience. "Camp was a wonderful reprieve, like heaven on earth. It was a chance to get away from a lot of the sadness in our lives."

Of course, during the mid-1960s a week at camp cost slightly more than it had some 40 years earlier. "I wanted my boys to go to camp, but it was expensive," Belle explained. Determined that they would go, yet literally penniless, she met with the Fresh Air Society and explained her situation. Fresh Air Camp offered the boys a full scholarship. Belle, proud and stubborn, refused to accept something for nothing. "She cut the deal with Fresh Air Camp," proudly recalled Michael. She paid $21 per child for each three-week session…$1 a day.

Michael and Barry Freedman have many cherished camp memories. But, Belle wasn't quite done with Fresh Air Camp. "Imagine me at 81 going back to camp!," she penned in a 1990 thank you note to the Butzel Senior Camp at Ortonville. "Last time I went to camp, mama packed my little bag including my toothpaste and a new toothbrush. This time I did my own packing including Maalox, Extra Strength Tyle-

nol and a can of fasteeth (sic) powder."

Her visit to Butzel aroused long forgotten memories. She recalled the noisy streetcar ride to the camp and the large dormitory with small uncomfortable cots. She remembered the hawk-like Venice Beach matrons making her finish her food and the treats delivered every Sunday by Eugene Sloman. And as Belle stepped off the bus, back home at Hechtman Federation Apartments, she also remembered how her mother would be waiting to greet her as she arrived back home from camp. Each time, Belle's 'mama' would cry, *"Gott Tzu Donkin,"* God Be Thanked.

Belle Freedman is one camper who has lived to see the total evolution of camp. She

Belle stands with her son Michael at his high school graduation. Michael attended Fresh Air Camp in 1961. Belle returned to camp as a senior camper in 1990.

experienced the beginning when camp was a respite for poor urban children. Her sons went at a time when camp was a great equalizing experience for suburban children and Belle had the chance to see the modern camp, full of varied activities for a variety of Jewish children from a myriad of backgrounds.

"I'll never forget Fresh Air Camp as long as I live. I owe a lot to them," said Belle. And, Fresh Air owes a lot to the Belle Freedman's of this world.

DAVID AND
NATHAN CARP—
—DAVID ATE A TOAD
NATHAN LATER BECAME
A CIRCUS PERFORMER

"Oh, the things you think are funny when you are 16." **Lillian Genser.**

MORNING FLAG RAISING

"I loved it at camp. When I got home, I was very unhappy." Irving Lash

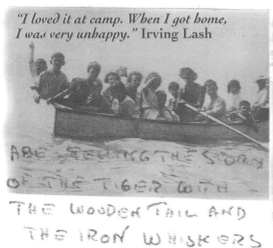

ABE SEEING THE STORY
OF THE TIGER WITH
THE WOODEN TAIL AND
THE IRON WHISKERS

"We were quite a group." Irving Rosen

*"The counselors were wonderful.
They did it because they cared."*
Belle Freedman (Kosofky)

A MOVE TO THE FRESH WATERS OF BLAINE LAKE

"What healthful fun it would be for these children to get far from the city, the automobile and the movie, to live for a while a truly rural life, to know the trees, the birds and the flowers and to roam at will over a large tract of land. May the time not be far distant when such will be the case."

Mrs. Edith Heavenrich, board president 1925

Every other week, a chartered streetcar carrying a new group of campers, their chaperones, and, often times, Blanche Hart, traveled out of the city eastward toward Venice Beach. With each clank of the wheel, the grime and buzz of the city faded as the colors, sights and smells of picturesque apple farms, acres of green pastures and miles of shimmering Lake St. Clair flooded into the crowded windows.

Returning campers excitedly chatted with old friends, plotting and planning their busy week ahead, while others sat stiff and motionless, silently facing a fear they had never known. Feeling abandoned, scared and insecure, these children, just like thousands that would follow them over the years, schemed of ways to quickly get home. Little did they know that once their gallons of tears were shed, they would taste independence for the first time and form bonds that could never be replaced or broken.

The tears of camp are timeless. Every summer, the pattern repeats itself. Tears of fear, shed in the beginning as children fearfully leave the security of home; tears of pain, shed in the clinic as a comforting nurse tends to a small wound; tears of laughter, shed among friends in the dark; and tears of sorrow as campers, counselors and staff are torn apart at the end of yet another wonderful season.

The Roaring Twenties, the glamorous, giddy time of prosperity and opulence, was a special time to grow up. Women won the right to vote and prohibition and speakeasy joints fostered an insatiable appetite for jazz. It was a time when baseball became everyone's

1922

The budget for the summer of 1922 included $500 for swimsuits, middies, bloomers and household supplies. A Board of Health nurse would examine each child's head before camp for head lice.

GUSSIE BROWN Much loved by campers, volunteers and Fresh Air Society Board members, Gussie Brown was the first director of Fresh Air Camp.

favorite summer pastime and children spent their pocket change on the newest snack sensations, Baby Ruth, Milky Way and Butterfinger candy bars. Everything was new and novel in a country filled with first-generation pioneers and immigrants.

The 1920s was also a time of great change within Detroit's Jewish community. A rash of open anti-Semitism, fueled in part by Henry Ford's virulent rhetoric, created an uneasy, all-too-familiar tension. Jews found themselves united in an all-out campaign to dispel the hatred and bigotry. Their efforts sparked an unexpected movement toward preserving and strengthening interest in Jewish culture.

Reform and Conservative Jews had begun their migration north to the 12th Street area moving into spacious homes on quiet boulevards. Children played in their own back yards or nearby parks, and a Sunday drive in the new family motorcar became the highlight of the week. Temple Beth El relocated to Woodward and Gladstone; Shaarey Zedek, which became Detroit's first Conservative congregation in 1913, rested on Willis and Brush. The new Jewish Center was located on Holbrook and Woodward.

Meanwhile, the Hastings Street area remained home to the *Ostjuden*, the East European, Orthodox Jews. Here, the roar of the '20s took on a different tone. Instead of jazzy music and rambling motorcars, the streets were filled with idle children growling with hunger and groaning from boredom. Their moans, however, became screams of joy when they found out that they were off to Fresh Air Camp.

1924

Miss Rose Meyers replaced Gussie Brown as camp director. Her salary was $350 for the season. That summer she reported that there were "541 little guests at camp. Twelve percent were unable to take heavy exercise, 11percent were undernourished and had been placed at a special diet table."

PHONES

Camp got connected to the outside world in 1927 when the first phone was installed at Brighton.

New Beds And Bathing Suits

The glittering summer sun beat a playful pattern against the freshly painted buildings of Venice Beach. In the summer of 1922, young campers like Mary Katz were treated to the news that a new bathhouse and two dormitories had been constructed. Inside, children found brand new beds and mattresses, purchased at a well-negotiated cost of $7.25 each.

Mary Katz came to Detroit from Russia in 1921 at the age of 10. Even 78 years later, she still could recall many wonderful camp experiences. Like most of those who attended camp in those years, Mary and her sister spoke mostly Yiddish, but quickly adapted to camp life and easily learned the new language. In 1999, Mary recalled her favorite camp cheer, a playful, melodic verse:

Give A Yell, Give A Yell
Give A Good Substantial Yell
And When We Yell, We Yell Like This
And This is What We Yell
Fresh Air Camp! Fresh Air Camp….

THE ROWBOAT
"We had a large risky-looking raft that was absolutely safe," recalled A.J. Levin. "They would pile into the boat and I would take them for a ride along the shoreline. While rowing I would tell them stories. We never got out of the shallow water."
(photo courtesy of Judy Cantor)

For three summers Katz's soul and body were nourished with the Fresh Air way of life. It was a welcomed respite from home. She was there in 1923, when the camp session was lengthened to two weeks and when children had to provide their own bathing suits. Katz remembers her camp days as a collage of arts and crafts, swimming, canoeing, hiking and picnics. Most of all, she remembers the plays.

"I liked to be in the plays. Outside they had seats and we would invite family and friends. We used to love that. We went for two weeks. I remember kids that were homesick. Visiting days were on Sunday each week. They would bring us goodies."[1] Katz and her fellow campers slept in a large dormitory with "rows and rows of cots." Her counselor was a high school girl who wasn't paid, but took the job for the fun of it.

The Fresh Air Society Brings Year-Round Support To The Hungry and Sick

With nearly 20 years of providing outdoor experiences to children, the all-female Fresh Air Society board had become adept at fund raising and administration of a growing program. Headed by the matronly Blanche Hart, the group enjoyed broad community support. Philanthropists such as Fred and Leo Butzel, Henry Wineman and others seemed always willing to be partners in furthering camp growth.

The women were a passionate, tireless group who, in addition to raising their own families, spent countless hours throughout the year meeting to plan and discuss camp operations and budgets, helping with camp enrollment and operating camp itself during the summer. And yet,

PARENTS

Early in the 20s, the board voted to completely ban parents from visiting camp. A few years later, they allowed parents to visit for two hours on the second Sunday of each session, and even later, during the Depression, the board considered allowing parents to spend Sunday nights at camp with children for an extra fee.

this was just a fraction of their work. Committed to providing for the health and medical needs of the struggling Jewish immigrant community, these women also spent their days visiting and nursing the sick, and feeding the hungry.

SHABBAT

While Saturday services had a great appeal for the children, Jewish leaders from the city didn't get to camp often. Hoping to improve their participation, Shabbat services were switched to Friday nights in 1926. Initially, no Rabbis or other dignitaries took advantage of the more convenient time.

Their year-round work led to the formation of a medical committee. One of its early tasks was to solve a perplexing dilemma. During the summer, the campers were well fed and practiced good nutrition and hygiene. Upon their return home, however, many of those health benefits were reversed so that by the following summer, the nutrition lessons had to begin again.

To correct this problem, the committee decided to follow camp families throughout the year, helping parents understand American hygiene and proper nutrition. They then secured informal commitments from the families that the good health habits would be maintained over the winter or the children would risk being refused for camp the following season. The strategy proved successful. Not only did the volunteers assist in maintaining the health of their campers, they also monitored younger siblings and caught more severe illnesses, such as tuberculosis, in early stages. All of this work led to the decision by the United Jewish Charities in 1922 that the Fresh Air Society would become the sponsoring agency for the North End Clinic, a free dispensary.

(l to r)
Mrs. Gurovsky
(2nd cook),
Mr. Gurovsky
(Maintenance)
and Mrs. Anna
Mintz (Cook)

THE COOKS
The duty of cooking was filled by hard-working immigrant women who lived at camp with their families. Pictured is the Mintz and Gurovsky families (l to r) rear: Sam A. Mintz, Joel Gurovsky; Middle: Anna Mintz and Mr. And Mrs. Gurovsky; Front: Mary Gurovsky and Frieda Mintz.

As concerned with children's health as the volunteers were, it was not until 1926 that a full-time nurse was employed for summer camp. Much like those succeeding her, Nurse Rachinsky spent her summer attending to plenty of cuts, bruises and sore throats. Twice a day, reported a devoted Rachinsky, she doled out "cod liver oil to the puny and undernourished children, most of whom show(ed) noticeable improvement in a surprisingly short while."[2]

A Move to the Clean Waters of Blaine Lake

"More and more one feels the present location of the Fresh Air Camp is too restricted, too close to the multitude," wrote board president, Edith Heavenrich, in early 1925.[3] "Such a thing as taking our children on an all day hike where they can learn to love and enjoy nature, is not to be thot (sic) of. Instead of tramping thru (sic) woods or over country roads, they must walk on highways or be chased from some farm where the cherries and apples are greatly coveted by our children, but not freely given by a hard worked farmer," continued Heavenrich.

The Board envisioned a new site far from the city; quiet, spacious and plush with flora and fauna. Their vision became reality in 1925 when Mr. and Mrs. Edwin Rosenthal donated 55 acres on Blaine Lake in Brighton. The United Jewish Charities tapped every resource available to amass the $90,000 needed to construct the site. Fresh Air Camp at Brighton, as it was formally named, opened in the summer of 1927.

Two hundred children were housed in four large dormitories with plenty of room to spare. The original camp structures also included a recreation hall, dining hall, administration building, garage, powerhouse, water tank, a women's building, two bathhouses and a dock.

CARS

In 1928, Mr. and Mrs. Leo Butzel donated a Cadillac that was later sold for a $50 credit toward the purchase of a new Chevrolet in 1931. Board member, Mrs. Max Berendt donated a Chevrolet, which was stored in her garage over the winter and cared for by the chauffeur of another board member, Mrs. Edwin Rosenthal.

LEGACY

In 1923, a gift of $3,000 was received from the estate of Mr. Leopold Wineman. Leopold was father to Henry and Henry was married to Gertrude, who became board president in 1920. Eighty years later, Gertrude and Henry's grandson, Henry II, became president of the Fresh Air Society.

SONG AND DANCE
Right from the start, campers adopted dancing and singing as part of camp life. Here is a group of giddy campers in 1927 showing off for a rare photo.

Sliding Pay Scale and Male Board Members
Signify a Change in Philosophy

Since the very first Belle Isle outing, it was commonly understood and accepted that Fresh Air would function on a deficit basis. No one ever disputed the invaluable service camp was providing to the poor. The United Jewish Charities and the Detroit Community Fund willingly covered operating shortages. With the opening of Brighton, however, deficits quickly increased. Pressure fell upon the Board to move toward becoming a self-sustaining agency. Pennies, and ultimately dollars, were saved, but finally it became obvious that the only way to bring in additional funds was to attract those who could afford to pay.

A sliding fee scale was implemented in 1928. Carolyn Eppstein, camp director, wrote that the camp was "breaking away from the pauperism idea." While the camp fee was raised to $13 for a two-week session, the average child paid only $4.[4] Full-pay campers and community agencies helped cover the cost of the "scholarship" kids. Income also was generated through weekend stays for camp alumni and other groups.

Minnie Bernberg (Cohen) considered herself one of the lucky ones. She came as a paid camper in the late 1920s. Her father was a brick layer and her family enjoyed the luxury of a car and a telephone. She often played in Palmer Park and on Belle Isle, but she and her siblings always eagerly awaited camp season. "I loved singing on the stage,"[5] remembered Minnie in 2000. "I went on to have a life long love of music. I didn't like the food, in particular the oatmeal with sugar," she chuckled remembering the taste she never forgot.

"They made me eat it!"

Whatever Minnie didn't eat, others did. Irving Lash, a camper in the mid-20s, couldn't wait for his morning bowl of oatmeal and slices of toast. "I got in line twice because I liked it so much."[6]

By the time 1929 rolled around, the camp had begun to move toward a focus on education and enrichment. Handicraft, woodcraft and nature programs were expanded. It was also in 1929 that Fresh Air Camp experienced yet one more radical change. The all-women board decided that "gentlemen be included on the board in addition to the ladies." The first men to serve in this esteemed group were Abraham J. Levin, the first boys' counselor, and Samuel Gilbert. Their timing was perfect. Several months after the two men accepted the position, the stock market crash ignited the Great Depression. While the women had managed to survive many financial hurdles, the Depression and the demands of operating a self-sustaining program would prove daunting.

MORRIS MINTZ
Anna Mintz, camp's cook, had three sons all of whom spent much time at camp. Her son Morris rode to Venice Beach on the John R bus and transferred to the suburban line for 10 cents. As a teen, Morris, who later became an ophthalmologist, was put to work as an assistant janitor. His pal was a junior counselor known as "Lindy," Irwin Shaw. On the back of the photo, Lindy penned this note to Morris, "Is that the way you sweep? Hurry up!"

COST OF CAMP

The per child expense of camp in 1929 was $17 for two weeks, including daily food costs of 43.5 cents. The average family paid $4 per child.

1929

Although the idea of building a year-round camp facility had been discussed early in the development of Brighton, no plans had been made. In 1929, the Children's Fund of Michigan financed a post-camp season for cardiac care children. The program was deemed worthwhile and planning began for a heated building on the grounds.

The North End
CLINIC

One would think that the creation of a free health clinic would have little to do with the running of a fresh air camp. Yet, put into the perspective of time and place, it is not surprising to find that the two were inextricably intertwined.

As the industrial boom of the early 20th Century got underway, Detroit was growing rapidly. Thousands of new residents and immigrants were pouring into the city, many of them Russian Jews who came empty handed. Their Jewish brethren organized numerous relief agencies all with similar missions; to help the new Americans become self-sufficient and gain a sense of independence and pride. The Fresh Air Society provided fresh air and nourishment to poor children, the Hebrew Ladies' Sewing Society sought to alleviate the distressed conditions of Russian exiles and the Hebrew Free Loan Society helped those in a financial emergency.

In the basement of the Hannah Schloss Building, the turn of the century equivalent to the Jewish Community Center, was a free dispensary, open three days a week, to provide medical care for the indigent. It was originally known as the United Jewish Charities Clinic and was funded, in part, by the Detroit Community Union (forerunner of United Foundation). First opened in 1905, it was expanded to an eight-room suite in 1908.

Although not a hospital (patients were referred to Harper, Detroit Receiving or Women's Hospitals), the clinic served the community well. Well and sick care, vaccinations, lice checks and even dental care were offered to residents in need. Gynecology, orthopedics, pediatrics and a surgery department also functioned in the small, but busy setting. And, late each spring, every child being considered for Fresh Air Camp went to the clinic for a free, general health examination and evaluation.

Helping to staff the clinic were the ladies of the Fresh Air Society whose services often duplicated those provided by the clinic. Both agencies visited the sick and hungry, supplied medications and taught lessons in hygiene and nutrition. The Fresh Air women took their task one step further and began visiting camp families over the winter months to ensure that the hygiene and nutrition lessons learned at camp continued at home. Soon the capable Fresh Air Society volunteers found themselves running the clinic.

Very visible within both agencies was Blanche Hart. As founder of Fresh Air, she maintained a high-profile position with the camp. As director of the United Jewish Charities, she carefully monitored its growing programs. When the Jewish community migrated north to the Oakland Ave. area, Hart, together with Dr. Harry Saltzstein, the future chief of staff of the clinic, went in search of a new location. They found it along Westminster Avenue, just east of Oakland Avenue. Two adjoining stores were cleaned and combined to form what would become known as the North End Community Clinic. Upon its move in 1922, Fresh Air Society assumed all responsibility for operating the clinic.

In 1923, the Fresh Air Society by-laws were revised to read that the Fresh Air Society was "organized to assist the sick and needy; to help with the maintenance of the United Jewish Charity Clinic, and to maintain the Fresh Air Camp during the summer months." Board president, Edith Heavenrich, in January 1925, wrote, "We realize that our Camp is a great factor in restoring rosy cheeks and animation to our boys and girls – although they are not really ill – then we are sure that the summer camp belongs properly to the health-giving agencies. From this viewpoint, the Camp and the Clinic are not so far apart."

Heavenrich and her fellow volunteers lovingly monitored the clinic. Board meeting minutes retell story after story of sickly children who were restored to good health, thanks to the work of the clinic and the camp. Dr.

Harry Saltzstein, at the time a young surgeon from New York, became an integral part of camp life frequently visiting the camp and attending nearly every monthly Fresh Air board meeting. He beamed with pride when the Society reported a camp season with few illnesses and plenty of weight-gain; and glowed with satisfaction when he reported that the clinic was improving the health of the general community. In 1924, for example, 2,033 people were vaccinated in seven days at a charge of 15 cents each.

Saltzstein was the first to recommend that a physician be on staff or at least come weekly to camp to examine the children and supervise sanitation of water, etc. He was also one of the leading champions of establishing a Jewish hospital in Detroit.

By the end of 1925, the North End Community Clinic had outgrown its quarters. When the Leopold Wineman Memorial Building opened in 1926, on Holbrook Avenue, the North End Clinic moved in. Considered a legitimate outpatient medical facility, the clinic operated with its own governing body and the Fresh Air Society women bowed away gracefully. Their own hands were full with a burgeoning camp program and the opening of Brighton.

The North End Clinic went on to serve thousands of low-income residents annually. By 1930, the clinic had a staff of more than 80 physicians, 17 dentists and dozens of others. Those who were able paid a small stipend for their care. Yet, even with this all-new Jewish medical institution, the city still lacked a Jewish hospital that served Kosher foods and helped foster the careers of young Jewish doctors. The move to establish a true Jewish hospital continued, in ebbs and flows, throughout the Depression and World War II. Finally, on January 15, 1953 Sinai Hospital opened its doors.

Two simple ideas…a day in the fresh air for the city's poorest Jewish children and a medical examination before their arrival at camp, led to two of the city's most beloved Jewish institutions: Sinai Hospital and Tamarack Camps.

The North End Community Clinic
(photo courtesy of Rabbi Leo M. Franklin Archives, Temple Beth El)

NORTH END CLINIC
The women of the Fresh Air Society were active volunteers throughout the Detroit Jewish community. Mostly members of Temple Beth El, they volunteered as chaperons for the children at camp, delivered medicine and food to the sick and hungry in the city, and were active with other relief efforts.

"There were lots of poor children, my family paid." Minnie Bernberg

Aerial View of Brighton

THE ORIGINAL TRACT
OF THIS CAMP SITE
WAS DONATED TO THE
FRESH AIR SOCIETY
BY
MR. AND MRS. EDWIN M. ROSENTHAL
JUNE, 1925

"I remember it was wonderful and we were very anxious to go back each year." Mary Katz

FRESH AIR CAMP

"When the board came to visit, everybody had to be up to measure." Lillian Genser (Mellen)

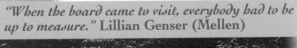

1920s

THE DEPRESSION
BUILDS CAMP STRENGTH

"I always loved to come up on the road and see the wide open spaces and buildings of camp. I could smell the new mown hay and remember the feeling of being back home."

Oscar Genser, camper/counselor 1933-1941

1930s

In 1930, daily camp life was simple and regimented. After a rousing 7:15 a.m. reveille, hungry, sleepy-eyed campers gathered around the flag post for the flag raising, then shuffled over to the mess hall to wait for breakfast. They talked in hushed tones, barely noticing the morning dew on the grass, the bright green lily pads that dotted the lake or the rich aroma of hot cocoa that filled the air. When the doors finally opened, the morning feast quickly began and within moments, noisy bedlam reigned.

After breakfast, counselors gathered their groups and tore off for that day's scheduled activities. Perhaps the day included a hike into the woods, where campers could discover more toads or snakes than the day before. Others went to the handicraft shelter to work with leather or clay, while a third group went to the field to play kickball or soccer. On special days, campers immersed themselves in preparing for the all-camp celebrations, such as the perennial favorite, Circus Day or rooting for the FAC baseball team when they played

ESTHER AND FRANCIS LOEWENBERG
Esther Loewenberg (r), an educator, worked at camp as a counselor during the mid 1930s. Like others during the Depression, the young woman was paid in script rather than cash. In 1939, Esther married Milton Maddin, once a camper himself. The couple became deeply involved in Fresh Air Camp, Milton serving as president of both the Fresh Air Society and the Tamarack Hills Authority during the 1950s. Their son, Michael, became one of camp's most generous benefactors and was Board president in the 1980s.

"IRV"
Irving Rosen had
a joyous ten-year
Fresh Air Camp
career. An artisan
and nature lore
expert, he put his
handicraft skills to
use numerous times.
There was the time,
in preparing for a day
hike, Rosen stole out
the night before and
strung oranges and
apples from a tree.
Once on the hike, he
told children that they
might find a magic
tree that bore
dangling fruit,
which, of course,
they did.

against a team from the city. When these games occurred, the whole camp came to watch.

Among those watching would be a group of children who could not play ball. This was the cardiac group. These children came to camp and lived a unique life. They were kids recovering from rheumatic fever, rapid pulses or heart disease. They usually stayed for the entire season, but their activities were quite limited. The healthier ones were allowed to toss around a softball and wade in the water twice daily. Actual swimming was forbidden. Conversely, the sickest were mostly restricted to bed, occasionally getting a brief walk around camp. A doctor and nurse from the T. B. & Health Society monitored the cardiac children, whose incentive was to eat, rest and get healthy so they could work up to more camp activities. Summers typically began with the majority of the cardiac children classified as Group 3, the sickest. By the end of the season, most had been upgraded to Group 1, those with the least restricted of activities.

After a game, if it was on a Sunday, cardiac campers and all were rewarded with a regular Sunday treat, an evening picnic on the grass. Fresh sandwiches and milk were served, followed by ice cream cones. It was a highly anticipated weekly treat, much like the Shabbat feasts that came later. After dinner, it was time for camp-fire songs and stories, and then off to bed. Campers were tucked in by their junior counselors (later known as CITs and then TSS), while the elders were given these nights for their own socials and events.

As camp negotiated with Detroit Edison to install permanent electric service, a disagreement arose over Brighton property lines and rights of way with a neighbor. The dispute was over a road that ran through camp. The neighbor – believing this to be his property – was refusing right of way. He intended to erect a fence and herd sheep across the Fresh Air campus onto his adjoining land. While attorneys haggled over the issue, the neighbor proceeded with his sheep herding. Some minimal grounds damage was incurred as a result of the "traffic," and the camp director and others were awakened many nights by the bleating of sheep.

1933/1934

Rose Lash (Simkovitz), a junior counselor in the early 1930s, remembered watching the children doze off, then heading into the screened-in porch area of the dorm where the counselors slept. "We didn't have any special responsibilities,"[1] recalled Rose, an only child who started as an 8-year-old camper and stayed until she was 14. "We helped out with the younger kids and watched them at night so the counselors could go out. I loved camp. Fresh Air gave me a chance to be with a lot of people, a lot of girls and just have fun."

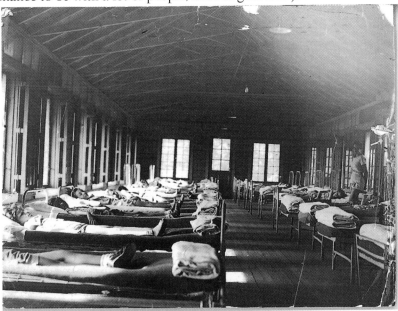

BUNK PRIDE
"We each had a locker and bed. We had inspections – you'd almost think it was the army – if you wanted to win, you had to have a neat, clean locker and your beds had to be made in a certain way," recalled Oscar Genser, a camper in the mid 1930s. At the end of each session, the bunk with the cleanest beds, lockers and floors won a special FAC award.

Board Members Take Extraordinary Measures As The Depression Hits

In 1930, the camp fee was $15 for a two-week session, a fee that was rarely collected.[2] Most camp families paid reduced sums ranging from $5 to $2 – or less – per week. Shortfalls were funded by various community agencies, including the Community Fund of Detroit, which relied upon Fresh Air to provide a much-needed healthy retreat for children while parents struggled to find work and food.

CANOES
Once the reluctant board of directors approved canoes, a fleet quickly appeared on Blaine Lake. Canoes were named by contributors. Pictured is a canoe donated by Harry L. Jacobson, one of the most passionate early canoeing advocates.

Camp director Carolyn Eppstein wrote in 1933, "Not only are the physical benefits and training of camping important, but also the spiritual values gained from an environment free from worry and tension. And for the child who has suffered from the lack of the bare necessities in the home, the camp is a means of keeping body and soul together, if only for a short period."[3]

Minor budget cuts were implemented while the board remained watchful as to how the Depression would impact camp. It soon became obvious that most families would be unable to pay even a small stipend. "All that can be done is to hope for the greatest possible income and still reach these children who need our care," wrote an optimistic Eppstein. Amazingly, in 1931, as one person in seven was on relief, Fresh Air posted a $1,000 surplus. While bread lines in the city were measured in miles and tuberculosis reached epidemic proportions, Fresh Air built a new dock and put a fresh coat of paint on the buildings. No one knew that this was the last coat

WHERE ARE THE GIRLS?

During the Depression, a noted change was attendance by fewer girls. Perhaps, mused executive director Eppstein, with more women seeking employment, the young girls were being kept at home to help with chores and childcare.

FOOD SHORTAGE

One of the many obstacles to overcome during the Depression years was the food shortage. With the camp at maximum capacity, and a charge to reduce meal costs by two cents per day per child, a dietician was employed in 1933. A vegetable garden, careful management of the kitchen and the use of a truck and driver who could travel daily to and from the downtown market reduced costs and kept food fresh. During the summer of 1933 campers gained an average of 2.2 pounds.

DAPPER DANS
This handsome group of counselors decided to have a formal evening of entertainment one night in 1937. They donned their Shabbat dress clothes and went out on the "camp."

(left)
SARAH SMITH (STEIN) AND IRVING ROSEN
These two popular counselors filled many a young child's heart with joy. Years later, Smith became active with the Fresh Air Society board and introduced Irwin Shaw to Frank Lloyd Wright, who almost designed the new Ortonville site.

(right)
CARNIVAL DAY 1938
This group of counselors eagerly awaited any chance to entertain the children. Here they are attired as circus performers. (l to r) Beatrice Fisher, Manny Simon, Ben Chinitz, Harry Fox and, lurking behind, is Reuben Isaacs. *(photo courtesy of Ben Chinitz)*

of paint the buildings would receive for many years.

The Depression came to camp early in 1932 when Fresh Air was dealt a surprising and devastating blow. The Community Fund was in the midst of its own financial crisis and elected to cut funding for all "non-essential" programs, including summer camps. Without this funding, it would be impossible for camp to open. It was an unprecedented predicament for the Board.

At the prestigious Phoenix Social Club of Detroit, the Fresh Air board members contemplated the future. In their typical resourceful fashion, they viewed this crisis as a glass that was half full. To fill the other half, they would have to take extraordinary measures, like a mother who will go to unimagined ends to save her child. They drastically cut expenses, eliminated amenities and cut back staff. They decided to only open two-thirds of the camp and reduce the number of campers. In addition, Board members personally guaranteed to fund any shortfalls. Determined that camp would survive, they implemented one more dramatic change. For the first time in its history, camp would focus some of its recruitment efforts on children who could afford to pay.

Support Builds For Pay Camp

"The idea of a pay-camp is something quite new to the Jewish group," wrote Eppstein in April 1932. She cautioned not to expect a large response. Yet, to everyone's delight, and within only a few weeks, it became evident that the community did indeed have the means to support a Jewish pay camp.

"We opened June 27th, with a group falling short of 100, the maximum number planned on," wrote Eppstein later that summer. "We filled vacancies with scholarship cases from lists referred by the Department of Public Welfare. Before the two weeks had passed, literally hundreds of requests were pouring in and registrations for the entire season of ten weeks were closed with a waiting list of over 100."

As things turned out, 1932 wasn't such a bad year. More than 470 children went to camp that summer with greater than 50 percent paying the full fee. The Community Fund allocated $4,000 to Fresh Air and the Jewish community responded to the crisis by sending in dozens of scholarship fund contributions. Over the next few years, Fresh Air Society became an affiliated agency of the Jewish

1934

The first Junior Unit was organized thanks to a large increase in campers ages six to ten. The unit had its own counselors, programs and activities.

CAMP RATES

Camperships were filled from three groups: full-pay, agency referral or no-pay. Full-pay enrollment was limited to the exact number of children needed to make up any deficit. Agency children were accepted at special rates and reduced-rate children paid only what the family could afford. The ratio of two-thirds no or partial rate and one-third full rate was consistent throughout the late 1930s and into the early 1940s.

DEPRESSION YEARS

It wasn't a miracle that opened the pockets of the Jewish community and saved Fresh Air Camp in the early 1930s. It was a combination of Jewish philanthropy, entrepreneurship and perseverance. The Jewish community fared better as a whole compared to other ethnic and geographic communities. The insulation, noted Sydney Bolkosky, a prolific chronicler of Detroit Jewish history, was that Detroit Jews were not totally reliant on the automotive industry for employment. More than 50 percent of Detroit's Jewish men were employed in "trade," non-industrial jobs such as retail and wholesale. Many others were employed in the white-collar professions of management, law and medicine.

Federation (1933), receiving funds from the Allied Jewish Campaign and United Jewish Charities. In addition, many referring agencies, such as the Department of Public Welfare, began to pay a reduced per-camper fee for those they referred.

This was the recipe for the camp's financial survival during the Depression, but they were hardly easy years. Each day was an ongoing struggle. Dwindling resources, staffing problems, rationing and children with increasing health problems took their toll on the camp and its director, Carolyn Eppstein.

Eppstein had been at the helm for ten years and was responsible for much of its tenacity and growth. She was the first to implement strategic growth plans, such as collaboration with schools, specialized training for counselors and leadership training. After a particularly hot and trying summer, Eppstein resigned in 1935.

Director Irwin Shaw "Lindy" Comes To Camp

Irwin Shaw, a strapping young man in love with the outdoors, took charge in 1936. He was no newcomer to Fresh Air. A decade earlier, at the age of 15, a young, eager Shaw sat in a bus headed for Fresh Air Camp at Brighton. It was a notable day, remembered Shaw, who in 1999, at age 89, remained involved with the Fresh Air Society. As the young teen rode toward Brighton with dreams of adventure and *ruach* (spirit), another young adventurer, Charles Lindbergh, fresh from his cross-Atlantic flight, was headed to Detroit for a ticker-tape parade.

"I remember 1927, my first and only year as a Fresh Air Camper,"[4] recalled Shaw in 1999. Like Lindbergh, Shaw was a lanky, mature-looking young man with a chiseled chin and deep-set eyes. That summer day, when he stepped off the bus, he stepped into his future. "The boys' head counselor came to the bus. I was 6-foot tall and weighed 150 pounds. He grabs me and says, 'Welcome Lindy!' He

LATE 1930s

A Ford Model T motor was rigged to a paddle wheel barge and used to rid the wading beach area of muck and weeds. After the water was cleared up, campers used the barge for pleasure.

IRWIN SHAW BLESSING THE PIGEON
When camp needed supplies from the city, it was common practice for Irwin Shaw to utter a *brucha* and send a pigeon from Brighton to Detroit. The pigeon belonged to one of the camp's maintenance men who lived in Detroit. Shaw fondly remembered the ritual, "He (the maintenance man) said, 'We'll bring the pigeons out here and after the truck driver leaves, if we have to give him a message, we'll send the pigeon to my house. When my wife sees it, she'll take the note." The wife would then contact the driver with the additional supplies needed.

said, you are going to be called Lindy and that's one of the require-
ments of you coming here."

The Lindy nickname stuck with Shaw, until it was discovered that
Charles Lindbergh associated with the Nazis. By that time, though,
the life-long camper already had created a legacy of his own. "Irv"
returned the following year to Fresh Air Camp as a junior counselor, moved on to other camps and, along the way, became
a Detroit schoolteacher. By the time he was tapped for the
director's position at Fresh Air, Shaw had become a passionate
advocate for Jewish education and innovative summer camp
programming.

The transition from the formidable Eppstein to the gentle-
manly educator came slowly for the well-seasoned board. The
idea of a man running their camp was uncomfortable, remembered Shaw. One of their chief concerns was the issue of girls
who would reach "womanhood" at camp. Would Shaw know
what was happening or what to do? Shaw convinced them he'd
be a compassionate learner.

Compassion would be only one trait used to describe Shaw
over the years, but in 1936, he had much else to do. The
Depression had taken a particularly hard toll on camp buildings, grounds and materials. With no handyman around during
the previous seven years, everything was in disrepair. Paint was
peeling and buildings leaking. The mattresses were shredded
and the beds were broken. Shaw submitted an expensive list
of camp repairs totaling $10,000 – a lot of money back then.
He told the board that they must agree to find the funds to fix
everything or he would not stay. "You know something," Shaw
proudly remembered, "they came through with the $10,000.
They replaced all of the beds and mattresses and made the
repairs."

OUCH!

In 1936, the cabin
floors were nearly
10 years old, and
had been left
unsanded and
unpainted for many
years. That
summer, the camp
clinic treated more
than its fair share of
slivers in feet. "The
floor areas around
the beds are so
rough that it is
virtually impossible
for a camper to
get his foot on the
floor while getting
out of bed without a
sliver," wrote Irwin
Shaw. By the
following season,
the floors were
sanded and painted.

In the early to
mid-1930s, camp was
divided into three age
groups (seniors, inter-
mediates and juniors),
three major activities
(waterfront, handi-
crafts and athletics)
and three periods.

A typical day went like this:
7:15 reveille
7:50 flag raising
8:00 breakfast
9:00 1st activity
10:30 general swim
12:00 lunch
1:00 rest hour
2:00 2nd activity
3:00 milk
3:30 3rd activity
4:30 general swim
6:00 supper
7:45 evening program
8:45 to bed

Irwin Shaw began to
implement more group-
based choices and
encouraged counselors
to plan activities for
their own groups.
This allowed for more
freedom, flexibility and
variety for campers
and counselors.

CAMP
SCHEDULE

One of the decade's greatest achievements was the development of a Kosher kitchen at Brighton. Originally constructed in a large shed – intended for a tool shop – the kitchen served Kosher-style food, but lacked the required separate kitchen areas. Recognizing the inadequacy, Shaw began to seek funding for a truly Kosher kitchen. He went to see Fred Butzel, a compassionate philanthropist who would become a life-long benefactor of camp. "When I told him the idea of two kitchens, milk and meat, Butzel laughed. 'What's funny?' I asked. Butzel told me that his parents came to this country during the Civil War. They never ate anything Kosher in their life." Shaw chuckled along with Butzel, but then reminded him about the people they were helping at camp. "He came through and gave money to build the kitchens. Fred Butzel continued to come to camp, every summer, until the year he died."

By the end of the decade, Shaw had implemented many other changes. He introduced waiters to camp, and constructed and opened a 12-bed infirmary. He also added the boys senior unit, which increased camp capacity to 250 children per session. The senior boys unit was the first foray into a trend that would prove itself in the following decade, the decentralized camp concept. Now, instead of always being with the larger group of campers, the senior boys and their counselors were located in a separate section of the camp, left to determine their own activities.

MRS. WALSH
One of the most beloved cooks at camp was Mrs. Walsh. A petite "chain smoker" who always ate cornflakes and milk, she cooked up a feast for the kids every Friday, and often during weeknights for staff and counselors.

SHABBAT 1937
Dressed in their whites are (l to r) Manny Simon, Harry Fox, Ben Chinitz and Irving Rosen. *(photo courtesy of Ben Chinitz)*

1936

The Jewish Welfare Federation purchased an additional 40 acres on Blaine Lake, increasing the Fresh Air acreage to 95, with lake frontage extending three-fourths of the way around the lake. By 1939, several additional buildings were erected on the property, including a senior campsite with three dormitories and a dining room/recreation hall. A 12-bed hospital wing and a 12-bed waiter's building also were constructed. All of these buildings became possible through a bequest from the Carrie Sittig Cohen Fund.

Camp Icons

They reign from different eras, hail from different ports, yet they share a common bond –
Fresh Air Camp, Camp Tamarack, Camp Maas. Blanche Hart, Irwin Shaw, Sam Marcus,
Michael Zaks, Allan Brown and Harvey Finkelberg all devoted their lives to camp. Their visions
becoming immortal footprints along its paths: Hart's camp for poor children, Shaw's
decentralized wilderness, Marcus' and Brown's tripping programs and outposts,
Zaks' spiritual Jewish environment and Finkelberg's dynamic Judaic outdoor recreation program.

Blanche Hart • Founder

Blanche Hart first escorted a group of immigrant women and their children to a picnic on Belle Isle in 1902. It was the first outing of what would become known, two years later, as the Fresh Air Society. In 1908, Hart purchased the first permanent camp location, a house in Roseville. By 1912, the fledgling organization had outgrown the small house. Hart secured a site on Lake St. Clair in an area known as Venice Beach. Among the quaint, white wooden cottages and the central dining hall, camp came unto its own. Each week, a new group of children and their chaperones stepped off a streetcar and into the fresh air.

She quickly became an influential, pioneering Jewish leader. She was the first superintendent of the United Jewish Charities, was chairperson of the Fresh Air Society and founder of the North End Clinic. The ubiquitous Hart remained an integral part of camp long past her departure as executive director. Born in Grand Rapids, Hart moved to Detroit in 1892. By the time Hart died in 1949, her passion for helping the indigent had led to the permanent establishment of Detroit's most enduring Jewish agencies and programs.

Irwin Shaw • Executive Director, 1936 - 1956

In 1927, Irwin Shaw went to Fresh Air Camp as a 15-year-old camper who paid his own way. One year later, he returned as a junior counselor, then went on to a teaching career with Detroit public schools. In 1936, just after the Depression, Shaw became Fresh Air Camp's first male executive director. The task before him was daunting. Repair a deteriorated camp, sustain the program and nurture its growth. Shaw did all that and more. With his wife, Lillian, and three sons by his side, Shaw lovingly carved out a camping program that fostered growth and independence not only in campers, but in counselors, as well. He relished watching young teens experience the unique kind of parenting counseling instilled. Lee Henkin, a camper in the late 1930s who, thanks to Irwin Shaw, was able to remain an extra session at camp when her mother was hospitalized, described him as "a man with *neshoma*, heart and soul."

Shaw led the charge to implement simple overnight canoe trips, more advanced senior camping experiences and specialized counselor training. He foresaw the baby boom before the term was coined and recognized that the Brighton campsite would never meet the coming demand. He made it his personal mission to find Fresh Air a new home, a woodsy place that could house a collection of self-sustaining, small villages. In 1950, he came upon a tamarack tree farm in Ortonville. By that time, Shaw had already presented Frank Lloyd Wright with his ideas of a camp that both communed with nature and allowed campers to live more independently. Although Wright did not design it, Shaw's dream came true.

In 1951, Shaw became executive director of the Jewish Community Center in addition to his Fresh Air duties. By 1956 the dual role had become too much and he resigned from Fresh Air. In 30 years as executive director, Shaw blossomed a camping program from a one-season, one-camp location to a year-round operation with two sprawling campsites.

Sam Marcus • Executive Director, 1956 - 1980

Even at age 81, Sam Marcus walks with determination. During the 24 years that he was executive director, beginning in 1956, "Sam" was always walking around camp – typically in a pair of khaki pants.

A camper in his youth, Marcus came to Detroit in 1949 after accepting a social work position with the 12th Street Council Center, a children's educational and recreational settlement house. A graduate of New York University, Marcus directed the Mother's and Children's Camp in Chelsea and eventually became director of the Jewish Community Center day camp program. In 1953, Marcus was appointed as staff liaison to the Tamarack Hills Authority, the Jewish Federation committee charged with the development and management of Ortonville.

Marcus and his wife, Irma, were passionate advocates. They helped transition camp into a place where Jewish children could connect with both nature and their heritage. Rather shy, Marcus was not the type to *kibbutz* with his campers. Instead, his joy came from seeing an idea blossom into reality and from working with others to make those dreams come true. He was a mentor to many and didn't tolerate counselors who broke curfew or ate cheeseburgers behind their bunks.

Ideas and visions became reality under Marcus' tenure. He cultivated camp's dynamic tripping and out-post program, helped build Silverman Village and worked with Children's Hospital to bring dialysis patients to camp for the summer. His passion for the arts encouraged experts in dance, drama, ceramics and song to come and summer at camp.

Twenty years after his retirement, Marcus visited camp in 2000. The magnificent sight of a heron flying over the lake reminded him of the spring ritual of tapping maple trees and the summer chore of cutting down a line of trees to make a fire break. He recalled going to the junk yard with a maintenance man named Floyd Young, who could weld just about anything, and watching his trusted friend, Allan Brown, the bound-less maintenance supervisor, cut wood for the children in the lumber mill. Marcus spent nearly 30 winters and summers at camp watching hundreds mature into seasoned campers, devoted counselors and nurturing parents. In a not-so-small way, his magic helped them grow.

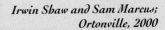

Sam Marcus

Irwin Shaw and Sam Marcus;
Ortonville, 2000

Blanche Hart   *Irwin Shaw*

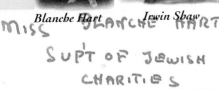

MISS BLANCHE HART
SUP'T OF JEWISH
CHARITIES

Michael Zaks • Assistant Executive Director, Executive Director, 1975 - 1983

Not too many people got to know the real Michael Zaks. Despite his short stature, tousled appearance and abrupt manner, Mike Zaks was really just a big teddy bear, playful and passionate. On first impression, Zaks was a strictly business sort of man, fervently pursuing his vision of camp, a Jewish camp for Jewish children: a place where nature, the arts and religion came together. His vision was often met with resistance, yet two decades later, his influence remains.

Preferring a hammer over a pen, Zaks was a hands-on leader. He loved to help campers paint a building, hammer nails into an Irving Berg sculpture or sing during an Oneg Shabbat. When it was lights out at camp, Zaks' day continued. Huddling with the Board, he'd plan the next move: a kosher kitchen, a scholar-in-residence program and a sanctuary at Butzel. Even as his health declined, Zaks kept going, pushing for camp to become a greater, more incredible place.

Born in 1946 in Florence, Italy, Zaks came to the United States as a young boy. He planned on becoming an electrical engineer and graduated from Lawrence Institute of Technology. Then, he landed a job driving a truck for Camp Tamarack. It changed his life. Zaks accelerated up the camp ladder, first working in the garage, then moving into administration. By 1968, he was both Administrative Assistant to the Tamarack Hills Authority and the Fresh Air Society. Camp became the center of his life, a position he, nor those who loved him, ever questioned. "Michael was camp," said Paula, Michael's wife, whom he met at camp.

Michael Zaks died in 1983, at camp surrounded by family and friends, just three short years after becoming its executive director. Yet, his spirit lingers. Just walk through Camp Maas to feel his presence. Hebrew words spoken around the flagpole, family camp weekends and the Irving Berg sculptures are a few of the gifts Zaks left behind.

Allan Brown • Maintenance Supervisor, 1959 - 1980

A few rare people on this earth have the gift of being able to envision something and then create it. Allan G. Brown, the only person at camp to earn the title of "Mr.", was one of those fortunate souls. His unfitting title was Maintenance Supervisor. True, he was in charge of the camp maintenance team, the group of devoted men who instantly responded to leaky pipes, blown fuses and broken equipment. But they, and Mr. Brown, did far more.

Brownie, as his friends called him, along with his wife, Olga, and children, Barney and Martha, found their way to Camp Tamarack in 1959. A World War II veteran, Brown worked for the West Virginia Parks and Recreation service where he created a campground from an area much like Ortonville. "I advertised in a forestry magazine looking for a maintenance man. I got his resume and it sounded fabulous," recalled Sam Marcus. It was the beginning of a trusting friendship and an amazing team.

When Brown first came to camp there were 35 buildings. In 1970, the Fresh Air Board honored his work in helping to build over 100 more. Brown could chop a tree, mill the wood and erect a new cabin in a matter of hours. He wasn't Jewish, yet nurtured camp as if it were his own. He took it upon himself to take an interest in every facet of camp, especially the outpost and tripping program, and closely monitored the conservation of the properties.

Most campers never got to know Brown, who retired in 1980, but the staff did. He was often referred to as a father-figure who "help raise a lot of these lost 60s souls," remembered Minda Tilchin, Agree's first woman supervisor who also became Brown's daughter-in-law. "He had a profound influence on us and helped us learn what being a human being really was." Mr. Brown passed away in 1993.

Harvey Finkelberg • Executive Director, 1992 - Present

At heart, Harvey Finkelberg is just a big camper in executive director's clothes. Up at the crack of dawn and asleep long after the rest of his staff, Finkelberg is obsessive about his life's work: making Tamarack a first class Jewish camping facility where kids go to bed each night completely and totally fulfilled and happy.

His education is that of a social worker, earning an M.S.W. at the University of Toronto, but his passion is camping. "He is truly a camp person, a bit of the P.T. Barnum of the Jewish camping world," fondly described Ed Lumberg, 1993 Board president.

In 1992, when Finkelberg became Tamarack's executive director, he inherited a camp reeling from a decade of inconsistent leadership, financial difficulties and stagnant enrollments. Tamarack had lost its competitive edge, but Finkelberg knew how to get it back.

With brilliant creativity and resolute determination, this father of seven reshaped camp. Every building was upgraded and an endless variety of programs and activities were implemented. Achievement awards moved from paper to coveted items of clothing and jewelry, and mezuzot were put on every door. A covered pool and gymnasium was built for rainy days and highly skilled staff were hired to nurture the children. He created Nachman Horizons and Horizons Avodah, programs that allow children with special needs to enjoy regular camp experiences. Ten years after his arrival, Tamarack had once more become the envy of the industry and the pride of the community.

Finkelberg judged camp's success differently. Each time a camper got up on water skis, bounded to the flagpole to receive an achievement award or returned from a camping trip bearing a grin wider than a tent, he felt a fatherly pride. He smiled contentedly every Shabbat as he watched the whole camp sing together with booming passion. When teary-eyed campers and staff boarded the buses home, Finkelberg knew he had succeeded. The friendships, images and memories formed over the past summer would never be forgotten and were the memories that would keep Tamarack alive for another 100 years.

Michael Zaks

(l to r) Allan Brown, Barney Brown,
Sam Marcus

Harvey Finkelberg

Camp Icons

"It was an opportunity to do something creative and constructive." Irwin Shaw

1930s

"Sometimes I think we had more fun with less, we always did things as a group."
Frances Malin
(Hartman)

STELLA B.

"The play was the greatest experience of my life. All the kids sang and we loved it." Harriet Berg (Warrack)

"Flag raising was always a treat." Ben Chinitz

"No one knew the scholarship kids from those that could pay." Lee Henkin

BRIGHTON GROWS UP

1940s

*These were people for whom a camp registration
meant well-balanced meals for an undernourished child …
a rehabilitating experience for a refugee girl; a boy's brief escape from
a seriously disturbed parent…It means that for at least three weeks
these boys and girls start even with the others, they live together
with normal youngsters;…they feel they belong, they feel secure.*

Irwin Shaw, executive director 1949

On a mellow summer night in 1942, a handful of staffers quietly gathered in the Fresh Air Camp recreation hall. "The lights were out and there was a fire in the fireplace. Then someone came up with the record album and phonograph and played 'Rhapsody In Blue.' It was an unforgettable experience,"[1] reminisced Sy Kalish, then a waiter. "Everyone should have their first exposure to 'Rhapsody in Blue' in such a setting," he wrote in a 1985 letter to Tamarack Camps.

The sounds of camp. For many, the memories of laughter, the crunch of feet upon dirt roads, the splash of water or the crackling of a roaring fire linger. For others it is the singing and the songs. "We'd sing 'em in the morning when we got up, and we sang them at the end of the day,"[2] fondly remembered Oscar Genser, a camper and counselor throughout the '30s. The songs sung around a campfire or along a trail, the songs blasting over the waterfront, or the songs that boomed in 1941 from the newly arrived jukebox, a gift of then Society president, Alex Schreiber.

"What I recall vividly," recalled Asher Tilchin, a former supervisor of the Brighton senior side, "is the singing. You'll find singing in many camps, but I think the amount, the enthusiasm and the extent of it was very great at Fresh Air Camp."[3] Although he is long past the camping age, Tilchin loves to croon camp tunes to his grandchildren, who are Tamarack Camp campers themselves. Among the Tilchin family favorites is the classic, 'There's A Frog At The Bottom Of The Sea.'

FOR THE SEASON OF 1939
FRESH AIR CAMP
ANNOUNCES A NEW SENIOR UNIT FOR BOYS FROM 14 TO 17

In addition to its regular facilities for boys from 6 to 14 and girls from 6 to 16.

The senior unit is located one mile from the camp proper. The plant includes 3 sleeping cabins, a dining-hall and a wash-house having accommodations for 30 boys and 4 counselors. An independent program will be planned and carried through by the boys themselves. Leadership will be provided by counselors trained and experienced in the handling of adolescent youth.

BLAINE LAKE - BRIGHTON, MICH.

BROCHURE
In 1939, Irwin Shaw created a new senior unit for boys ages 14 to 17. The unit was located on the "other side of the lake" and the boys lived a much more independent life than the rest of camp.
(Image courtesy of the Jewish Federation Community Archives collection)

Canoeing Comes to Camp

Since the dawn of Fresh Air Camp, slow-moving, flat-bottomed rowboats have been a daily part of camp life. Canoes, on the other hand, slid into camp but not without a bit of a struggle. In 1940, camp director, Irwin Shaw, decided it was time to bring canoes to camp. The matriarchs of the Fresh Air Society Board protested, saying the venture was too risky, too dangerous. Nonsense, insisted Shaw and fellow board member, Harry Jacobson, who had dubbed themselves official "canoeing chairpersons." The two men argued persuasively and finally convinced the Board to give the sport a trial.

With canoes (most of which were obtained by Jacobson) in the water, Shaw decided to prove the merits of the sport to the Board. So, with the able-bodied help of some senior campers, he staged a little demonstration.

1943

Isadore Sobeloff, Executive Director of the Jewish Federation, wrote to the draft board asking for an exemption on behalf of Alvin Skelly, who had replaced Irwin Shaw. "Mr. Skelly is the only person available under whose direction the camp could operate," wrote Sobeloff. "Should Mr. Skelly be called to induction prior to the opening of camp season, we would have no alternative but the closing of camp. Your board is fully aware of the government's strong desire to continue the operation of such summer camps during the war period."

"The women were appalled (at the notion of canoeing). We had already gotten the canoes, so I invited them to come out to the waterfront and we created a little piece of dramatics,"[4] remembered Shaw. "We got a couple of campers to get into a canoe and then they tipped the canoe over. The women screamed, 'get them, get them!' I sat there with my arms folded and didn't move." Sixty years later, Shaw sat once again with his arms folded and laughed at the memory. "They were screaming to get them out of the water. I said, 'Nah, I'm not going to get them." The kids continued to play as if they were about to drown. Finally, they righted the canoe and everyone, well almost everyone, enjoyed a good laugh. Canoeing thus became a permanent part of camp life.

SHERUTH LEAGUE

During the 1940s, 50s and 60s, the Sheruth League became one of the most significant benefactors of Fresh Air Society. Sheruth, which means service in Hebrew, was organized as a service and philanthropic organization for young Jewish married women from Northwest Detroit. At its peak there were 200 members who primarily devoted themselves to supporting camp. Seemingly always a phone call away, Sheruth responded to some of the more mundane, routine requests for funds. They provided camping scholarships, and often clothing, for hundreds of poor Jewish children. They purchased tents, games and sports equipment. In Brighton, their funds established the library and constructed and furnished a counselor's cabin. The Sheruth Lodge was among the first buildings constructed in Ortonville. Sadly, by the 1970s, there weren't enough women to keep up the work, so the Sheruth League disbanded. As a last gesture, the league took an active role in funding and establishing Silverman Village. Bertha Chomsky, who devoted nearly 30 years of her life to the league, says it was all worth it. "I'm the one richer for it," she recalled. "When you do things for a community, the return you get is ten-fold. You feel connected, you realize we are all connected."

The War Years

Days before the end of the 1939 camp season, a young boy, Emil Wolok, frantically darted across the green spans of the campground. "I vividly remember Emil running across camp and into our bunk, shouting that war had broken out,"[5] recalled Genser, then a counselor.

Emil was right. The Germans invaded Poland on September 1, and on September 3, France and Britain declared war on Germany. By the drop of the ball that New Year's eve, most Americans regarded the brewing tensions in Europe cautiously. Despite the horrific stories of Hitler's reign of terror, few thought the United States would become directly involved. Of course, in 1941 all those doubts were put to rest. Pearl Harbor was attacked and America entered the Great War.

The War permeated every crevice of American life. No person or place escaped, including Fresh Air Camp. In case of a direct attack upon Detroit, the Red Cross would commandeer all camp equipment and supplies, such as cots, bedding and fire-fighting equipment. The camp was listed as a possible evac-

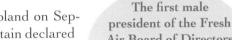

1939

The first male president of the Fresh Air Board of Directors was Harry L. Jackson. He served from 1939-41.

MOISHE LAST
This young camper came to the U.S. from Poland in 1936, at the age of six. In 1942, he came to Fresh Air Camp as a scholarship camper. Forever grateful, Last ultimately became a counselor in his teens, then as an adult, was a song leader, guitar instructor and artist-in-residence.

OFF TO CAMP
Carrying suitcases, campers boarded buses from the Jewish Community Center. Wearing clothes that aren't exactly his size, the boy standing in the front and center of this photo was probably a recent immigrant.

uation center and its trucks were registered with the war department. Commodities became scarce and expensive, and rationing made obtaining gas, fuel and food difficult.

One remedy was to cultivate a victory garden. Caretaker Richard Haas, who lived with his family at camp year-round, tended the 2½ acre plot where corn, cantaloupe, watermelon and lots of potatoes were grown. "We had a bumper crop of potatoes," recalled Haas in 1993.[6] "The campers would bag potatoes and sell them to visitors, which helped us buy a small tractor that came in handy for camp chores." Campers helped tend the garden that provided close to half of the camp's fresh vegetables. Still, in 1942, camp spent $206.52 on produce.[7]

Reaping the harvest from the garden was one of Shaw's last duties as camp director. Later that year, young Shaw was called to serve in the Navy. Board members, staff and others soon followed. Counselor recruitment became a nightmare as more and more young Americans were called to serve. As a result, less experienced counselors were recruited at a younger age. In the summer of '42, the average counselor age was 17½, one year younger than in '41 and two years younger than in '40.[8] Because of their youth and inexperience, these unpaid counselors were given menial tasks while all of the significant guidance

BOB LUBY
Bob Luby was Irwin Shaw's assistant from 1946 to 1955. Luby loved the relaxed summers at camp. Later, his children, Ellen and Richard, would complain they never had a real summer vacation.
(photo courtesy of Robert Luby)

RE-FORESTATION

A re-forestation and farm project was started in 1942. With a loan of nearly $900 from the Jewish Federation, over 2,500 seedlings were planted that spring and an additional 1,500 were planted in the fall.

SHABBAT

By the 1940s, the Friday night Shabbat tradition was well established. Dressed in their Shabbat whites, campers gathered together for a fine meal and, most certainly prayed for the safety of the soldiers and peace in the world. Lou Shulman, a waiter in 1940, befriended another waiter, young Irving Berg. Berg remembered Friday night services and his friend Shulman, "When Lou left for the army, he handed me his beautiful white, full-length Friday night supper shirt he knew I admired – with the promise that when he returned safely, I would return it to him. Sort of a guarantee that he would come back. I was happy to return it to him a few years later."

and decision making was handled by the overworked and underpaid section heads, positions held mostly by women.

With Shaw gone, staff and supplies difficult to secure, funds scarce and the world at war, there were rumblings of closing camp for the 1943 season. Such thoughts were quickly put to rest. The war was tearing families apart, sending fathers overseas and mothers to work. Children were often left unsupervised. Juvenile delinquency was increasing at an alarming rate and nutrition was once again an issue. It was obvious to the board, the community and even the U.S. Government, that summer camps helped protect the welfare of children. All became committed to keeping camp open.

Two changes were made to overcome the financial shortage. First, full-pay camp prices increased to $16 per week in 1943, then to $18 in 1944. Second, instead of five two-week sessions, camp instituted three three-week sessions. During those years, children of servicemen and wounded or deceased veterans were considered "urgent requests." Their camp applications were never turned away, regardless of their ability to pay.

Alvin Skelly, a colleague of Shaw's in the Detroit Public Schools and an assistant director at Camp Tamakwa, took over the helm when Shaw was called to duty. Behind the scenes, Skelly and the Board went to

1949

Nearly 700 young children attended camp. Fifty-nine were children with special emergency needs – children of war widows, refugees, broken homes, agency clients. Those with special health problems were allowed to stay for more than one three-week session. Over 500 applicants were turned away that summer, including children who requested scholarships. It was the first time the underprivileged could not be accommodated.

REGISTRATION 7:30 a.m. Sunday, May 4, 1947; It was an annual rite of passage, parents would line up at the crack of dawn to register their children for Fresh Air Camp. It was not until 1953 that mail-in registration would alleviate the long lines.

great lengths to ensure a smooth operation. To obtain meat, dairy products and vegetables, camp had to first obtain the necessary number of ration points from the local ration board, then make frequent trips to the city to assure an uninterrupted flow of supplies. To get gas for these trips, Skelly or one of his volunteers went through a special appeals process before the Office of Defense. Campers were asked to bring in their own ration coupons.

Camp Life Goes On

Of course, all of these exercises were shielded from the children. Together with their fellow bunk mates and counselors, campers immersed themselves into their busy summer routines. The handicraft shelter was bustling with creative energy and the nature center was forever expanding its population of frogs, toads and snakes. Thursday was the cook's day off, which meant it was cook out day. All 200 campers would hike about five miles through pastures and along Highway 59 to a favored picnic spot. Armed with their own compasses and "mess kits," campers learned the art of making a campfire and cooking over an open flame. On their way, they'd identify trees, have a treasure hunt or tell a story about the legendary Paul Bunyan. Senior boys eagerly prepared for their overnight canoe trip down the Huron River.

Evenings were filled with a myriad of activities. Socials, folk dances, occasional piano recitals, and of course, plays and skits. Everyone got into the act. In 1943, counselors and staff brought the war into the mess hall with a program called, "Fresh Air Camp

1946

Directions to camp: Drive out Grand River Avenue, U.S.-16. At Five Mile Rd. check your mileage and continue on U.S.16 for 30 miles to U.S. 23. Turn right at the State Police Post on U.S. 23 for six miles.

1949 WAITER AND KITCHEN STAFF By some accounts the camp kitchen was the best place to be. Young teens found the food and fun of working a summer at camp purely enjoyable. From left, Leonard Krause, Howard Steinmetz, Jerry Katz, Sol Chicorel, Fred Findling, Bill Marwell, the cook, Alvin Ring, the cook, Gerald Anchor, Fritz Sieferheld, Sheldon Iden, Ralph Siporin. *(photo courtesy of Howard Steinmetz)*

Armed Forces." In addition to a tribute to the armed forces, each bunk participated in a radio drama written and directed by "Pvt." Morrie Weiss (then assistant camp director) called, "He's my Sergeant in the Army but he's my waiter at F.A.C." Dorm I was the WAGS, Dorm II the Army, the senior side the Marines and so on. Mrs. Walsh, the head cook, treated campers to a special evening meal highlighted by chopped liver, Southern Fried Chicken Ala Walsh, peas, apple pie and wild cherry punch.[9]

1946

In 1946, camp instituted a policy of accepting only Detroit-area children.

Full House

By the mid-1940s, the 20 green and yellow camp buildings of Brighton were filled to the rafters three times a summer with bug bitten campers, dirty clothes and postcards from home. One hundred girls and 130 boys could attend camp in a single session. In 1946, all of those who wished to attend camp on a "scholarship" were accommodated plus another 284 full-pay campers. With room for no more, however, 400 youngsters were turned away and by the summer of 1949 more than 500 applications – both from those who could afford to pay and those who could not – were rejected.

One child who did attend that year was Eugene Applebaum. It was his third and final summer as a Fresh Air camper. "I loved camp. I wanted to keep going, but you had to stop after being a senior," recalled Applebaum in a 2000 interview.[10] The bright-eyed philanthropist and founder of Arbor Drugs, who in 1998 generously endowed his name upon a village at camp, was an eager young camper.

"My parents knew – somehow – that going to camp was the right thing for me. I really enjoyed the camp experience. The day was simple. You got up, you went out, you came in for lunch. You came back out. You didn't have a lot of choices, but the day flew by."

Applebaum was a scholarship camper. His parents paid $3 a week. As an adult, he knew he wanted to give back. "I hold camp very dear. It gave you an opportunity to get away from home, to learn to live with others. You got to know the idiosyncrasies of people." People like fellow camper, "Pepper" Barton. "He put pepper on everything!," laughed a tender-hearted Applebaum.

EUGENE APPLEBAUM
Eugene Applebaum went to camp from 1947-1949. One of his most vivid memories is the summer his parents came to see him on visiting day. They brought him comics, a treasured possession at the time which remained a precious memory some 50 years later. *(photo courtesy of Eugene Applebaum)*

By the late 1940s, there were four Detroit-area Jewish camps: The Fresh Air Camp and Council Camp were overnight camps, Chelsea Mother's and Children's Camp and Camp Habonim were day camps. All four were bursting at the seams. In 1946 a special subcommittee of the Jewish Welfare Federation was formed to study camping needs and trends. A foresighted Shaw noted that these camps would be unable to accommodate the volume of campers "born between 1932 and 1939, a period of the lowest birthrate in recent American history." What is going to happen, he pondered, when children born past 1940 would come of camp age? "It behooves us to anticipate a greatly increased demand for camping in the period from 1947 to 1960. These years will reflect the rapidly accelerating birthrate which began in 1940 and is continuing."[11]

INDIAN LORE
The connection between camp and Native American life has always been strong. On the first and last night of camp, the Fresh Air Camp Tribal council would convene. Mesmerized campers and serious counselors stepped away from one reality into another as rules were read, awards given and new legends made.

FRANK LLOYD WRIGHT

Even as the search for a new campsite continued, plans were being made to update and expand Brighton. Helen DeRoy, an ardent Fresh Air Camp supporter and automobile magnate's Aaron DeRoy's widow, donated $6,000 toward the construction of an individualized girl's village. Irwin Shaw wanted the Helen DeRoy Village to be a model of modern camp architecture designed as a self-contained village. In preparation, lumber was cut from the Brighton woods. Shaw, unable to locate any local architects who shared his vision, sought the services of the premier architect of the time, Frank Lloyd Wright. Shaw wrote Wright in April 1949.

"Personally, I do not believe we must use the Indian's wigwam or the pioneer's log cabin just because we want to have youngsters live in the woods and participate in a varied and creative camping program… I would like to see a new type of camp architecture: one which would use indigenous materials which would fit into the natural surroundings, yet one which would embody a more artistic form and modern engineering concepts…On the slim chance that you would be at least willing to advise us, I am writing this request for an interview."

Frank Lloyd Wright took up the challenge, but the project came to naught. Wright was sent aerial photographs and detailed surveys of the campgrounds. He drew a rough schematic of the area and corresponded with Shaw for nearly one year. In that time, the plan to build at Brighton was abandoned in favor of purchasing and developing Ortonville. Despite an interest in designing the new campsite, Mr. Wright's proposals were rejected by the Board. Among his ideas was the notion of a footbridge spanning the lake. The loss of the great architect's input is a bittersweet memory for Shaw.

IRWIN SHAW 1948
Irwin Shaw, pictured
with his wife, Lillian,
became executive
director in 1936. He
spent his summers at
camp and his winters
teaching with Detroit
Public Schools.
During his tenure,
Shaw implemented
overnight canoe
trips, found the
Ortonville campsite
and began the
Shabbat tradition.

1949

The first outpost camp was
established at Kensington Park.
That summer, thanks to a $500
gift from the Sheruth League,
nearly 75 senior boys and girls
cooked their own meals, slept in
tents, hiked and canoed.

10,000 Miles Later

His figures may be a bit exaggerated, but Irwin Shaw made it
his mission to find Fresh Air Camp a new home. Between 1947 and
1949, Shaw added 10,000 miles to his odometer searching for the
right location. He wanted a site far enough away so campers would
forget the feel of the city yet close enough to obtain supplies in a rea-
sonable fashion. He found it when he came across a private, 600 acre
wooded tree farm surrounding two lakes near Ortonville.

The land was ideal, except for one small detail. Tamarack Farms,
located only 50 miles from the city, was over the budgeted expense of
$25,000. Shaw approached Isadore Sobeloff, Jewish Welfare Feder-
ation executive director. The conversation couldn't have been easy.
"Sobby, I got some good news and some bad news," recalled Shaw.

1949

To celebrate the new independent state of Israel, camp began teaching Israeli dance.

BEST BED
Building children's self-esteem and pride have long been an important aspect of camp life. For many years, campers were awarded for making their beds in a perfect manner. This page from the scrapbook of a camper named Joyce Kaplan demonstrates how proud she was of her own efforts.

"The good news is I found what I think is the ideal camp. The bad news is that the campsite will cost us $100,000."

Sobeloff was shocked. But the persistent Shaw prevailed. Soon, a camping committee comprised of Shaw; Sobeloff; more than a dozen influential Federation members; Barney Smith, Fresh Air President; and his immediate successor, Milton M. Maddin, became passionate champions of the land acquisition. They obtained the needed funding, but with a few conditions.

Tamarack Farms would house the Fresh Air Society's children's camping program, but the property would also be available for use by other agencies serving other age groups. Winterized buildings would allow the Jewish Community Center, schools and other organizations to use the facility year-round. It was an exceptional agreement, and plans to purchase the land moved forward.

No one expected what happened next.

"I went out to inspect the property again and discovered that one corner of the property belonged to another landowner," said Shaw. "It was 20 acres including 15 or 20 feet of lake frontage, which meant that anybody could get on the lake from the other site. The property became worthless."

A man named Oscar Green owned the land. He prudently recognized that his property had suddenly become very valuable. Shaw can't remember the exact amount, but Green asked a very high per-acre price, far more than what the larger landowner, John Binkinz, was getting. Combined, the two prices exceeded the stringently approved

$100,000. Green held steadfast to his price, so Shaw and his allies appealed to Binkinz to intervene on their behalf. In the end, after many hours of haggling and negotiations, both men came down in their price and an agreement to purchase both lots for the budgeted $100,000 was reached.

Late one March afternoon, Shaw drove out to Pontiac to meet Green and sign the final papers. "Something told me I had better go on Thursday," recalled Shaw. "Green had made the deal, but all of a sudden he wanted to back out. The purchase agreement expired on Friday, and the transfer of property had to be registered with the county." Green reluctantly signed the papers and Shaw drove to the county office. "The weather got terrible. I barely got to the office in time. The snow fell and fell and fell. By that night, all the roads were closed. If I waited until the next day, I would have never made it. Green wouldn't have signed and we never would have acquired Ortonville."

And, so it was that Fresh Air Camp became a two camp family with a baby sister in Ortonville.

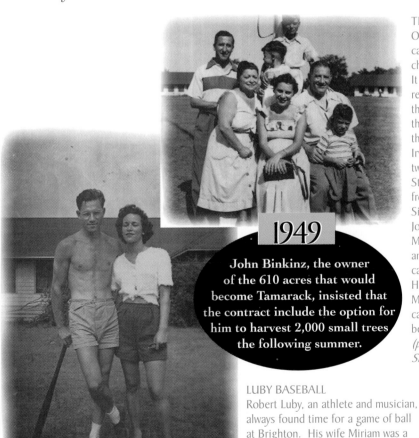

1949

John Binkinz, the owner of the 610 acres that would become Tamarack, insisted that the contract include the option for him to harvest 2,000 small trees the following summer.

THE LASH FAMILY
On Sundays, parents came to pick up their children from camp. It was always a happy reunion. Here are three generations of the Lash family. From the left, top row, Irving Lash and his two sons Harvey and Steven. Bottom row from left, Masha Simkovitz, Rose Lash, Joe Simkovitz and Mickey Lash. Rose and Irving were campers in the 20s. Harvey, Steven and Mickey were all campers and later became counselors. *(photo courtesy of Steve Lash)*

LUBY BASEBALL
Robert Luby, an athlete and musician, always found time for a game of ball at Brighton. His wife Miriam was a counselor before they married. *(photo courtesy of Robert Luby)*

Songs of Fresh Air Camp

Not an hour goes by when someone, somewhere at camp isn't singing.
Camp and singing and song.
The words are synonymous.
Here is a tiny sampling of songs from over time:

Village Songs and Chants

1915: (from A.J. Levin)
Hurrah for Fresh Air Camp
Hurrah for its joys,
Now all together –
Let us make a great big Noise.

Oh, the poor Detroit kids,
They sure are hot,
Three cheers for our camp,
We sure are not.

■

1930s:
(Tune of Gloworm)
We are the girls of Fresh Air College
All we do is gather knowledge
Eat gefilte fish and knaidlach
Don't you think we're Kosher maidlach?

When we graduate we will marry
Izzi, Ikey, Jakey, Harry
Don't you think we're grand?
We're the girls of Fresh Air Camp.

■

1934:
(Tune of Flying Trapeze)
We came to Fresh Air Camp in search of some fun
To better our health and to play in the sun
The meals they are swell, the counselors are fine
The swimming is right in our line.

THE FRESH AIR GOAT

The Fresh Air Goat was feeling fine – ate three red
shirts right off the line,
A boy named Jack gave him a whack and tied him to
a railroad track.
And when the train came roaring by that Fresh Air
goat was DOOMED to die,
He gave three shrieks of awful pain, coughed up
those shirts and flagged the train.

■

LEVISON (1970s)
(Tune of Green Acres)
Camp Tamarack is the place to be
Levison Village is the place for me
I just adore a balcony view
Keep suburbia just give me that countryside.

■

SHERUTH VILLAGE
Sheruth girls are full of fun
We're the ones that get things done
(da da da da)
We're the best in all of Tamarack
We swim with ease
The boys we please
Every job is just a breeze
(da da da da)
We're the best in all of Tamarack

Our spirits never dwindle
Our friendships are so true
A special light is kindled
And Levinson thinks so too, wooo, woo!

BERMAN

Are you from Berman?
Are you from Berman?
From the home we love on top of the hill
So glad to see ya', So glad to see ya,
'cuz we always give you a thrill
If you're from DeRoy, Levison, Hermelin or Pioneer
The Bermis will take care of you so have no fear
Let's give a cheer now, let's have a cheer now
'cuz we're from Berman tooooo
B-E-R uh M-A-N uh
Berman, Berman, yeahhhhh, Berman

L&M, L&M, L&Mdiago, Sandiego, Ishka pishka , hit them in the kishka.
Cod, liver, mustard, relish, this is what we yell-Goooo Berman!!!

■

THE EUPHORIA CAMP

Written by Steve Guggenheim 1981
(Tune of The Irish Washerwomen)

When the sun goes down low and mosquitoes are feasting
On campers and staffers all covered with bee stings
We'll build up our fires and not mind the least thing
Because we are from the Euphoria Camp.

So what if our pancakes can be somewhat greasy
U4EA campers will never get queasy
We'll pitch up our tents and make it look easy
Because we are from the Euphoria Camp.

No, if you're from Dorm 4 or one of the rest
And you think your camp group is really the best
We'll laugh for the truth is, if put to the test
Someday you will come from Euphoria Camp.

■

MODELL 1987

(Tune of My Girl)
We got sunshine
Every single day
No matter rain or shine
You'll be sure to stay – cause

We're from Modell
The village that you know so well
Modell…Modell…Modell
Talking 'bout Modell…MODELL

We have good times
The whole summer long
When we're just playing sports
Or if we're singing songs, cause…
(chorus)

We've got Flatbed
And he runs the show
And the Berman girls
they all love us so, cause
(chorus)

■

PIONEER SONG

Pioneer, Pioneer
There is nothing in this world that we fear
We are brave and strong
We can do no wrong
We're the leaders of the camp called Pioneer

So give a cheer….for Pioneer
Maybe someday the bugs will disappear
We're a fearless band
Under our own command
And so living here is great in Pioneer
P I O N double E R
Pioneer is the best by far
(chorus)

Pioneer!
Pioneer, the best of all the rest
Pioneer, we're better than the best
Pioneer, the bugs are really thick
Pioneer, camp food just makes us sick.

We all live way out back
In a camp called Tamarack
(chorus)

P uh I uh O uh N uh E what? E uh R uh Pioneer!

Folk and Hebrew Songs

MORNING SONGS (1940s)

Father, we thank Thee for the night,
And for the blessed morning light,
For rest and food and loving care,
And all that makes this world so fair.

Help us to do the things we should,
To be to others kind and good,
In all we do in work or play,
To grow more loving every day.

NOT BY MIGHT

Not by might and not by power
By spirit alone shall we all live in peace
The Children sing, the children dream
And their tears may fall
You can hear them call
And another song will rise (3X)
(Repeat chorus 5X)

Not by might and not by power
Shalom

BLOWING IN THE WIND
©Bob Dylan

How many roads must a man walk down
Before they call him a man?
How many seas can a white dove sail
Before she sleeps in the sand?
How many times must the cannon balls fly
Before they're forever banned?

The answer my friend is blowing in the wind
The answer is blowing in the wind.

How many years can a mountain exist
Before it is washed to the sea?
How many years must a people exist
Before they're allowed to be free?
How many times can a man turn his head
And pretend that he just doesn't see?
The answer my friend is blowing in the wind
The answer is blowing in the wind.
How many times must a man look up
Before he can see the sky?
How many years must one man have
Before he can hear people cry?

How many deaths will it take till he knows
That too many people have died?
The answer my friend is blowing in the wind
The answer is blowing in the wind.

MIRIAM'S SONG (late 1990s)
©1988 Deborah Lynn Friedman

Chorus:
And the women dancing with their timbrels
Followed Miriam as she sang her song
Sing a song to the One whom we've exalted
Miriam and the women danced and danced the whole
night long

And Miriam was a weaver of unique variety
The tapestry she wove was one which sang our history
With every strand and every thread she crafted
her delight
A woman touched with spirit, she dances
toward the light
(chorus)

And when Miriam stood upon the shores and gazed
across the sea
The wonder of this miracle she soon came to believe
Whoever thought the sea would part with an out-
stretched hand?
And we would pass to freedom and march to the
promised land.
(chorus)

And Miram the prophet took her timbrel in her hand
And all the women followed her just as she had
planned
And Miriam raised her voice in song she sang with
praise and might
"We've just lived through a miracle, we're going to
dance tonight."
(chorus)

IM TIRZU

Im Tirzu (2 times)
Ayn zo agadah (2 times)
Lih'yot am chofshi b'artzeinu
B'e—retz, tzi—on V'rushalayim

If you will it, it is no legend
To be a free people in our land
in Zion and Jerusalem

LEAVING ON A TAMARACK BUS
(Tune of Leaving on a Jet Plane)

Well the summer's over and It's time to go
The leaves are falling and the sessions flown
It seems so soon for us to say goodbye
But our bags are packed and we're ready to go
We're standing here outside our bunk
Already we're so lonesome we could cry.

Chorus:
So kiss me and write to us
Tell us you'll be back with us
Camp Memories will never let you go
Cause you're leaving on a Tamarack bus
Don't know when you'll be back with us
Oh campers, please don't go.

Arts and crafts and swimming too
Sports and trips to name a few
Treasures now – always to remain
Everyplace we go we'll think of you
Till you come back things won't be the same
(Chorus)

Now it's time for you to leave us
Friendships made we'll carry with us
One last thing and you'll be on your way
Dream about the things to come
And the things we've done
Goodbyes are always hard for us to say
(Chorus)

■

BOI KALLA
Boi kalla boi kalla
Boi kalla, boi kalla (2 times)
    L'cha dodi likrat kalla
    P'ney Shabbat n'ka-bla (2 times)
Boi kalla, (2times)

*Enter, O Bride! Beloved, come to meet
the bride; beloved come to greet the Shabbat.*

■

TAPS
Day is done, gone the sun
From the lakes, from the hills, from the sky.
All is well, safely rest,
God is nigh.

TWISTED CANDLE
The twisted candle brightens our hearts
As together we watch the Sabbath depart
We smell the spices and taste the wine
As the stars in the sky begin to shine.

Chorus:
Shavua Tov may you have a good week
May you find the happiness you seek
Shavua Tov may your week be fine
May it be as sweet as the Sabbath wine.

We say goodbye to a special friend
As another Shabbat has come to an end.
Shavua Tov are the words we speak
To say, May you have a happy week.
(Chorus)

■

LO YISA GOY
Ai---- Oh ---- Oh ---- Ai

Lo yisa goy el goy cherev
Lo yisa goy el milchama

Don't walk in front of me I may not follow
Don't walk behind me I may not lead
Just stand behind me and be my friend
Together we will stand in Jerusalem.

*Nation shall not lift up sword against nation.
Nor ever again shall they study of war*

■

HINEI RAKEVET
Chug chug chug chug chug chug chug chug
Chug chug chug chug

Ding a ling toot toot Ding a ling toot toot
Ding a ling toot toot Ding a ling toot toot

Hi-nei re-ke-vet she-mis-to-ve-et
Al gal-ga-lim al gal-ga-lim al gal-ga-lim toot toot

Here is a train which goes around on wheels

Barbara Littky
Fresh air Camp
Brighton Mich

THIS SIDE OF CARD IS FOR ADDRESS

Mr. & Mrs. Littky
18237 Littlefield
Detroit 21, Mich.

Dear Mother
I want you
to write me
or I will not
write you.
we had liver
for lunch today

I LOVE you

BARBARA
ANN

1940

"The amount of singing and
enthusiasm was very great"
Asher Tilchin

"When you got there, you had
the feeling that you were safe,
you were home." Irving Berg

"I spent the happiest days of my life at camp, especially as a kid." Lee Henkin

"In our eyes Fresh Air Camp was … was putting on the Ritz! Just the best." Marvin Littky

1940's

"We had wonderful campfires. And we would walk along back roads to eat our picnic." Robert Luby

TWO PLACES
TO CALL HOME

1954

1950-1965

*"Camp is where an immigrant kid became Americanized. It was
the place of equalization. It was away from our parents who
were Old World. We could really learn American ways and make
friends, which for an immigrant, is the greatest challenge."*

Barbara Steinmetz (Bandler)
1950s camper who emigrated from Hungary in 1945

If an aerial camera snapped a photograph of Fresh Air's new Ortonville property on a summer day in 1950, the virgin acres of deep-green tree tops and fields of wildflowers and grass would have been broken only by a narrow dirt path that wound through its middle, two lakes – one clear and large, the other smaller and murky green – and a cottage or two on the outskirts of the property.

Serene and quiet, Ortonville was ready, patiently awaiting its new occupants. Slowly, they came. Senior Brighton campers used Ortonville as an outpost declaring a barren field as their base. Irwin Shaw organized a work camp for boys ages 15 to 17 who came ready to work and prepare the grounds for the coming cabins and villages. In 1951, a small group of senior girls spent a few weeks in one of the cottages and in 1953...

"We called ourselves the Un-Holy Six,"[1] recalled Beverly Salasnek (Abel). Ortonville's first counselors, a group of six inexperienced college students in charge of 42 campers, lived in newly built cabins that, one year later, would be dubbed DeRoy Village. "We had no more business being there than the man in the moon,"[2] remembered another of the six, Lenore Rosa (Rhinestone). "But we all had fun."

Bunks traded turns handling various chores while each counselor accepted responsibility for a different aspect of programming. Lenore tackled arts and crafts while Beverly supervised the sports department. Despite their lack of wilderness training, the crew created a wonderful summer experience for their campers. On Wednesdays, they had some extra help.

Each week outpost campers, their counselors and food supplies for the girls, were bussed in from Brighton. Henry "Hank" Baskin, then a 19-year-old college student in charge of Dorm Four, rode along. "Every Wednesday we had to drive up U.S. 23 to Fenton and over to this new thing called Tamarack,"[3] began Baskin. "The camp was peopled by women that first year. The administration decided that they would have to truck some guys over there. So we'd go over and have social evenings, forced social evenings."

Forced maybe, but the gang clearly enjoyed themselves. Pasted into Salasnek's scrapbook, preserved forever, rests a little rhyme the girls dreamed up, "Sunday – frustration; Monday – aggravation; Tuesday – anticipation; Wednesday – men; Thursday – can't get up in the a.m.!"

THE UN-HOLY SIX, 1953: Cool, calm and collected this veritable group of college freshmen await a bus ride from Brighton to Ortonville. They called themselves the Un-Holy Six, and at age 18, were the first counselors at the newly opened Camp Tamarack. L to R: Nina (last name unknown), Beverly Abel, Phyllis Koppelman, Shana Geller, Marilyn Borin, Lenore Rhinestone. *(photo courtesy of Beverly Salasnek)*

1953

A mail-in registration system was implemented, eliminating long, frustrating registration lines.

Baby Boomers Come to Camp

Camp administrators did not have to fret – too much – over the interactions of the Un-Holy Six and their male visitors. After all, it was the 50s, the very end of the age of innocence and the beginning of the age of Rock 'n Roll. It was a time when clean-shaven young men and neatly primped young women could sit around a campfire, hold hands and quietly steal away into the woods to passionately exchange kisses. No one had to worry about drugs or alcohol, sexual harassment or birth control. It was the dawning of the age of blue jeans and poodle skirts, and when color television sets dotted the living rooms of a fortunate few.

At the start of the decade, most campers and staff lived in the Dexter-Davison area, although the population shift away from the "old neighborhood" and into the new was underway. Northwest Detroit, the area that spanned 6 Mile Road to 8 Mile Road and Livernois west to Evergreen, was quickly developing as the new center of Jewish life. By 1958, 62 percent of Detroit's Jewish families lived in Northwest Detroit, while just a few had discovered Oak Park.[4]

Parents could send their child to Fresh Air Camp for $25 per week. Less than half paid the full fee, easily qualifying for reduced

ORTONVILLE'S FIRST RESIDENTS
In 1951, the very first summer that the Ortonville property belonged to Fresh Air Society, a group of female campers came and lived in a cottage on the property. Pictured here is Lenore Altman.
(photo courtesy of Barbara Steinmetz)

fees or full scholarships. Campers didn't have to pack much: a suitcase, shorts and slacks, and rain boots. Luxuries were few, a pair of long underwear which cost around $1.44, a 5 cent box of Luden's Cough Drops or, the most coveted possession, comic books.

"The big thing was not music back then. Comic books were a huge, huge thing," reminisced Barbara Steinmetz (Bandler). Steinmetz arrived in America in 1945 from Hungary. Like many young immigrants, she learned the English language courtesy of "Archie and The Gang," "Captain Marvel," "The Vault of Horror" and "Wonder Woman." In 1951, Steinmetz was

MAINTENANCE MEN

Sam Marcus swears that Camp Tamarack would never have been able to succeed without the maintenance men. Under the direction of Allan Brown, they built nearly every building on the property and could "stretch a dollar into $1.25." Some of the men were provided with a home located around the perimeter of Ortonville, then doubled as camp's own security team, constantly vigilant against intruders, fire and other hazards. "They had a stake in the camp. The people of the community knew we were tough. We had children to protect," said Marcus.

one of the senior campers to live in the Ortonville cottage. "At rest time everyone would pull out their comics. There was no scheduling because there were no organized activities. We were 14. At that age, there was nothing we liked better than just hangin' out…reading, talking, taking hikes and swims."[5]

Early Ortonville

Irwin Shaw instinctively knew how Ortonville would function and how it would look. Twelve self-contained villages scattered idyllically throughout the woods, a dirt road connecting them all. Within every village was a central meeting place, a family room of sorts, where villagers would come together for meals and special activities. Children slept on small cots, facing each other head to toe. Those same cots would later be converted to bunk beds and were still used well into the 1990s.

Where Brighton had a central flagpole and pre-printed activity sheets, Ortonville had an industrial kitchen and late night planning meetings. Bellowing choruses of the *motzi* were replaced with quiet chants in the lodges. The bunk was the family, the village the community.

1953

Second session: 55 children arrived with elevated temperatures and infected throats. Third session: A record 150 children arrived with fevers and sore throats. That summer, one of the major camp activities was the twice-daily clinic call.

"At Tamarack things changed," explained Morris "Moishe" Last, a counselor and song leader who taught dozens of young campers to strum the guitar. "Suddenly, counselors were programming based on their own original ideas and the kids' abilities and limitations. If the counselor wanted to plan an Indian day, then the arts and crafts directors would assist by helping build drums from logs, or the program director would help plan the music."[6]

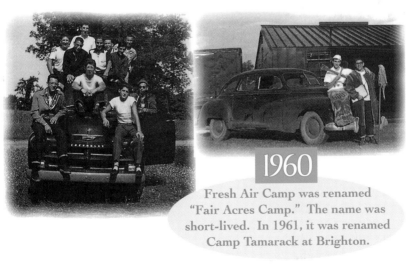

1960

Fresh Air Camp was renamed "Fair Acres Camp." The name was short-lived. In 1961, it was renamed Camp Tamarack at Brighton.

MOB MOBILE Brothers Myles (seated) and Steve Lash both worked in the kitchen during the early 1960s. The kitchen crew delivered three meals a day, washed the dishes and, in between, jumped into the Mob Mobile, a 1948 Dodge Hydromatic. The unlicensed vehicle was used to escort the crew around camp and, as Myles Lash recalled, it was always a fun challenge to see who would be among the eight lucky occupants in the car. *(right photo courtesy of Myles and Linda Lash)*

Sam Marcus

Slowly, like a late summer sunset, Camp Tamarack transformed itself into a living, thriving camping community. It was a massive undertaking. Sewage treatment, water, electricity, communications, roads, living quarters and support services all had to be developed while preserving ecological and natural settings. A devoted team nurtured the process: Irwin Shaw, of course; a sharp New Yorker named Sam Marcus and the Tamarack Hills Authority.

Like Irwin Shaw, Sam Marcus found the idea of the decentralized camp invigorating. A camper in his youth, Marcus came to Detroit as a social worker in 1949. He rose through the ranks of the Jewish Community Center (JCC) and by the time Ortonville was purchased, Marcus had become the JCC day camp director. At the same time, in 1951, Irwin Shaw became executive director of the JCC, overseeing both agencies. Although Sam Marcus was Shaw's employee, he quickly became his peer.

By 1953, an additional 124 acres of Ortonville property had been acquired. The task of managing the construction and maintenance of the campsite, raising the capital needed to sustain the growth, accumulating additional property and coordinating usage of the land by various agencies was put into the hands of a special committee created by the Jewish Federation. The Tamarack Hills Authority was an influential group of Jewish leaders including Nathan Silverman, Milton Maddin, Bert Smokler and others. The committee had one employee, Sam Marcus, and operated with its own budget, its own agenda and very little red tape impeding its progress.

CANOEING ON KENSINGTON
For years, camp canoe trips were taken along the Huron River. While looking for a larger camp facility in the late 1940s, Irwin Shaw discovered the newly opened Kensington Park had ideal base camp facilities. Immediately, campers began taking longer overnight canoe trips, setting up tents at Kensington.

BRIGHTON DORM FOUR 1951 or 1952
Home to the older Brighton campers, Dorm Four became a very special place for counselor Henry Baskin. Many of the kids were new immigrants and could only speak Yiddish. "At the end of each 10-week period, we would be just exhausted and swore we would never go back. By mid-winter, we were ready to go back again," remembered Baskin. *(photo courtesy of Henry Baskin)*

The Not Quite Perfect Food System

Key to the individual village concept was the decentralized food system. In 1953, a 60-foot-long "temporary" food factory was built. Intended to handle only three or four villages, the kitchen ultimately remained in service for more than 20 years. Three times a day, "kosher-style" meals were prepared, packed in vacuum containers and shipped to the villages along with the appropriate dishes and tableware. It was a massive operation.

"The food service was difficult," grimaced Marcus as he recalled the countless times one village was shorted while another received too much. "The instructions were, you put in more than they need, because you don't want them to be short. If you put it in too hot, it would continue to cook. You didn't want that, so you had to try to get your food to undercook a little bit,"[7] he said. Some foods shipped better than others, prompting various adjustments. Soggy toast, for example, led to the purchase of toasters for each village.

"It was a mind boggling operation,"[8] attested Steve Lash, who worked in and managed the Ortonville kitchen between 1959 and 1965. "You'd be working on lunch and dinner at the same time. We'd serve up to 80 tables of 10 people!

"You had to fill up a truck, packed. It would start at Kfar Ivri, then to Pioneer, then back up to Berman, up to Sheruth, down to Fishman and down to DeRoy all in about 30 minutes so everyone could start eating at the same time. Then we'd pick up everything, get it back to the kitchen, wash it and start it all over again," said Lash.

The kitchen staff lived a life much different than those they fed. "We were much freer than the counseling staff," recalled Myles "Mickey" Lash, Steve's older brother. "We were more roguish and we played the role up quite well."[9]

"Can you imagine being 16 years old and being on our own!" said Steve, who claims to have been the fastest egg cracker in Tamarack history. "We had our own lunchroom that sat 20, our own bunk house and we could come and go as we please." Inevitably, their free time was spent around the girls. Both Lash brothers nourished lifelong camp romances.

The camp registrar mused, "The process of registration is complicated by the fact that we have two camps and three periods. Getting the right number of girls and boys requires the wisdom of a Solomon." That year a true sliding scale was introduced with all campers required to pay a minimum of $25, as this was the amount the family normally saved when a child was at camp. Exceptions were made for the poor.

MARVELOUS MARV
Marvin Berman, pictured here with pie on his face, began his camp career in 1955 in Ortonville. By 1960 he was program director. He is pictured here with a fellow counselor named Marilyn. Berman was instrumental in camp's development until he left in 1994. *(photo courtesy of Marvin Berman)*

THE BRIGHTON COOKS

Everyone loved Mrs. Mintz, the Brighton bubbie who could cook up a storm. Henry Baskin remembered when, "one night someone came upon 32 pounds of shrimp. We decided to cook the shrimp and have a party in the mess hall. And, we did. We couldn't decide what pots to use, the milk or meat. She found out and was just livid."

DAY HIKES
Many a lazy summer afternoon, campers and
counselors hiked along U.S. 23 to nearby ponds, lakes
and farms. The Fresh Air sign was a welcomed site.

FRIDAY NIGHT CLUB
Dressed in their best, 1957 counselors
(l to r) Henry Baskin, Sam Davis, Barry Elias,
Al Goldberg and Sam Weiner.
(photo courtesy of Henry Baskin)

1961

2,000 tree
seedlings
were planted
on camp
property.

Brighton Becomes Home To The Younger Set

As Ortonville grew, Brighton comfortably settled into its niche
of being home to the younger campers, the seven to ten year olds.
"The significant thing for me as camp director, was how to orient the
younger children," said a soft-spoken Marvin Berman, who started
as a counselor in 1955 and went on to have a 40-year camp career.
"Make sure they felt safe and knew what to do when something
strange happened."

Mention Brighton, and people remember it with a smile. Picnics
on the lawn in front of the dining hall and corn roasts with big
cans of melted butter; the magical transformation of camp on Circus
Day, hikes up U.S. 23 to wild blueberry fields and canoe trips up the Huron
River. And, then there was Blaine Lake. To swim across Blaine Lake was
a milestone every camper dreamed of. "If you got to be a lake swimmer, that
was something," said Barbara Steinmetz, who went on to become captain of
her championship Central High School swim team. Her winning edge, she
claimed, came from her summers on Blaine Lake.

**Ortonville's villages and new buildings took shape
throughout the 1950s.**

DEDICATIONS

Helen L. DeRoy Village 1952
Nathan and Meyer Fishman Village 1954
Sheruth Village 1954
Robert John Maas Memorial Health Lodge 1954
Maurice H. Sobell Waterfront Shelters and Docks 1955
Mina and Theodore Bargman Crafts Building 1956
Julius Berman Village and Lodge 1957
Additional cabins in DeRoy, Fishman and Sheruth 1958
Sidney and Phyllis Allen Amphitheater 1958
Joseph G. Mahler Trip Center 1959
Sheruth Athletic Fields 1959
Emanuel M. Rosenthal Nature Shelter 1960

Brighton's greatest charm, however, was the innocence of its young campers. Every summer at least one youngster would get the ingenious idea of hanging an undergarment on the flagpole or trying to climb the *verboten* water tower. Frogs often ended up in shoes, snakes in the beds, or beds with snakes in them relocated to the middle of the campground.

"I guess the worst thing you could do back then was sneak out of the bunk," confessed Carol Lash (Stutz). She was a Brighton camper back in 1953. "We just didn't do much to cause trouble." Ten years later, Carol returned as an Ortonville counselor. This time, she didn't have to sneak out of her bunk, she strolled out to meet her beau, the young egg-crackin' cook, Steve Lash. The pair tied the knot in 1966.

Henry Baskin recalled the time when Dorm Four counselors conducted their own biology lesson. "We would collect these Mississauga Rattlers with butterfly nets. Being cold blooded, they would come out to warm up. Our beds were high up and we would put them on the floor and taunt them to see what we could find out about the venom. Bob Luby walked in one day and thought we were absolutely insane."

Robert Luby was Brighton's director from 1952 until 1955. Among his favorite Brighton traditions were the Color Wars. The camp would be divided into four teams, each wearing its own color. "We would have competitions…athletic contests, volleyball, softball, soccer, touch football, swimming events and canoe races. We would play fast-moving, fun games and egg toss and mock wrestling." As the day wound down, teams would huddle together to create a celebratory song, chant or "yell." Later, they all gathered around the campfire to perform their innovations – each group trying to outshout, out-yell or out-sing the other.

QUEEN FOR A DAY Maureen Schiffman (Greenwald) (l) came to Brighton in 1959 as an 8-year-old, continuing until she was 12. At camp she discovered her knack for making children laugh when she won the honor of "Queen for a Day." In 1997, she reflected on her winning presentation. "My sob story (to the judges) involved me talking with a funny voice while making a goofy face the whole time on stage. The judges liked my silly antics more than my story." As an adult, Maureen came back to camp, to entertain children with her puppets. She is pictured with her friend Eddie Elson. *(photo courtesy of Maureen Schiffman)*

DEAR MOM AND DAD...

"I arrived at camp. How is Jane? How is Bobbie? Tell Mother to stop crying. Dot"

"I am having fun. Come take me home. Joan"

"Your worries are over. I am really growing up.
I'm in a tent with older girls and all we
talk about is boys and sex.
Please send me a water pistol…"

THE
SIDNEY J. ALLEN
AMPHITHEATER
When it was decided
to construct an
open-air auditorium
for camp gatherings,
Sam Marcus
envisioned a serene
water-side location.
The idea was
rejected. Instead, the
Allen Amphitheater
was nestled in a
clearing by the
woods. Designed
by Louis Redstone,
Marcus monitored
the 1958 building
project. "I remember
the poison sumac
that was all around.
The workers got so
ill some had to go
to the hospital." The
acoustics were per-
fect, remembered
Marcus. "We never
used the micro-
phones and speakers
we installed."

My Camp Is Better Than Your Camp

For every nail hammered into a new wall or porch in Ortonville,
a smattering of glue or paint was being applied to patch a wall or
floor in Brighton. Despite new bathrooms and hot showers in each
of the Brighton dorms, loveable, old Brighton, like the Velveteen
Rabbit, was no longer the apple of the Fresh Air eye. The discrep-
ancy showed in subtle ways.

"Tamarack counselors were more elite than the Brighton group,"
recalled Baskin, who felt that what
Brighton lacked in amenities, it
more than made up for in
people. "They had more
land, better facilities…
but we had a nice little
spread. Four dorms,
the administration
building, recreation
hall, little nature
huts and what not.
It was a perfect
place."

Marshall Hersh,
who started his camp
career in 1957 as a CIT,
and ultimately became the
Assistant Director of Ortonville

BED WETTERS

Every year there are campers who, for one
reason or another, have to be awakened at night
and taken to the bathroom. They are dubbed the
'bed wetters' and these 1950s and 60s counselors had
a myriad of ways of assisting them.

"Our bunk arrangements were…you put the bed wetter next
to the pyromaniac." *Aaron Goren*

"We had to walk the bed wetters at night. We'd listen to their
problems, talk to them one-on-one about their unhappiness
and their fears, why they were having nightmares and why
they couldn't sleep." *Henry Baskin*

"You put them in front of the urinal. You would say
to them, now sink the submarine, then they
would go. They never remembered."
Moishe Last

in 1971, felt the rivalry showed up in counselor attitudes, especially when the two camps would compete in a rousing game of softball. "It was not an open rivalry. They would come to visit us, or we would go to Brighton to visit them. They said we were looking down upon them, we said they were looking down upon us."[10]

There was a far greater rivalry, however: the one that existed between Fresh Air Camp and its private camp competitors.

In November 1964, a tersely worded telegram was sent to Fresh Air Society president, Peter Shifrin, M.D. Ten private Michigan camps, all catering to Jewish children, expressed their concern over Fresh Air Camp's deficit-supported, non-profit status. Specifically, the telegram stated, "We feel that the present fee structure … subsidizes camping for children who could well afford tuition fees in line with actual costs. While we are in hearty agreement that camping should not become 'class camping' only for the disadvantaged we do believe that reexamination of present policy is in order."[11]

At the time, Fresh Air rates began at $115 and increased to $170 for a three-week session, depending on the family's ability to pay. Comparatively, the private camps were charging between $575 and $650 per eight-week session.

The two groups met. The private camp owners accused Fresh Air of creating a dynasty that threatened their existence. They wanted Fresh Air Society's tax-exempt status revoked and accused the camp of accepting higher income families in preference to the indigent. They urged Fresh Air to increase fees or refuse to accept families whose income exceeded $15,000 annually. The Fresh Air committee put up a sensible counter. They pointed out that the number of private camps had increased by 50 percent at a time when families were spreading to the suburbs and taking advantage of country club memberships. They also cited a large increase in the number of day camps and families taking their own vacations. Fresh Air recommended that the private camps examine their own program offerings and facilities before blaming Camp Tamarack.

The tension between the two groups simmered for some 20 years. By the 70s, the private camps were booming and it would not be until the mid-1990s, that Fresh Air Camp would once again directly compete with the private camps.

1962

Where campers lived: 947 lived in various Detroit zip codes (56% of total); 513 Oak Park; 72 Huntington Woods; 64 Southfield; 43 Livonia; 27 Birmingham. More than 120 program staff and counselors worked at camp that summer.

RATTLESNAKES AROUND THE FLAGPOLE Although their bite was harmless, Brighton's snakes rattled a few. Morris Last remembered the morning when Al Tendler (pictured), slowly dragging along behind his campers on their way to the flagpole, suddenly screamed. "Everyone looked back and saw Al being attacked by a rattlesnake. No one had stepped on it, no one had seen it, but somehow the snake found Al. You think of 50 people walking over the same area, and it picks Al! He got duped for that the rest of camp." (photo courtesy of Barbara Steinmetz)

Kfar Ivri and Pioneer Village
Create An Expanded Attraction

As the 1960s got underway, Jewish life in America was beginning to undergo a revolutionary change. Intermarriage rates and divorce rates began increasing dramatically, while the number of Jewish families affiliated with a synagogue began to decrease. Suddenly, there developed an intense interest in strengthening Jewish culture at camp and teaching Israeli life and rituals. Jewish programming became as important as nature lore. The goal, said Gail Gales, camper, counselor, supervisor and later, Jewish program director, was to "make kids feel very positive about Judaism, positive about their roles in society as Jews. We helped kids know that religion is not a spectator sport. It was a more open way to celebrate Judaism, to celebrate with music, song and drama."[12]

Camp could not only develop a sense of one's heritage, it could also teach it. That was the idea behind the United Hebrew Schools' (UHS) proposal to create a special unit where campers would live and play in an entirely Hebrew atmosphere. In 1963, Kfar Ivri, the Hebrew Village, opened.

The first group, 28 boys and girls between the ages of 13 and 16, selected from the UHS student body, attended a four-week session. They slept in tents, ate in a newly built lodge and had their own bath house. A staff of four counselors, a supervisor, a cook and dishwasher completed the unit. Later, as the program grew, cabins, more staff and facilities were added. Kfar Ivri, completely Kashruth, was an idyllic setting for the Hebrew immersion. Campers acquired fluent Hebrew conversational skills, studied the bible and debated contemporary Israeli issues. They participated in daily and Sabbath services, davenned every morning and swam every afternoon. Kfar Ivri operated until 1987.

At the same time, Jewish lead-

STINKY BOYS!

Gail Gales recalled the night in 1964 or 1965, she and her fellow junior counselors sneaked into the empty boys' junior counselor and service staff bunk. The girls hid under the beds, anxious to anonymously observe the chaps. Unaware of the intruders, the boys returned, jumped into their beds for lights out and promptly initiated a "farting" contest. Unable to contain their own giggling and gagging, the girls dashed for the door. The chase that ensued lasted long into the night.

THE WATER BALLET 1958 The Brighton senior side male staff performed annually for campers in their own version of the Nutcracker Ballet. The laughable event was always followed with a festive party. *(photo courtesy of Marvin Berman)*

ers noticed that there were no organized summer teen activities. Tamarack's Pioneer units were created to fill this void. The first Pioneer unit, in 1959, was strictly for girls. One year later, a boys' unit was added. Pioneer campers, ages 13 to 15, were treated to expanded overnights and fewer tethers to the organized camp life. They cooked meals over an open fire, worked on long-term conservation projects and had their own waterfront, the Alvin M. Rodecker Beach. Dave Eason, in 1960, supervised the first boys' Pioneer unit. He recalled nude nighttime swims and the closeness of the group. "Every night, we had a quiet time when we'd have a 'good and welfare of the house.' Everyone sat around and said what was on his mind and we talked about it as a group. It was a very nice time," he said.

The Pioneer units were just the beginning of the trend toward special programming for older campers. In stark contrast to the "Leave It To Beaver" era, the late 1960s became a time of tremendous *tumult*, and teens were at its center. Determined to pave their own way, young adults found that rebellion gave them a voice and their voice could effect change.

The hippies were about to arrive at camp.

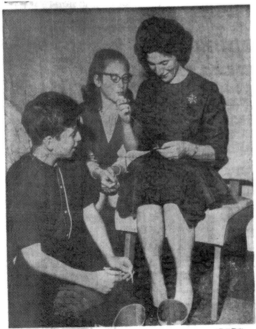

THERE'S MORE to sending children off to camp than a kiss and a knapsack. One of the jobs that Mrs. Samuel Chapin started well in advance was name tagging for both her children. Neil leaves June 28 and Elise on July 14.

DETROIT NEWS CLIP
Mrs. Samuel Chapin, Anna, was more than mother to these two eager campers, she was also a loyal camp patriot. President of the Sheruth League, the women's service organization that adopted Fresh Air Society, and employed at the Jewish Federation for 25 years, Chapin harbored a deep love for the Fresh Air Society, serving on its board for more than 20 years.

 1963

An additional 97 acres were purchased from landowner, Oscar Green, for a price of $23,625. The plot became known as the Newlands, the site of many future camp adventures.

 1963

153,000 meals were served, 102,000 cookies were baked, 575 campers mastered beginning swim tests, and 33,084 quarts of milk were drunk.

From The Heart

Benard Maas

"When you save a soul,
you save the world."

Mishna Sanhedrin 4:5

Every gift to Fresh Air Camps – no matter what size or form – touches campers in some way. The smile plastered across the face of a camper eating a cookie delivered by Eugene Sloman 90 years ago is just as big as that of a 2001 Silverman Village camper playing with the sports equipment donated by the Women's Division of Jewish Federation. The $25 a family donates toward a scholarship brings the same joy as did Benard Maas' $1 million dollar bequest.

Generous benefactors enabled streetcars to be chartered and picnic baskets to be packed in the 1900s. The United Jewish Charities (Jewish Federation of Metropolitan Detroit) took the Fresh Air Society as one of its own in 1904, launching a nearly 100-year-old relationship between two of Detroit's oldest Jewish agencies. Since then, Federation has funded deficits, enabled land purchases and helped raise the millions of dollars needed to run the camp and provide summer camping experiences to children who could not otherwise afford them.

In 1927, Mr. and Mrs. Edwin Rosenthal donated 55 acres on Blaine Lake. It was Fresh Air's first large donation. In the 1940s and 1950s, two philanthropic organizations, the Montefiore Lodge and the Sheruth League, provided scholarship money for the underprivileged. Montefiore, a fraternal order of about 80 to 100 men and women, maintained a cemetery, supported widows and orphans and chose the Fresh Air Society as one of their primary benefactors. The Sheruth League, a women's service organization, initially funded camp scholarships and eventually directed all of their fundraising efforts toward the Fresh Air Society. They ultimately funded a village in Ortonville.

It was in the 1950s, that a philanthropic mindset changed camp forever. With the purchase of Ortonville, and as more acreage was acquired, the chore of efficiently managing the property and funding its growth was put to the Tamarack Hills Authority, a special committee of the Jewish Federation. Irwin Shaw modeled the committee name after New York's Triborough Bridge Authority, an autonomous organization that raised the money and oversaw the construction of the famous bridge. The Tamarack Hills Authority (THA) was the bridge that connected the Jewish philanthropic community

Charles Agree

Milton Maddin

Helen DeRoy

Nathan Fishman

Smokler Family

to the Fresh Air Society.

The THA was responsible for improving and protecting the property, and providing support for the property's primary tenant, the Fresh Air Society. During the off-season, the THA oversaw the rental of the property by other agencies, ran the outdoor education program and the Butzel Conference Center.

Initially the THA was "an old boys club," a group of prestigious Jewish men, and later women, who had connections. "Federation picked heavy weights. People who could get things done," recalled Lester Burton, THA's third chairperson and a builder who often called upon his own connections to get a roof onto a building or a road paved.

To understand the people connected to the THA, one need only walk around Camp Maas. The children of Nathan and Esther Silverman, THA's second chairperson, endowed Silverman Village. Bert Smokler, one of the original THA board members, and his wife Toba funded numerous programs, buildings and the Smokler Pioneer Skills Village. Milton Mahler funded the equestrian program and Michael Maddin, named the Milton M. Maddin Physical Fitness course in memory of his father's work as THA chairperson during the 1950s. Charles Agree, the committee's first building chairperson, went on to provide the funding for the Agree Outpost in Wawa, Ontario.

It wasn't just the THA members that funded their way to the doorposts of camp. "I went with my little tin cup," joked Burton, sitting in his easy chair 50 years later. He went, like his co-board members, to their peers within the community. "You were always afraid you would be asking for too much," he said seriously. Rarely were they turned down.

For nearly 40 years, the Tamarack Hills Authority dealt with camp's big and little deals. From repairing toilets that refused to flush to flushing a new project with capital, their input and brilliance built the camp.

It wasn't until 1997 that the Fresh Air Society launched its first capital and endowment campaign, a $2.7 million drive, chaired by Jack Robinson. "There was a need to improve the facilities, to bring camp into the 21st century," remarked Edward Lumberg, board president at the time. Six months after it began the committee proudly announced it had raised $4.1 million. The addition of a new multipurpose indoor facility housing a pool and gym, two dining halls, a glatt kosher kitchen and additional endowments were cemented.

Philanthropists give for many reasons. Many, like Burton, are deeply committed to maintaining a Jewish camp. Once they hear the stories of children who have been to camp or see a Havdallah service, their hearts are satisfied. Others endow because they are grateful. Eugene Applebaum, the child of immigrant parents, benefited as a youth from camp. As an adult, he funded a village.

Other gifts come for less obvious reasons. Richard Komer, board president between 1988 and 1991, caught a five-pound bass in 1960 when he was a Brighton counselor. He was the talk of camp that night. Years later, he set up the Harry & Lillian Komer Memorial Fishing Fund to help buy equipment for the camp's fishing program.

There is an old Talmudic story that David Harold, board president 1997 – 2000, loves to tell: An old man was planting a tree when a stranger passing by stops and asks, "Why are you planting this tree? You are not going to be around to see it mature." The old man says, "As my father and grandfather planted for me, I will plant for my sons and grandsons and daughters and granddaughters." Harold believes that all those who give to camp do so because they, like the old man, are "picking up from the past, carrying it forward and laying the seeds of the future."

Jack and Aviva Robinson

Lois Shiffman

Marcia and Eugene Applebaum

Doreen and David Hermelin

Camp Maas (1981)
Benard L. and Rosalyn Maas Recreation Area
Benard L. and Rosalyn Maas
Specialty Village (1997)

In 1981, Benard Maas, an auto industrialist, pledged $1.5 million to Fresh Air Society. A grateful community renamed the property the Benard L. and Rosalyn J. Maas Recreation Area and the camp, Camp Maas. The gift was the culmination of the couple's long history of generously supporting camp. In 1954, after the death of their eight-year-old son, the Maas family devoted themselves to helping children's organizations. Fresh Air became one of their favorites. The Maas's provided the funds to construct the John Maas Memorial Health Lodge and later its renovation. They also endowed a Scholar-in-Residence program and the naming of Maas Specialty Village. Mr. Maas was often at camp, showing delight in the many children who bestowed upon him big, heartfelt and thankful smiles.

The Villages and the Facilities

Helen L. DeRoy Village (1954)
Rodecker Beach (1961)

Mrs. Helen L. DeRoy, wife of automotive magnate Aaron, generously bestowed camp with her time, money and visions. The Tamarack Hills Authority honored her devotion by naming the camp's first village after her. She donated $10,000 toward the winterized village's construction that became home to 4th and 5th grade boys. In 1961, Mrs. DeRoy provided funds for the construction of Rodecker Beach in honor of her nephew, Alvin M. Rodecker. Mrs. DeRoy died in 1977. Alvin's son, Arthur, continues to support camp, the upkeep and upgrading of the beach.

Nathan and Meyer Fishman Village (1955)

These two brothers emigrated from the Soviet Union in 1920 and quickly began to build an American legacy. Their small garage housed their fledgling hardware business that eventually grew into Star Steel Supply. They provided the funds for this winterized village, home to 4th and 5th grade girls. Nathan Fishman served on the board of directors from 1955-57 and died in 1985. His brother Meyer died in 1992.

Julius Berman Village (1957)

On the occasion of his 75th birthday, the family of Julius Berman: Mr. and Mrs. Bert Smokler, Mr. and Mrs. Mildred Pregerson and Mr. and Mrs. Mandell Berman, named this village in his honor. Julius Berman was a well-known real estate developer and community leader. The village is the summer residence of 7th and 8th grade girls and in the winter is used for retreats and school camping.

Sheruth Village (1954)

The Sheruth Women's League was formed in 1944 with its primary purpose to help underprivileged children come to camp. In its heyday, nearly 200 women volunteered for the organization that gave countless gifts to the Fresh Air Society and its campers. Sheruth Village is winterized for year-round use and in the summer is home to 6th grade girls.

Sydney, Robert and Sharon
Levison Village (1965)

The Tamarack Hills Authority worked with many philanthropic Jewish residents and convinced them that their Fresh Air Society donations would be a *mitzvah* in every sense of the word. Levison Village was named in honor of three generations of Levisons: Sydney G., founder, president and chairman of Michigan Typesetting and Printing Company, his son, Robert, and Robert's daughter, Sharon. Levison Village is home to 6th grade boys.

Theodore and Mina Bargman
Arts and Crafts Program (1960s)
Theodore and Mina Bargman Staff Housing;
Hiking and Tripping Program (1997)

A childless couple, the Bargmans directed their philanthropic gifts toward organizations that were important to the community. Their first gift, in 1961, enabled camp to purchase a 10-foot trailer for use on Teen Travel trips. By the end of the decade, both Theodore and Mina had passed away. As Trustee of the estate, attorney Joseph Jackier continued to support programs that had interested the couple. Fresh Air Camp's arts and crafts programs, hiking and tripping programs and sports fields have benefited from the continued support of the Bargman Foundation, currently under the direction of Larry Jackier.

Nathan and Esther Silverman Village (1972)

One of the most active chairpersons of the Tamarack Hills Authority, Nathan Silverman often came to camp with Sam Marcus to discuss the design and construction needs of the growing campsite. Silverman Village is home to approximately 100 emotionally impaired children each summer. This village was named in their parent's honor by their children: Mr. and Mrs. Gil Silverman, Mr. and Mrs. Jack Alspector and Mrs. and Mrs. Joel Herschman.

Shirley Harris Barnett Staff Recreation and Mass Media Building (1990)

The children of Mrs. Barnett, a 1950s board member, chose to honor their mother and father's 40th wedding anniversary with a lasting gift. That gift enabled the construction of a much-needed staff lounge and communications building.

Jack and Aviva Robinson Family Pioneer Village (1997)

Jack Robinson, founder of Perry Drugs, and his wife, Aviva, first became involved with camp when their children attended in the 1970s. Their daughter, Beth, met her husband, Steve, when she was a counselor in Pioneer Village. In 1982, the Robinsons provided funding for the first Alaska trip. Jack Robinson then chaired Fresh Air's $2.7 million capital and endowment campaign in 1997 which raised over $4.1 million. An additional gift from the Robinsons enables 8th grade boys and girls to continue Pioneer trips.

Eugene and Marcia Applebaum Village (1997)

Originally called Frontier Village, this home for 2nd and 3rd grade boys was renamed in 1997 when Eugene Applebaum generously gave back to the camp that once welcomed him as a young scholarship camper in 1947. Applebaum, founder of Arbor Drugs, has never forgotten his fabulous summer get-aways at Fresh Air Camp.

Dr. Milton and Lois Shiffman Family Village (1997)

Originally built in 1994, this village is centrally located with bathrooms and showers in each bunk and roomy cubbies, it is perfect for camp's youngest girls. Dr. Shiffman, a surgeon and businessman, and his wife Lois, lovingly endowed this village in 1997. Dr. Shiffman passed away in 2000.

Doreen and David Hermelin Village (1997)

To celebrate David's 60th birthday, Gil and Lila Silverman named this village in honor of the Hermelins, their friends and a couple considered ultimate *mensches*. When the village was dedicated, the Hermelins spent an enjoyable day with the village's 7th and 8th grade residents. Mr. Hermelin, former ambassador to Norway, died in 2000.

Ruach Field (1997)

There was a tremendous spirit among the members of the Fresh Air Society board during the capital campaign of 1997. Each decided to make a contribution in honor of the team that worked so hard to raise $4.1 million. This soccer and baseball field was named in their honor.

Michael and Donna Maddin Family Camp (1997)

Michael Maddin, board president from 1983 to 1985, noticed the community lacked a place where Jewish families could spend quality time together in an enriching environment. He and Donna generously endowed the Family Camp program thus allowing it to grow from an occasional weekend retreat to a year-round operation. Families spend weekends at the Butzel Conference Center with Tamarack staff leading the merriment. In 2000, the program was expanded to the Grand Resort at Mullett Lake. The Maddins also funded the Maddin Fitness Center and Physical Fitness Course and the waterskiing program at Camp Maas.

Clara S. and Harvey Gordon Scholar-In-Residence Program (1997)

Mr. Gordon was Fresh Air Society president between 1977 and 1980 and was associate chairperson of the 1997 capital campaign. He and his wife chose to provide funds for a Scholar-In-Residence program that brings scholars from across the globe to enrich the lives of campers.

The Gifts

Irving and Sarah Mahler
Dining Facility (1997)
Irving and Sarah Mahler
Senior Adult Camping (1983)

Irving and Sarah Mahler provided a generous gift in 1983 to underwrite some of the costs associated with the senior adult camping program at Butzel. Twenty-five years later, Mr. Mahler chose to honor his wife with a lasting gift, endowing the long-awaited dining facility at Camp Maas.

Radin Lake (1997)

In the midst of the 1997 capital campaign, Meyer Radin overheard Howard Rosen, a board member, discussing camp. Radin mentioned that he had gone to camp and a subsequent conversation led Radin to designate funds for the upkeep of Phipps Lake.

Lee and Gerson Bernstein
and Sonia and Hyman Blumenstein
Sailing and Windsurfing Program (1998)

Penny and Harold Blumenstein discovered that each of their parents had been to camp as youngsters. They endowed the windsurfing and sailing program in their honor and memory.

Warren and Margo Coville
Nature Center (1998)

For years, one nature center serviced the entire camp population. In 1998, the Coville's provided funding to create a junior side nature center for Camp Maas' youngest campers.

Immerman Teen Travel Program (1998)

Stanley Immerman, a successful business owner and bachelor, became a Fresh Air supporter after his friend and advisor Joseph Jackier described Tamarack Camps' vital role in the Jewish community and its impact on children. When Immerman died in the 1970s, leaving his trust to Jackier, the Immerman Foundation continued to support Fresh Air. Larry Jackier, Joseph's son, furthered the legacy by directing funds toward the esteemed teen travel program.

Charles and Sadie Grosberg Village (1999)
Joseph O. Grant Field (1965)

The need to have an extra village on camp property, for visiting guests or other area agencies, led to the creation of this village in 1999. Merwin Grosberg named the village in honor of his parents, Charles and Sadie, long-time Fresh Air supporters. Charles provided the funds to build a cabin in Pioneer Village in 1961. In 1965, he honored the 50th birthday of his son-in-law, Dr. Joseph O. Grant, with a gift that became a ball field.

Sam and Jean Frankel Cabins (1965)

Located in Specialty Village, these cabins were originally funded in the 1960s by Sam and Jean Frankel, who gave generously once again during the 1997 capital campaign.

Stephen and Nancy Grand
Multi-Use Indoor Facility
Stephen and Nancy Grand Resort (2000)

With up to 1,200 campers in a single session, a large covered facility for events, plays and parties became necessary. The multi-purpose gymnasium provided covered shelter while the addition of a covered pool complimented the swimming instruction program.

In the waning years of the 20th Century, family camping had become wildly popular. The Butzel Conference Center was adequate, but camp longed to offer families a more luxurious setting. That opportunity came in 1999, when Stephen and Nancy Grand generously donated the Silver Lodge, a 13-cabin resort on Mullet Lake in Cheboygan. Tamarack Camps operate the family camp center that became known as the Stephen and Nancy Grand Resort.

Henrietta and Herbert Charfoos
Administration Building (2000)

In 1954, when Ortonville opened, an office was built that 40 years later was still being used year-round. Ron Charfoos, a long-time board member and camp supporter, together with his father, Herbert, chose to fund the new administration building in memory of Henrietta, Ron's mother.

The Gifts

Fund	Purpose
Adler, Rabbi Morris	Family Camping
Agree, Arnold & Marilyn	Scholarships
Agree, Charles N.	Outpost Camp
Alumni Campership	Scholarships
Applebaum, Eugene and Marcia	Applebaum Village
Bargman Foundation	Arts & Crafts
Bargman, Theodore & Mina	Hiking & Tripping
Barnett, Henry & Edith	Cabin Maintenance
Barnett, Henry & Edith	Library
Barron, Ethel Memorial	Operations
Berman, Bill & Madeline	Berman Village
Birnkrant, Loris	Scholarships
Bittker, Dr. Irving J.	Scholarships
Blitz, Donald R.	Scholarships
Blum, George & Joyce/Zuieback Lillian	Camp Maas
Blumberg, Louis & Edith	Scholarships
Blumenstein, Ricky & Carol	Waterfront
Blumenstein, Penny & Harold	Sailing & Windsurfing
Briton, Mitchell Allan	Arts and Crafts
Brodsky, Betty & Sarah	Scholarships
Brown, Sadie & Harry	Operations
Burtman, Samuel & Molly	Burtman Camp
Chapin, Anna W. Memorial	Scholarships
Charfoos, Ron & Lynda	Administration Building
Cohn, Irwin I.	Silverman Village
Coville Foundation	Nature Center
Danto, Marvin & Betty	Senior Citizen
Davidson, Donald Memorial	Scholarships
Davis, Bernard & Goldie Memorial	Scholarships
DeRoy, Aaron & Helen	Scholarships
Dickman, Frank & Dorothy	Silverman Travel
Dodge, Charles	Tennis
Farber, Billy	Scholarships
Feldman, Dr. Barry & Leslye	Horizons
Ferber, Fred & Miriam	Music
Fink, David	Scholarships
Finkelberg, Sharyn	Music
Finkelberg, Shirley	Family Camping
Frank, Ben	Cabin
Frank, William	Silverman Village
Frankel, Sam & Jean	Scholarships
Friedman, Samuel & Isabelle	Operations
Ginn, Marcus	Scholarships
Gold, Hyman & Dora	Scholarships
Goldberg, Marilyn & Darryl	Family Camping
Gordon, Harvey & Clara	Scholar-in-Residence
Grand, Stephen & Nancy	Multi-Use Indoor Facility
Grosberg, Charles & Sadie	Grosberg Village
Gutterman, Dr. Meyer	Scholarships
Haddow, Rita & John	Overnight Camping and Waterfront

"As you sow, so shall you reap." Leviticus Rabba 25:5

Fresh Air Society Endowment Funds

Handler, Lou-Kraft, Esta	Day Camp
Harold, David & Susan	Horseback Riding and Clinic
Helman, Peter & Shirley	Scholarships
Herman, Leonard & Ophelia	Scholarships
Hermelin, David & Doreen	Hermelin Village
Himelhoch, Israel	Drama
Himmel, Clarence & Jack	Operations
Holtzman, Jean	Silverman Village Book Fund
Horace Haber Memorial	Scholarships
Horne, Louis	Butzel
Immerman Foundation	Teen Travel Trips
Immerman, John & Ella	Communications
Jacob, Joel & Lauren	Mountain Biking
Jacobson, Nancy & Joseph	Scholar-in-Residence
Kasle, Robert	Operations
Katz, Norman & Ann	Waterfront
Katzen, Ruth	Silverman Village Learning Center
Komer, Harry	Fishing Fund
Kowalsky, Edith & Larry	Bubbie Zadie Camp
Kepes, Brian & Fern	Scholarship
Klein, Emery & Diane	Floor Hockey Rink
Knopper, Judith Lowe	Playground
Krugel, Dr. Richard & Sally	Scholarships
Kunin, Marc	Operations and Scholarships
Lax, Sheldon	Ball Field
Layton, Charles	Operations
Leipsitz, Harry	Scholarships
Levine, Edward Memorial	Scholarships
Levison, Syd & Robert	Levison Village
Lieberman, Arthur & Rochelle	Scholarships
Lipsitt, Seymour & Gertrude	Needy Child
Lowe, Maxwell M. Memorial	Scholarships
Lumberg, Edward	Scholarships
Maas, B. & R.-Scholarship Loan	Staff Loan
Maas, Benard L. & Rosalyn J.	Operations
Maas Foundation	Specialty Village
Maas	Scholar-in-Residence
Maddin, Michael and Donna	Family Camping
Maddin, Milton M.	Fitness
Mahler, Irving & Sarah	Dining Hall
Mahler, Milton K.	Equestrian
Marcus, Samuel	Scholarships
Marx, Edwin I. Memorial	Scholarships
Masserman, Theodore	Scholarships
Maurice, Winston Memorial	Operations
Meistrich/Lenter, Phyllis & John	Scholarships
Michigan Sports Foundation	Scholarships
Milstein, A. Freda & Max	Playground
Milstein Family	Scholarships
Mintz, Anna	Scholarships
Montefiore Lodge	Scholarships

"As you sow, so shall you reap." Leviticus Rabba 25:5

Fresh Air Society Endowment Funds

Nachman, Allan & Joy	Horizons
Newman, Louise Camp Scholarship	Scholarships
Opperer, Pam	Teen Travel
Ormond, Dennis	Tripping Equipment
Phillips, Sydney	Scholarships
Pitt, Murray & Ina	Basketball Court
Popkin, Irving	Waterfront
Posner, Irving & Helen	Judaica
Rapkin, Ellen	Radin Lake
Robinson, Aviva & Jack	Robinson Pioneer Village
Rodecker, Arthur	Memorial Beach
Rohlik, Sigmund & Sophie	Scholarships
Rosen, Betty	Scholarships
Rosen, Bruce & Rosalie	Vehicles
Rosen, Howard & Jo	Zip Line
Rubin, Thomas Memorial	Scholarships
Saferstein, Sadie	Silverman Village
Schembeck, Rachel	Scholarships
Schiff, Benton A.	Scholarships
Schreiber, Alex	Operations
Schwartz, Leonard	Art
Schwartz, Oscar D.	Clinic
Shalit, Dr. Ivan	Visual Aids
Shapiro, Lindsey Ann	Scholarships
Shenkman Judaic	Judaica
Shenkman, Jack & Miriam	Maintenance
Sherman, Donald	Staff Training
Sheruth League	Scholarships
Shiffman, Milt & Lois	Shiffman Village
Shifrin, Peter & Esther	Operations
Shufro, Arthur & Norma Jean	Music Fund
Shulevitz, Abraham & Elizabeth	Scholarships
Silverman, Esther & Nathan	Silverman Village
Silverman, Gil & Lila	Silverman Village
Simon, Bertha & Meyer	Scholarships
Skillman Foundation	Scholarships
Smokler, Bert & Toba	Pioneer Skills
Sobell, Maurice H.	Waterfront
Sugarman, Marcus & Elenore	C.P.R.
Surnow, Jack	Scholarships
Tanner, E.	Scholar-in-Residence Music Fund
Tronstein, Steve & Barbara	Scholarships
Victor, Steve & Arlene	Scholarships
Weingarten, Irwin J.	Scholarships
Weinstein, Bertha & Fred	Elderhostel
Wineman, Henry & Trudie	Scholarship
Winer, Sydney & Melba	Fine Arts
Wolk, Ida & Morris	Scholarships
Wolok, Helen	Scholarships
Yolles, Ron & Julie	Theater Arts
Zaks, Michael	Zaks Amphitheater

"As you sow, so shall you reap." Leviticus Rabba 25:5

Fresh Air Society Endowment Funds

"It meant so much to get mail." Iris Kramer

"I lived for camp. The year was simply in anticipation of camp." Chuck Wolfe

"It wasn't only homesickness, it was child-sickness" Marshall Hersh

"The lake in the morning, the trees, scenery and serenity." Moishe Last

"Camp has never stopped for me. These camp people never go away." David Eason

THIS BUILDING GIVEN AS A LIVING
MEMORIAL TO THE SACRED MEMORY OF
ROBERT JOHN MAAS
SO OTHER CHILDREN MAY LIVE AND
ENJOY LIFE AND HAPPINESS

BY HIS PARENTS
MR. AND MRS. BENARD L. MAAS
AND
BROTHER BENARD, JR.

"We met at camp, our friends went there, our kids went there." Howard Steinmetz

"The staff would put on really funny skits." Richard Komer

"The ground was so wet from the dew, we had to wear boots to breakfast." Diane Klein (Yura)

"Favorite food, Joe Bender's chocolate chip cookies." Steve Lash

BOOMER TIME

1965-1979

*"Camp was not always as Jewish as it is today, but it created
a deep impression on those who went there. We'd be a poorer
community without it. It has created life-long friends, marriages
and has fed a lot of leadership into our community.
It is part of our weave and fabric."*

Allan Nachman, board president, Fresh Air Society 1980-1983

By 1965 the baby boom was over. Eighteen years after the first post-war baby let out a healthy cry, the generation had grown to 78 million strong. The oldest boomers were living on college campuses; the youngest were just learning to walk. In between was a vast expanse of children and each summer nearly 2,000 of them came to Camp Tamarack.

Margaret Leipsitz was eight years old when she arrived as a first-time Brighton camper in 1969. "I had no idea how homesick I would be,"[1] she recalled. "I was a closet thumb sucker my first year at camp. I remember getting up early while all the bunk was asleep, staring up at the tall angular ceiling of the dorm and passionately sucking my thumb. One morning I looked at the girl next to me. Much to my amazement I found her busily sucking her thumb. It made me feel so good to know I was not alone."

Leipsitz returned again in 1970 and again and again until her last summer at Tamarack in 1981. "I remember my first overnight in Brighton. There were no tents. We strung a tarp between trees and used two blankets for a sleeping bag. We practiced putting up the tarp before our real overnight. We'd make the shelter and then someone would come and dump water on top of it to make sure it would stay dry."

WINTER CAMP

Winter weekend camping began in earnest in 1966. In 1967, two winter weekend camps were conducted serving a total of 105 children.

Over her camp lifetime, much would change. Tents and sleeping bags replaced tarps and blankets. Hobby hours – camp-style electives – gave campers the opportunity to individualize their camp experience and camp enrollments reached all-time highs. Whatever equipment, building or program camp administrators needed or dreamt up, a prosperous community happily funded it.

But if the 60s and 70s were, in some respects, the golden age

BERMAN 1965
Bunks 5 and 6 teamed up for an afternoon hike and found some juicy apples along the way.
(photo courtesy of Jim Grey)

of Camp Tamarack, they also brought darker undertones.   As
Bob Dylan crooned 'The Times They Are A-Changin,' camp supervisors and administrators were suddenly coping with social problems
unheard of ten years earlier.   Drugs and politics entered camp in
the backpacks of camp staff and by the end of the 1970s, marketing
and camp's Jewish identity became hot topics around the boardroom
table.

Build It And They Will Come

In the mid 1960s, Ortonville had grown to six villages. Brighton
still had its four long dorms, the senior side cabins and a tent unit.
In 1964, Tamarack's Camp Kennedy, in Michigan's Upper Peninsula, began running an all-boys wilderness program, and Eastern and
Western trips were booked solid. Camp was flush with counselors,
staff and money.

Enticing campers to stay with camp until they became staff was
the job of the senior camp personnel, men like Marvin Berman and
Allan Brown, along with many creative supervisors and counselors.
Collectively they fashioned a range of camping experiences that mag-
netically lured campers toward the ultimate Tamarack experience,
teen travel and tripping. Teen travel trips ventured east and west,
and wilderness exploration adventures to Lake Superior Provincial
Park began in 1966.

The same year that America celebrated its first Earth Day and
Neil Armstrong walked on the moon, Fresh Air Society acquired
the Charles N. Agree Outpost Camp in Wawa, Ontario. Set
upon the shores of Lake Kabenung, Agree was located in the
completely untamed wilderness of
northern Lake Superior. The only
people who lived in the vicinity
were French-speaking lumberjacks
and Native American Indians.   In
1969, the handful of 20-year-old,
long-haired boomers who ran the

DUDES

In the early 1960s, the Canadian government
built a road around Lake Superior that
terminated near Ely, MN and provided access
to a virgin area of lakes, mountains and natural phenomena. Wawa, Ontario, located half-
way between the beginning and end of that
highway, became an annual Tamarack destination for older campers. Escorting them was
a hearty group of counselors. In 1966, Pete
Bolgar, Jim Grey, Howard Davis, Joel Konikow
and Jan Mayhew had the pleasure. *(photo
courtesy of Jim Grey)*

camp thought they were in commune heaven.

Younger boys, aspiring to become trippers themselves, enrolled in the Explorers program (A note about language. Trippers were the young men, and later women, who guided hiking and canoe trips. It is purely coincidental that they were dubbed the same name given to many within the drug culture). Created in 1970, Explorers were given the mission of their life-time: to romp through rocky terrain, roll down winding rivers and chart the hikes and trips for future campers. They charted courses around the Agree camp and the base camps, Mesick and Mio, that were acquired in 1971. Forty years later campers still followed those original trail maps.

Meanwhile, 8th and 9th grade Ortonville Pioneers were sleeping in tents and on hammocks and were being taught advanced canoeing and hiking skills to prepare them for their camping future. It was fine for the boys, but the girls, as Sam Marcus explained in 1969, were in need of variety. Added to the Pioneer agenda were concen-

CATTLE TRUCK
Campers traveled to the base camps in a big, open steak truck. Everyone just piled their gear and bodies in the back and headed north. No seats, no seat belts and no roof. "The road trip was always a great bonding experience," recalled tripper Howard Davis. *(photo courtesy of Jim Grey)*

JOE KREPSEY

Where were you when you first heard Joe Krepsey? Legend has it that the Krepsey story first surfaced in 1964 when Eli Greenbaum, a counselor, told the story to his DeRoy campers. His version was tame. The horrific variations came soon after.

Jeffrey Appel remembers being a camper and hearing the story for the first time. He didn't sleep a wink. "You never forget the night you heard Joe Krepsey," said Appel. A counselor in the early 1970s, he told the full Krepsey to his Ortonville campers, always leaving some seaweed behind. His intense eyes and gruff voice gave the tale a note of authority, and a bright, red birthmark on his left cheek attested to the horror of it all…

"In the Newland, across the road, lived Joe Krepsey, his wife and kids. One day Joe was in the fields and saw a fire. He ran back to his home and tried to save his wife and kids. It was too late. His body badly burned, he went crazy and ran into the Tamarack Swamp and was never seen again. Every once in a while though, Joe Krepsey will come into the cabins when we are asleep and look for his lost kids. If he sees someone who looks like his children, he will take you with him…and you will never be seen again. You know when he has been here because there will be seaweed left behind."

trations in dance, dramatics, advanced pioneering and ceramics. Modeled after Kfar Ivri, these were the first Specialty campers. Their mornings were spent within their chosen avocation and their afternoons enjoying other camp activities. In 1970, 224 girls registered for Pioneer.[2] That year, the ceramics group acquired an outdoor kiln. By 1975, a waterfront specialty was added and the program had become co-ed.

HIPPIES

In the late 1960s, the Board referred to long hair as a "new dimension" in staff relations. The style of dress and appearance should not be a concern, they noted, as long as the "hippie" does not try to impose his or her attitude and values on the campers.

Michelle Rose's experience as a Ceramics Specialty camper in 1973 shaped her future. For four weeks she was immersed in a fine arts environment, a passion that would become her career. "All we did was work in the ceramics shop. It was great," she recalled. "I was a shy kid, but being at camp had a big impact on who I am today. My strongest memories are in the ceramics studio and the canoe trip to the Manistee River."[3]

The After Midnight Crowd

In the late 1960s, most campers carried their own hard-sided luggage. It was quite a sight to see them, especially the little ones,

STRING ART
Arts at camp took many shapes and forms. Paula Zaks, BFA and MFA, introduced fine arts to camp (batik, silk screen) in the 1970s. Intertwined with their String Earth Sculpture is one of the arts teams from the late 1970s, (l to r) Miriam VanNess, Lori Zukin Burkow, Paula Zaks, Sherry Gunsberg, Hannah Zamler.

clumsily maneuver toward their bunks. Waiting to help were the counselors, college students with long hair, braids, beads, well-worn t-shirts and frayed blue jeans (holes in the knees, peace sign and ban the bomb patches on the rear end). They were a colorful bunch, passionate about anything and everything from the war in Vietnam, to the ecology, to what time they should go to bed. And, so unlike any generation that preceded them, the hippies loved to openly challenge authority.

Susie Zaks was a counselor in the early 1970s. "There was one time when the counselors had the kids make protest signs and protest lunch. The kids would walk around with their signs and wouldn't go in (to the lodge). It was all in fun, all in jest, but the kids wouldn't eat their macaroni and cheese that day,"[4] said Zaks. Thirty years later, Zaks continued to work with camp counselors as camp's Assistant Director. While the counselors of 2000 often looked like their hippie predecessors, it is unlikely they would have been found standing around with protest signs.

"We slept very little at camp," recalled Howard Davis, a 60s tripper – the wilderness kind – and the apple of many a female counselor's eye. His pal, Larry Gussin, elaborated, "There were vast numbers of people moving through the woods after midnight. We played this cat and mouse game with Marcus and Berman. Everyone knew their way around camp without flashlights."[5]

CIRCLE OF FRIENDS
The counselors and CITs of Fishman 1971 create a fun photo moment. *(photo courtesy of Roz Blanck)*

MARIJUANA

Barely was there a night when the woods did not bear the distinct odor of marijuana. Not only were counselors smoking, older campers were also. Dealing with it was an emotional roller coaster for administrators. "There were times when I had to put my head in the sand and try to ignore it," said a 67-year-old Marvin Berman, "but it was so widespread among young adults at that time." Many were fired or sent home, some were warned and a lot of them never got caught.

STIHL-MOBILE
Rob Morrison and Denise Landau model a new base camp vehicle, the Stihl Mobile. With absolutely no gas required, the two capable counselors used the vehicle to demonstrate the efficiency of human power. One summer later, Morrison and Landau led the bike trips across the U.P. *(photo courtesy of Denise Landau)*

Knowing how to get from one end of camp to another without flashlights and without using main roads became imperative.

Merrill Gordon was an expert. "I'd roam camp until about two in the morning," he proudly recalled. "I'd go and see whoever was CD (counselor on duty), go to the auditorium, to Sheruth and Berman. I'd get back to my village and fall asleep. Then, I'd get up at 6:30 and go to Rodecker and swim for a half an hour."[6] Arriving back in his village just as the kids and Mark Turbowitz, his co-coun-selor, were waking up, Gordon realized that, "Mark must have thought I never slept!" laughed the attorney and father whose bedtime later became much earlier.

1970

2,961 total campers:
24 teen trippers,
49 Kennedy campers,
29 Wilderness campers,
35 Agree campers.

39.5% (836) from Southfield
31.6% (669) Oak Park
11.5% (243) Detroit
3.5% (75) Birmingham
1 camper each from
Grosse Pointe Woods,
Highland Park,
Southgate

Like many other late night roamers, Gordon fre-quented the kitchen. A sign, BBB&F: Bender, Bender, Bender & Friedman hung over the door. Inside were the bakers, Joe Bender, his two sons and, camper turned baker, Harold Friedman. Friedman, who left his baking career in the dust to become a cardiologist, absolutely loved his four years by Bender's side. "People would smell the rolls baking and come by. We had a big pan of melted butter, so we'd cut a roll in half, brush on the melted butter and people would just go crazy,"[7] remem-bered Friedman. It was a great camp job. His day would start at about 4:30 p.m. and end when the baking was done. "We got it so sometimes we'd be done by 10:30 and that was when all the action (in camp) was happening."

Even the bakers were in on an elaborate 1969 prank organized by two counselors, Larry Gussin and Mike Bossin. It was known as the Great Escape. The plot included secretly parading all of the campers out of main camp, hijacking the food truck and a supply of food. "We started to pick up the kids at 3:30 in the morning," modestly recalled Gussin. "Pioneer campers were the lookouts and helped escort kids through back trails to the meeting point, which was past the kitchen in the woods. To get the campers back, we arranged to have a ransom note put in Marv Berman's scrambled eggs." The con-tents of the note have been forgotten, but as

MICHAEL ZAKS
Hands on and always around, Michael Zaks was camp's associate director through 1980 when he became executive director. He loved the time he spent working hand-in-hand with campers and staff.
(photo courtesy of Paula Zaks)

he remembered Berman's shock, an embarrassed smile came to Gussin's face. "It all ended in typical camp style. There were about three hours of games." Then they hiked back to camp and everyone went to bed early.

Not all of the late-night antics tested the will of senior staff. Beth Stone (Katz), an endlessly happy camper in the 70s, and counselor throughout the 80s, remembers lots and lots of after-bedtime activities. Late one 1973 night, a gang of counselors woke Stone and her Sheruth villagers. "They told us we were being attacked and had us paint our faces black. We had to go with one little tiny flashlight to the beach. It was pitch black. We were all holding hands," she lovingly remembered. "There were boats coming across the lake. They separated us into groups and said it was the kick-off of Color Wars."

Stone had many late nights at camp, one of her most memorable was as a Berman camper. "The counselors woke us up and took us to Berman field. They had popcorn and blankets out so we could watch the meteor showers," she reminisced. "It was great. I can still remember lying there, everyone saying oh my G-d they are amazing"

MENINGITIS

85 campers cancelled their summer experience in 1972 when two cases of meningitis were diagnosed at Brighton. More than $18,000 in camp fees were refunded that summer.

The Modell Puppet Program

In 1968, Marcus launched a program he originally described as an experiment. David Ben Shalom, one of Israel's most highly regarded puppeteers, came to Ortonville. Together with an enamored group of teens, he created the Marionette Puppet Theater, a summer troupe that studied Shalom's original scripts, hand-crafted their own puppets and performed for campers, senior citizens and children's agencies throughout Michigan. Shalom spent the summers of 1968 and '69 at camp. His campers set up shop in a remote area of camp in a tent village known as Modell. Marcus described Shalom in a *Tamaractivities* newsletter: "Those who knew him will never forget him. We are the richer for having him in our midst. And he has left us with tangible and concrete evidence of his great talent: a puppet theater, dozens of marionettes and scripts to satisfy talented youngsters for several summers."[8]

Many of those marionettes now hold places of honor in the homes of the children that went to Modell. One, Monica Sageman (Steinmetz), remembers Phil Molby and Pat Sutton, the two men who took over where Shalom left

MODELL PUPPETS
In 1968, David Ben Shalom, a puppeteer from Israel's Bubatron Theatre, came to camp to launch a dramatic arts camp, the Modell Puppet Camp. Campers crafted their own puppets, worked from Shalom's original scripts and performed at camp and throughout the state. *(photo source Tamaractivities December 1967)*

off. "It was a great human experience working with these two men,"[9] she recalled of her 1973 experience. Campers began the loving transformation of a piece of wood into a nearly life-like puppet as soon as they arrived. "We rehearsed the whole time we were making the puppets," said Sageman.

Like the Specialty programs, Modell campers worked their craft in the morning and spent afternoons enjoying the rest of the camp.

They broke from their routine to enjoy AuSable River overnights and won special praise for their entertaining work. By the end of the decade, however, the program was closed and all that remained was the Modell lodge, the memories and the puppets.

The Beginning Of An Evolution

In 1967, a young man was hired to drive a camp truck. Somewhere between tinkering with its engine and sitting quietly on Shabbat, he found that Camp Tamarack was his home. That young man was Michael Zaks, who spent the next 17 years sculpting a new kind of camp.

Zaks arrived at camp when America was undergoing a sea of change. Organized religion, including Judaism, was under philosophical assault from the "make love, not war" generation. The old-world ways that emphasized cultural uniqueness, clashed with the emerging culture: "C'mon people…everybody get together and love one another," was one of the lyrics of the day. Intermarriage rates soared and the number of young couples joining a congregation and integrating Judaic culture into their lives dropped. Divorce rates were increasing and single-parent households were becoming commonplace.

But camp was a way to reinforce Jewish identity. "We tried to project the Jewish way of life," remembered Marshall Hersh, Ortonville's assistant director in the late 1960s and early 1970s.

CIRCUS DAY
Circus Day at Brighton arrived once a session in grand style. It was an event that campers, staff and alumni anticipated with cotton-candy eyes. Giant giraffes and elephants, clowns, games, music and ringmasters filled the day. When exhausted campers went to bed that night, the circus quietly left town. *(photos courtesy of Marvin Berman)*

"We had the kids develop the Shabbat services. It was something they created, not an official read-the-book service. Even on a Saturday morning, we would get together around a table or in beautiful area and talk about the wonderful things we see in each other and around camp. It was a time to reflect."

"It was a camp for Jewish kids," commented Bob Lipsitz. "A place to give kids an outdoor experience, a place where Jewish culture could be tasted." Israeli scholars-in-residence visited and traditional dances and songs were taught. In 1968, the first Israeli staff arrived and introduced children to the Israeli way of life. Marvin Berman, at the time Ortonville's director, remembered, "Our camp was probably one of the least Jewish camps in the country, yet it was among the first to participate in the program of working with Israeli counselors."

Zaks, who quickly graduated from trucks to clipboards, brought a different vision: He intended to make camp a Jewish haven, a place for children to informally experience their religion in a natural setting. He became the propellant behind the Judaic fire – but not without struggle.

At a time when being religious was considered "uncool," Zaks battled a number of staff and community members who feared a Jewish camp would turn off more campers than it would attract. He moved forward anyway. Zaks hired staff who would fulfill his vision, added more Hebrew songs and prayers to the Shabbat service, incorporated Jewish themes into arts and crafts and integrated Jewish words into regular camp dialogue. "Instead of it being that Jewish kids went to this camp, it became a Jewish camp,"[10] said Mark Rosenwasser, counselor and supervisor throughout the 1970s.

Brighton followed suit under the equally passionate leadership of Lenny Newman. Bouncing around in his colorful socks, this skinny resident

1978

The Tamarack Hills Authority desperately sought funds to dredge Phipps Lake in Ortonville. "The weeds and muck in our lake at Ortonville had grown to such an extent that swimming and other water sports became severely restricted. Worse, there is concern that swimmers might become entangled in the weeds with possibly unpleasant consequences."

BEST FRIENDS
Paula Zaks (Steinberger) was an art student at Eastern Michigan University when a friend convinced her to come to Camp Tamarack for a summer counseling job. She landed in Sheruth Village and "I was in heaven. Camp was full of all these Jewish guys," she reminisced 30 years later. That summer she met Michael Zaks, who would become her husband in 1974. This photo was taken in 1974 when Zaks was supervising arts and crafts. (Top to bottom) Elaine Zaks, Paula Zaks, Shirlee Wymann Harris and Shari Maniloff Korenstein. *(photo courtesy of Paula Zaks)*

director was on a constant charge to find ways to astound and educate young campers. Jewish themes found their way into bedtime stories, Shabbat services and around the flagpole. Children could take Hebrew lessons in the woods and learn Jewish cooking. The Maccabi games and all camp themes further entrenched a Jewish flavor into camp life.

Meanwhile, Kfar Ivri, the Hebrew village, filled each session with campers who wanted to enjoy a unique Jewish environment. Marty Levinson was a 1971 Kfar Ivri counselor. Years later, he became one of camp's most devoted pediatricians. The village had a very special charm, he recalled. "There were two separate groups within Kfar, the Orthodox and secular. The kids interacted very well. It was probably the only time in these people's lives that they interacted so closely with the other group."[11]

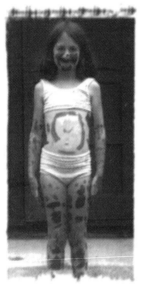

PAINTED AND PROUD OF IT! A proud Marilyn Schulte (Jonas) adorned in body paint stands in front of Brighton Bunk I in 1974. That summer she urged her mother to send candy, games and Caladryl for mosquito bites.

Kfar Ivri's food was prepared in its own kosher kitchen. The meals, which never traveled further than a few hundred feet, were far better than what the rest of the camp was eating. "I'm sure the biggest reason the rest of camp staff treated us so well was our food. We had a kosher caterer who came and cooked for us. It was a real honor for someone to be invited to eat in our camp," said Levinson.

Camp Magic

When he was 16, Cliff Cantor was one of three Ortonville nature specialists. It was 1971. That year, Cantor remembers, they built a huge pyre of logs for an all-camp program. Cantor entered the

WHERE WERE YOU WHEN:

1967: Detroit Riots - Marc Shindler, camper: "We heard that Detroit was on fire and they were killing people. My father's store was on 12th and Clairmont. The riots started right next door. They didn't burn us down." The next year the store was looted, his father closed it and bought Brody's in 1969.

1969: Neil Armstrong landed on the moon - Mike Bossin, counselor: His group, on a canoe trip along the Manistee, came out of the woods at a trout hatchery and saw a bunch of people shooting a commercial for a 1970 Oldsmobile. "We lumbered out of the woods to see Armstrong walking on the moon. They had stopped shooting to watch."

1974: Nixon resigns as President - Minda Tilchin, head counselor, Camp Agree: "We were building one of the new cabins and were on the roof when a neighbor came running to tell us that Nixon had resigned. We were so detached from things. We didn't see newspapers for weeks at a time."

TRIP CENTER CREW
Stationed in front of
the Yellow Dawg, the
in-camp utility vehicle
(an old mail truck),
these men
provided the
tripping food and
equipment for
Tamarack campers in
1974: (top l to r) Mike
Binder "Pickles" and
Mark Adler "Sup."
(bottom l to r) Dale
Cohen "Dutch,"
Gary Torf "Zambina"
and Bob Goldschmidt
"SchmitLab."

amphitheater with a bow and lighted arrow. "Everyone was sitting
in a semi-circle around the pyre,"[12] he explained. "I made it look like
I was going to shoot a flaming arrow into them. Then, my co-nature
specialist came out and tackled me." The two staged a struggle and
the arrow was shot high over the heads of the group, off into the
woods where the third member of the nature trio hid. He came
stumbling into the theater, the arrow seemingly shot through his
waist and dropped dead next to the pyre. Cantor pulled a string
attached to a drum of fuel and the great fire ignited.

An old camp adage, Ortonville was for the counselors and
Brighton was for the kids, made sense. Ortonville campers
were older, wiser and fooled less easily. Counselors needed
to dig a little deeper into their black bag of magic tricks to
impress them. At Brighton, the kids were so young and so
in awe of their counselors and surroundings, that impressing
them required little more than a bit of charm and a dose of imagination. "Brighton was a magical place,"[13] said Julie Steinmetz,
a Brighton counselor between 1975 and 1977. "We'd take the kids
on a hike to this swampy, muddy place in the woods and tell them
it was Dinosaur Land. We'd build it up and turn it into a fantastic
adventure. The focus was on meeting the needs of the little kids."

"We went to camp in an age of innocence," reflected Beth Stone
(Katz) in 2001. "We loved the all-camp activities like the Color Wars,
we'd play spin the bottle and shriek with excitement. We couldn't
get enough lanyard and we loved the milk and cookies. We'd sit
around the campfire and sing 'Blowin' in the Wind.'" Long past her
own camping years, Stone paused and thought of her own young
daughters. "Kids today know too much, they would never be as easily
enchanted."

SAILING

In 1967,
Ortonville's
sailing program got
underway thanks to
a fleet of four sail-
boats donated by
Mrs. Helen DeRoy
and Dr. Peter G.
Shifrin.

Boom Winds Down

"Brighton is outmoded and dorm living is not accepted as being desirable,"[14] declared Robert Kasle in 1974, just before becoming board president in 1975. "A new site for children would create excitement and revitalize camping." The 50-year-old campsite was showing its age, and worse, the number of Brighton campers was dropping.

Brighton's problems weren't exclusive, camp enrollment was declining everywhere. "The ravages of inflation and an economic recession have wreaked havoc with our planning... Enrollment appears directly related to the state of the economy..." wrote Kasle in 1976. The boom was over.

BRIGHTON

Brighton was slated to close in 1976. That winter an unexpected increase in applications revived the doomed camp. The camp was updated in 1984 and remained open until 1994.

The board and senior staff racked their brains trying to overcome a growing fiscal deficit and increase enrollment. They questioned everything: Was the amount of Jewish education at camp turning people away? Were they not offering the right selection of programs? How much were the changes in lifestyles and the increase in community summer recreation programs biting into their enrollment?

"We never knew from marketing," said Berman. "We used to have waiting lists. By my last years we spent hours and hours talking about marketing and advertising. We would agonize over it."

A deeply committed group worked to put Tamarack back on the map. Lenny Newman created the Winter Jamboree, a mid-winter JCC festival of all that Tamarack had to offer. For the first time, camp opened enrollment to areas outside of Detroit. Children from Flint, Grand Rapids, Lansing and Alpena experienced Tam-

BRIGHTON DORM 4 1979 Many of these young he-men later returned as counselors. For Jeff Metz, their counselor in 1979 who later became Brighton's resident director, that was the greatest compliment to his efforts as a leader. "Camp was a change agent for so many kids and who they became years later," said Metz.
(photo courtesy of Jeff Metz)

arack. Board members conducted telephone telethons to recruit campers and targeted programs to attract specific populations were created: a sports camp, a weight-loss camp, a farm program and additional family camp weekends.

Adjustments were made to accommodate the lower enrollments. In Brighton, the senior side was closed and campers slept in a tent village behind Dorm 4 called Euphoria (U4EA). Dorms merged. In Ortonville, Sheruth, Berman and Specialty villages became co-ed. Counselor pay took a dip. As maintenance costs were slashed, buses began breaking down as often as they were started. In 1977, the board requested a $20,000 loan from the Jewish Federation to help pay for new buses. Federation, feeling its own crunch, offered only $12,000 leaving Board President Kasle to make an unprecedented request. He asked parents to "make a contribution of $10 for each camper."[15]

Fortunately, these struggles stayed in the office. Outside, camp was still camp. The smells and the experiences were the same: the musty cabins, the first morning scent of pine and watery dew, roasting marshmallows, fluttering fireflies and late-night crackling campfires. Being boy crazy, being girl crazy and skinny dipping on Rodecker Beach. Swatting mosquitoes all night long, playing baseball on a hot afternoon, walking around camp singing village songs, drinking bug juice, cold milk and cookies, and opening mail.

No financial crisis could take away the Tamarack magic. The feeling of waking up with a smile knowing that the day ahead was going to be better than the one just past, and the happiness of being with your very best friends.

BOYS AND GORP
In 1975, these Berman campers got their first taste of GORP, Good Old Raisins and Peanuts, on their canoe trip to Mio. "It was the best trip," remembered Sherri Ketai (Kay). "They worked us, but we learned about taking responsibility for ourselves and others." (l to r) Debbie Ernst (Alexander), Sherri Ketai (Kay) and Pam Balbes (Silverman). *(photo courtesy of Lisa Elconin)*

GENDER GAP

Almost consistently, more girls came to camp than boys. The camp application statistics from 1970 show this trend:

Agree, Pioneer & Advanced Pioneer Boys -203
Pioneer girls-224
Camp Kennedy boys-48
Camp Kennedy girls-67
Teen trip boys-34
Teen trip girls-42
Wilderness boys-26
Wilderness girls-11
Total camp enrollment boys-1352
Total camp girls-1609

HANGIN' OUT
1975 Brighton staff (l to r) Bruce Shaffer, Avi Noam Caspi and Dennis Zaretsky take a break from erecting a circus day tarp, Shaffer assured "we were hard at work… or hardly working." *(photo courtesy of Shaffer family)*

Tales and Fables

For every generation of campers, there was a story, a legend or a fable that was told to all.
Many were tied into Indian lore, the early American wisdom that permeated much of camp,
from the grand opening night ceremony to drama, crafts and hikes.

On the first night of Brighton camp, the Grand Indian Council convened. With campers seated around
the fire pit and tom-toms beating, counselors and supervisors, their faces decorated with elaborate war paint,
solemnly marched into the ring.

As the tom-toms stopped, the tribal leaders (counselors), dressed in authentic Native American costumes, began their chant. The Medicine Man rose. In a great voice he sang, "Wa-kon-da-de-du wa-pa-din
a-ton-he. Great Father, a needy one stands before thee, I who speak am he." He chants another verse, then
lights the great fire. The tribal Chief and four braves join the Medicine Man and celebrate the fire. Then,
they seat themselves and the tom-tom starts again. The story teller advances and the tribe hears his tale:

The Legend of Blaine Lake

"Many moons ago, there lived a great old Indian chief who ruled over a mighty Indian nation. This great
chief had two strong sons and the three were very happy. They would go out into the fields and forests and
stalk game. The father taught his brave sons the unique ways of the Indians. After many years, the great chief
became old and tired and very sick. Soon, the chief died and went to the great Indian hunting ground.

The boys knelt over their dead father in mournful sorrow. Then they slowly rose, clasped hands and
promised that they would carry on the leadership of their father's nation. And this they did for many years.

One afternoon, the brothers spotted a deer in the forest. Quietly, they drew closer, took out their arrows
and shot. They found only one arrow in the dead animal's body. One brother said, "It is my arrow! I am
always the best shot." The other shouted, "No! It is my arrow, I have always been the best shot." They argued
violently. Finally, one brother slapped the other across the face. They looked at each other and then parted
ways, vowing that if they ever saw each other again they would fight to the death.

One brother gathered his followers and went to the site where the Senior side now stands. Here he
settled and built his own tribe. The other brother remained on the grounds where the main side rests today
– and here he built his own tribe.

Each brother led their tribes for many years in peace and prosperity, but they never saw each other. Then,
one winter there was a great famine. Each brother had been very resourceful in the previous years and had
enough food to last the winter. But, each thought the other had nothing.

One dark and moonless night, each set out for the other side of the lake carrying a sack of corn to leave
behind. They passed each other by inches, but did not see one another. The next night, they again set out,
but again it was a moonless night and did not see each other.

On the third night, the clouds moved and the moon shown through. The two brothers saw each other,
dropped their corn and began a deathly combat. Round and round they went – viciously fighting, ready to
deal a deadly blow until suddenly a bright beam of moonlight lit their faces.

In that moment, they realized they were each trying to help the other. They broke their spears, embraced
and walked off together, hand-in-hand and built one great Indian brotherhood.

Marvin Berman loved to tell campers stories. His camp career began as a DeRoy village counselor in 1955. Over the next 32 years, Marv sat with campers spinning fables that sparked the children's imaginations. "Storytelling was part of camp," he said. One of his favorites was the Tamarack Tree, a tale told as campers sat under a tree and gazed at a Tamarack tree, the great evergreen that lent camp its name. After telling the story, Berman would say to the kids, "that sometime during your camp stay, you may be hiking, get tired and sit under a tree. Who knows, it may be a Tamarack Tree and by sitting under it, you too may have a life of fulfillment, wisdom and success."

The Tamarack Tree

"This is a story about an Indian boy. Back then, instead of Bar Mitzvah, boys and girls had to go through a rite of passage in order to take their place among the elders of the tribe. Those boys and girls would be on the very site where you children sit today. One boy, White Pine, was the son of the tribal Chief. It was particularly important for him to pass the test, because if he did not, he could not follow his father's footsteps.

With just a knife, leather thongs and sparse clothing, the boy had to spend a cold northern winter alone in the woods and survive on his own. Now, this was a bit harder than a Bar Mitzvah. After awhile, the boy, tired and hungry, found shelter in a cave. He should have known that this was a cave where bears were hiding, but he fell asleep exhausted. Pretty soon, the growling of an angry bear woke him. (How would you like it if you fell asleep for four or five months and all of a sudden someone woke you?)

The bear attacked the boy, but the boy warded off the bear with his little knife. The bear took a last swipe at White Pine and wounded him seriously. White Pine made his way out of the cave and sat under a big tree with lush limbs, ready to die. Then, something strange happened. A young girl from his tribe spotted him and came to care for him under that tree. It was a huge Tamarack tree that sheltered him. White Pine got better, returned to his tribe and became a wise chief. The Tamarack tree had sheltered him."

"Shabbat was a special time. Tranquil, quiet and peaceful." Howard Rosen

"Two things were always present, music and bugs." Jim Grey

"Everyone went to Camp Tamarack. It was the place to go." Mark Rosenwasser

"We had the best food fights." Eli Greenbaum

"You learn to live with people from all walks of life." Nancy Triest

"It felt like such a better place, like you were in utopia for a while." Laura Berman

"I thought I'd meet my husband at camp." Paula Zaks

Danny Raskin's
LISTENING
POST

PARKING LOT AT Northland Theater was jammed with cars . . . as loading time arrived for Camp Tamarack . . . Like most of the others, 10-year-old son Scott was eager to get away . . . Bad error by counseling supervision had first bus he was in jammed like sardines . . . It was a small one originally intended for the not too large number of 8-year-olds who, because of the boo boo, had a big half-empty bus to themselves . . . Scene wasn't too unlike other camp goingsaway . . . some parents crying and some saying they should be the ones going to camp instead of the kids . . . or "Nobody ever sent us to camp!" . . . and "Now starts OUR vacation! . . . In the meantime, the youngsters could care less . . . as away they went for a good time.

"A certain kind of person is attracted to camp and camp helps nurture that person." Aaron Goren

"A counselor's job was to recreate the magic that we as campers experienced." Jeffrey Zaks

"Camp was a way of life. It was ingrained into our every fibre." Marvin Berman

"It was fun. You ate what you wanted and mom wasn't there to tell you to change your socks." Marc Shindler

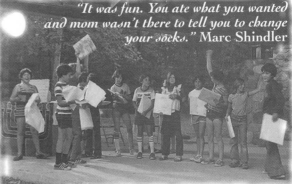

"The road trip was always a bonding experience." Howard Davis

"We were separate from what was going on in the world." Diane Klein

TRADITION AND CHANGE
USHER IN A NEW CENTURY

1980-2000

WELCOME TO
THE GROOVY
GANG!

"Everyone always wonders why Jewish geography works
so wonderfully. Well, camp is probably 70 percent of the reason.
I knew people from all these other schools
and my schoolmates didn't understand how.
Camp Tamarack absolutely shaped my life from respecting nature
and the environment, to respecting people and making friends."

Marty Maddin, camper 1980s

The summer IBM celebrated the fifth anniversary of its personal computer, 10-year-old Lisa Kopelman packed her little stuffed animal, Roofy, sunglasses and bathing suit and headed to Brighton as a 1982 Girl Pioneer. Tucked inside of her duffle bag was a sock stuffed with candy, "so it wouldn't get taken away from us," she recalled. She missed watching Punky Brewster on television, but was never homesick and loved making friendship bracelets, singing songs and walking around camp.

In 1999, talk of the Y-2K problem threatened the 53 million households with computers, but hardly bothered 10-year-old Eric Wolfe as he pulled out his Gameboy for the bus ride to Ortonville. Eagerly anticipating the baseball games, rock climbing and go-carting that awaited him, he peaked into his backpack to check his essentials: a picture of his mom and dad, a lucky $1 bill and a sock full of candy. Candy? "You sneak it in. It is a camp tradition!" he exclaimed.

In the course of nearly 20 years, much has changed at camp and much has remained the same. In 1982, postage was 20 cents and Brighton campers chose two Block activities, hobby electives, per session. Campers ate together in a large dining hall and slept in dormitory-style bunks. Two decades later, Ortonville campers spent their days water skiing, jet skiing, kayaking and horseback riding. Postage was 33 cents, but many campers opted to fax home their letters.

1980s FOOD

Carmen's, which became Annie McPhee's, was a restaurant located 10 minutes from camp. The breadsticks were the best, a treat every counselor and camper coveted. As for camp food, the reviews were mixed. Delivered by food trucks, favorites included soggy grilled cheese and meatloaf that would inevitably be followed the next night by tacos.

A Downward Trend Reverses

In 1980, just as the recession was beginning, Michael Zaks became the fifth executive director of Fresh Air Camp. Michael Maddin, board president in 1980, outlined the challenges ahead: a declining population, children's higher expectations, attraction of pri-

BERMAN 8 BUNK (l to r) Gillian Leonard, Erin Lowen, Amy Friedman, Lisa Blanck and Hallie Farber were 8th grade Berman bunkmates in 1996. Erin Lowen remembered, "We were one of the two Berman 8 bunks, so there weren't very many of us. And we loved our cabin... it was one of the new ones and it was definitely the biggest. It still smelled like new wood, not like old dirty cabins." *(photo courtesy of Erin Lowen)*

vate camps and the inability to increase fees nor depend on Federation for subsidies.[1]

Fifty years earlier, around a different board table, a group of women, and a few men, persisted in the heat of a Great Depression to overcome their own financial hurdles. Using their own wit and creativity, they stretched pennies to make sure camp wouldn't suffer. In that same spirit, Zaks, his senior staff and board members, put up an equally gallant fight. From a magic bag of tricks, the team – Zaks, Bob Lipsitz, Lenny Newman, Marvin Berman, Elliott Sorkin and Jeff Metz – became masters of marketing, parading into the community to promote camp. They held dynamic Jamborees and even built a temporary winter camp inside of Tel-12 Mall.

Slowly the numbers increased, but it wouldn't be until a decade later that camp would once more begin to see black on its books and full bunks and cabins. In the meantime, camp went on.

The Newlands

Sometime around 1980, junior Ortonville campers began taking overnight adventures to the Newlands. Located across from the old kitchen, on the other side of Grange Hall road, the undeveloped area was a perfect place to introduce the overnight experience.

"They put you in a truck that you couldn't see out of and drove you around for 45 minutes,"[2] reminisced Aric Melder, a Levison camper in 1982. "You'd hike about 10 minutes to this site where tents and all your food was waiting … to this area with a fire pit and water. They told you helicopters just dropped this off – and you'd buy it!"

Rick Goren, who later became Melder's best friend and camp's development director, was also a victim of the Newlands gag. Goren accompanied a 1989 Newlands trip as a junior counselor. "They would drive campers around to give them the sensation of being far away. Then campers would bushwhack their way to the campsite using compasses. They had no idea they were just across the street from camp."[3] That is, of course, until the next morning when the bus picked them up. Goren's trip was one of the last. "It was horrible," he remembered. "We had kids stung by bees, we had wild dogs at our camp site. We

HORSES

In 1980, horseback riding came to camp. At first there was a surcharge, but after businessman Milton Mahler came for a 1981 visit, he fell in love with and endowed the program.

FRONTIER 95
When Brighton closed, the youngest boys came to Ortonville to live in Frontier village. In 1995, their counselors were two British soccer fanatics, Alan Lado-Devesa and Simon Barbarash. Bunks were referred to as *Kujis*, and pictured here are the kids from Kuji 2. *(photo courtesy of Alan Lado-Devesa)*

had hail….just on us. It was horrible."

So much for the Newlands. The site became an occasional day hike area and overnight spot for older Ortonville campers. The thrill and importance of overnight experiences, however, remain central to the Tamarack experience.

The Transition Years

Under Zaks' leadership, Tamarack Camps began an important transformation process. Believing that camp should be a model of how nature, culture and Judaism could coalesce in a living environment, he began to increase the amount of Judaic programming and arts at camp. Sadly, almost before he got started, Michael Zaks passed away in July 1983, after a difficult battle with cancer.

After his death, camp went through an agonizing period. Despite a senior staff committed to carrying on the good of the camp, theirs was an uphill battle. Finances were unstable and enrollments stagnated. After a long search, in 1984 the board hired Steve Makoff, a camp director from California. He served for only two years as executive director before Sam Fisher, an Israeli, took his place. Both men implemented new ideas and strategies but neither succeeded in bringing camp back to the forefront.

In 1992, Harvey Finkelberg set foot in Ortonville. The executive came with an impressive record and a demonstrated "vision, drive and business sense,"[4] explained David Harold, board president in 1998. Four years earlier, Finkelberg had revived another camp, the Y Country Camp in Montreal.

"The Y Country Camp was almost a replica of Tamarack,"[5] explained Finkelberg, an M.S.W. who always carried camping in his heart. "During the 1960s and 70s, times were great. Camps were full and the economy was good. By the late 70s and 80s, camps started to close and enrollment went down." Less than 600 kids a summer

1981

A $1 million dollar bequest was received from Benard and Rosalyn Maas. After much debate, Camp Tamarack at Ortonville officially became Camp Maas.

1981

Who Slept Where:
6th grade boys **DeRoy**
6th grade girls **Fishman**
7th grade boys **Levison**
7th grade girls **Sheruth**
8th grade boys **Modell**
8th grade girls **Berman**

SPECIALTY 1986
(l to r) P.J. Cherrin, Fred Lusky, Jason Klein and Lee Bernstein were Specialty campers in 1986. They are pictured here on the Mackinac trip. Jason Klein remembers main camp where "I was a white cap every year, but we always stayed in the red water. Back then, how much fun could you have if you couldn't touch the ground. Red water was where the party was."
(photo courtesy of Jason Klein)

1996:
Lisa Zaks grew up
at camp. Jeffrey,
her father was camp
doctor, and her
mother, Susie,
became Assistant
Director. In 1996
Lisa (pictured with
camper) supervised
Kadima and Frontier
Villages, the youngest
kids at Ortonville.
"It was great. Those
little kids are so
young. They were
calling me mommy!
I tucked them in
every night." One
year later, she
supervised Sheruth,
home to sixth grade
girls. "They deal with
more mature issues
like boys and friend-
ship conflicts.
I was a role model
to them."
(photo courtesy
of Lisa Zaks)

attended the Y Country Camp when Finkelberg began. Four years later, as he packed for Michigan, 975 kids enrolled. He was confident he would do the same for Tamarack.

A no-nonsense talker with an imagination as bright as his red hair, Finkelberg spent his first summer getting to know Tamarack Camps. "When I came to this camp, I saw kids playing floor hockey with the goalie wearing two pillows for kneepads," he said. "That is the image of a scholarship camp. The Board wanted to rebuild this camp and bring it back to the top. So, you spend the $25 for knee pads."

A marketer would call it repackaging; Finkelberg called it a transformation. Tamarack went from black and white to technicolor. In his first years, he raised fees by 20 percent and obtained funding to build new basketball and tennis courts and floor hockey facilities. Jet skiing, tubing and waterslides were added. Informal Jewish education became a priority and achievements, small and large, became milestones celebrated with beaded bracelets and awards ceremonies. Tamarack became an affordable, first-class outdoor recreation facility with excellent programming that attracted Jewish children from all backgrounds.

"Harvey brought camp back to the campers. He looked at their needs and wants and desires. He wasn't always liked for that, but we supported him,"[6] said Jonathan Haber, board president in 1992. Finkelberg shook camp up as it had never been shaken before. Some of the changes were long overdue, some were emotionally difficult and some were just plain fun.

GOLF CARTS

Senior staff had the luxury of golf carts as their in-camp travel mode beginning sometime in the 1980s. The carts were also an efficient means of transportation for campers too. "Borrowing" the carts was a favorite pastime of campers like Lisa Goren. "We could take a paper clip or a barrette, put it in the ignition, and ride those things all over. Up the Berman steps, anywhere you weren't allowed to go, we would go. If you saw a golf cart, you jumped on it. It was a great way to make 10 new friends."

On The Land, In The Water, Sports Thrive

In 1982, a runner named Andy Krafsur became the sports supervisor at camp. He already had a long camp history, including being excluded from the 1978 Western Trip because he "mooned" his counselors. As sports supervisor, however, he kept his pants on. "In those days, sports was a very small part of camp,"[7] he remembered. "We didn't have particularly good facilities. I used to beg Marv (Berman) to put lights on the basketball courts so the staff would have something to do other than go to Carmen's for breadsticks."

By the time Finkelberg arrived, the courts were even worse. The same year that the Dream Team dazzled the world at the 1992 Barcelona Olympics, Camp Maas campers had to wait in line to shoot baskets on cracked courts into hoops that were barely netted together. Two years later, eight full courts, one fully lighted, and two half courts, kept campers busy all summer.

It was hard to tell who enjoyed the facilities more, Finkelberg or the campers.

"Everyday I play basketball with the senior side," Finkelberg said. Three to five players from one of the villages form a team and play against the big boss until they lose. There is a risk and a reward. If the group wins the first game, they get extra *keebood*, candy, if they win the second, it is pizza; the third a movie and the fourth, a night in a hotel. "You can keep going until you win it all, but if you lose, you lose it all," explained Finkelberg.

A lot of kids won the candy and the movie, but only on rare occasions did a team stick with it and win the grand prize.

"It wasn't exactly the easiest thing to beat Harvey,"[8] boasted Evan

1998 PIONEER
WHITE WATER RAFTING
Andrew Landau (l) couldn't wait to try white water rafting and neither could his cousin, Adam Leeb. "It was scary, but we did it and it was definitely worth it! When you accomplish something like that you feel you have reached something other people haven't. You knew you gave it all you could and did your best job," rightfully boasted Landau. *(photo courtesy of Andrew Landau)*

Schwartz whose Robinson Pioneer team beat Finkelberg in 2000. "He played really hard, he didn't want to lose. But, he did and Schwartz's village was taken to a nearby hotel where they stayed up all night watching infomercials.

1978-1983

Stablex, a hazardous waste processing company, submitted a request to construct a hazardous waste plant just north of Grange Hall Road. Up to 500,000 tons of waste would be transported into the plant annually. The county and the township, partnering with businesses and residents in the area, fought a successful battle to block the plant.

Reflective of an era when kids were less likely to play a pick-up game of Frisbee, and more likely to excel in an organized sports setting, Finkelberg vastly expanded both the land and water sports programs. What had been a one-person land sports department in the 80s, grew into a 12-person sports department by the end of the 90s. Roller hockey, mountain biking and tennis had been enhanced and golf, go-carting and gymnastics programs had begun.

Once quiet and serene, the waterfront morphed into a vibrant center of activity. In addition to upgrading canoeing, water skiing and sailing, kayaking and jet skiing were added. The two beaches were updated, too. Each side boasted the Log, a replica of the old, wooden-log-in-the-water game; a water-slide; and the Blob, a 12-foot climbing tower with a giant, inflatable pillow below.

Foxfire Fair

The Bert and Toba Smokler Pioneer Skills Center opened in 1984. This authentic old-western-style village features a one-room schoolhouse, a log cabin, a blacksmith shop, a general store, windmill and barn. Campers step back in time to learn and live pioneering skills. They make wax candles, spin wool, press cider and learn the 'Cotton-Eyed Joe.'

"P Skills" is also where the infamous Foxfire Fair, the second Sunday of each session, is held. It is a day "when you dress as cowpeople,"[9] explained Jenna Blanck, a nine-year-old 2000 camper. Adorned in overalls, bandannas and pigtails, Foxfire is the most anticipated social event of the summer. Remembering the freckles she'd paint on her face every Foxfire, Lisa Blanck, Jenna's big sister, swore "that Foxfire was always the hottest day, which made the lemons dipped in sugar perfect," she recalled.

1984

Anyone hungry? Each week campers consumed 3,000 lbs. of hot dogs, 4000 lbs. of hamburger and 900 lbs. of chicken.

"I wish I could be in a helicopter looking down on Foxfire day, to see 1,000 kids having such a good time,"[10] said Donna Bloom, a counselor who began her six-year camp career in 1993. "The music, the booths, water fights, it is a free for all. It is one of the most magical times at camp."

A giant barbecue loaded with 1,000 hamburgers and hot dogs sizzles as campers and staff play long-forgotten games, such as turtle races and log rolling. In between rounds of singing, everyone gets a chance to bob for apples, make donuts and throw wet sponges at grinning counselors. There are carnival games, fireworks, dancing and live music. The grand finale is the pie-eating contest. One lucky counselor from each village participates. They line up, each with one freshly baked blueberry pie and dig in. The image of these counselors, faces totally covered in pie, makes for plenty of sweet camper dreams that night.

FOXFIRE
Teamed up for a rip roarin' good time on Foxfire Day, is 2000 Fishman Bunk 4. Hannah Blume remembered, "Spraying my hair with sparkles, getting a tattoo, and playing lots of games with my bunkmates." *(photo courtesy of the Blume family)*

Brighton's Final Farewell

After many years of debating its feasibility, the Board finally closed Brighton in 1994. It was an emotional time for campers, counselors and alumni.

"As difficult as it was to face, it was obvious Brighton had to be closed,"[11] sadly recalled Helayne Shaw, a Brighton camper who became Brighton's Jewish programming director. "Besides the well running dry and the septic system not functioning, houses were encroaching on the property. There was a house that was built right next to the senior side bunks. Our fifth grade boys were looking into the kitchen and watching TV."

It is not that Brighton suffered in its last years. Actually, the camp enjoyed a late rally. Narrowly escaping a permanent closing

WINTER CAMP

Winter camping became popular in the 1980s as a way for parents to introduce their children to camp, and provide them with a fun winter break experience. In 1984, 212 campers participated in Winter Week programs.

in 1975, camp enrollment climbed, and in 1982 the Jewish Welfare Federation, the Sam and Mollie Burtman Foundation and the United Foundation funded a massive $500,000 renovation project, completed in time for Brighton's big 60th birthday bash in 1987.

Every Brighton project, every outing was gilded for the children. Dinoland swamp walks were preceded by wonderful stories, clowns came to breakfast and jovial Rabbis sang at dinner. Even teaching children trivia was kid-proofed. Shaw hosted Jewish Double Dare, a game based on Nickelodeon's Double Dare. The kids would mix green food coloring into cold instant mashed potatoes to make the

MARKETING

In an effort to reach out to a different sort of camper, and help increase enrollments, camp began offering one-week sports camps: basketball, soccer, softball and gymnastics. In 1982, Kent Benson and Terry Tyler, two Detroit Pistons, led a two-week clinic. Detroit Lion Al "Bubba" Baker also led a one-week football sports camp.

CIRCUS DAY ORTONVILLE STYLE
In 1993, Harvey Finkelberg brought the circus to camp… literally. Complete with high wire acts, juggling and live elephants. Campers learned to arabesque in ways they only thought possible in a dream. Sarah Roth (Meyers) wowed campers, flying through the air and landing safely in the net a few moments later.
(photo courtesy of Matt and Sarah Roth)

SIBLINGS

Assistant camp directors, David and Cheryl Miller, first arrived in Ortonville in 1993. This brother and sister team soon became a summer fixture at Tamarack Camps. Together they launched more boats, comforted more homesick campers and brought more smiles than any other duo at camp.

slime, and if they got the question wrong, they got slimed. "I still hate the smell of mashed potatoes," laughed Shaw.

"Everything at Brighton was playful, fun and magical," remembered Jeff Metz, Brighton's director from 1985 to 1989. Metz would greet campers every morning around the flagpole for the ritual *Bokar Tov*, an exchange of corny jokes and occasional skits. One of Metz's favorites was the Lost and Found Man.

"Whoever was up at the flagpole for that day would come dressed in every single item of lost clothing that had been found. It was a fun way to get the clothes back to kids."

By far, the most incredible Brighton event was Circus Day. "It was the best," remembered Metz. "The kids would go to sleep. When they woke up, the whole camp had been transformed into a circus. We'd stay up all night getting the camp ready. The flagpole was a 30-foot-high giraffe, there were giant elephants and bears. When it was over, the kids would go to bed and the circus left town."

The circus left Brighton for the final time in 1994. At the end of that summer several old and new campers and staff convened at the Brighton amphitheater to say an emotional good-bye. Elaine Schonberger (Malin) was a 10-year-old Brighton camper in 1962. "It seemed so small, especially after so many years,"[12] recalled the second-generation camper. Schonberger's mother, Frances, who attended camp in 1931, accompanied her daughter to the closing ceremony. "We walked over to Dorm 1. As we stood there, we realized that both of us had been Dorm 1, Bunk 5 campers. So many rich memories came flooding back. It was very emotional."

The Village Life

With Brighton closed, Camp Maas, for the first time in its 50-year history, became home to the youngest campers. As they had in Brighton, juniors led a simpler life than their elders. Holly Swartz was a 2000 Fishman camper.

"We did the Polar Bear Hunt in Fishman,[13]" she said. "We went near the DeRoy waterslide and looked for white stuff, anything white. Then we cooked our own pancakes on a campfire and found sticks and logs." Obviously, emphasized Holly, they found no polar bears, but they certainly enjoyed the chocolate chip pancakes cooked over an open flame.

Every village has its own history and every bunk its own stories. If only those walls could talk! At the beginning of the season the bunks are quiet and musty, the beds neatly arranged and the cubbies are bare. Then, the campers arrive. The little ones unload stuffed animals and markers while the older ones organize their make-up, razors and Walkman CD players. Cabins look empty at first, but within a week they look worse than a trailer park after a tornado.

Some may think bunk living is downright

NEW AMERICANS

At the turn of the century, Russian immigrants flooded the New York shores and dispersed to find new homes in America. In the 1940s, German refugees came to this nation and into the arms of distant family members who were grateful to see their gaunt faces. In the late 1980s, Russian immigrants began once again to flock to this country, this time to escape an impoverished, threatening environment. In each of those eras, camp became a respite for immigrant children, these "New Americans." In 1994, 80 New Americans came to Tamarack. By 1999, the numbers had dwindled to less than 12 per year.

luxurious compared to calling a tent home for the summer. But not Jason Zaks. As a 7th grade Modell camper in the mid-1980s, he slept in a soft-sided castle with a flap for a door. "Everybody had a nickname, I was Boone. I lived in a platform tent with my two best friends. We put carpet on the floor, little battery powered fans and we hung lights. We thought it was the coolest place in the world.[14]"

One year later, Zaks and his fellow 8th grade campers participated in the dramatic game of Exodus, an adventure that has become a camp tradition. "You start in canoes and pretend you are fleeing Egypt. Then you try to make it back to your village without getting caught," explained Aric Melder. Campers have about one hour to go from Sobell Beach back to their lodge. A camper is caught when a flashlight tags him. "I was hiding in the bushes, without a watch, for what I thought was 10 minutes. It turns out half the camp was looking for me because I was there for an hour. Just sitting in my little bush hiding, hoping no one would find me."

Jeffrey Grey played the game in 1993. His parents had both been campers and his mother, Ruth, was Camp Maas' long-time associate director. He knew every nook and cranny of the property and thought he was a shoe-in to win. "They get sooo many counselors out there because they don't want anyone to win,"[15] he recalled. "Usually

DANCE BARN

Sidney Winer, board president 1973-1975 and his wife Melba, a local dancer and actress, provided the funding to build a dance barn on camp property in 1983. Together, Melba, Irma Marcus and Allan Brown visited barns in the area and designed the structure. "I wanted it to look like a barn. I wanted benches under the trees and lights focusing on the dancers," remembered Melba.

no one does. When I was a camper the counselors were worried. I had been at camp longer than most, or maybe all of the counselors. I had knowledge of paths that didn't even exist anymore." Despite his confidence, Grey was caught.

While older boys experienced the thrill of a daring Middle-eastern escape, younger DeRoy boys went off to chase chickens. At least they did in 1995 when Evan Schwartz was at camp. "We had a mascot, a rubber chicken. One night it was stolen,"[16] he remembered. The next day the village searched the entire camp-grounds for the lost chicken. When it was finally located, the poor bird had been ripped in half. An elaborate funeral was held featuring a slide show of the chicken's brief but happy life. It was a night worth remembering.

The final stop on the Camp Maas trail is Maas Specialty Village.

"We asked ourselves how we could impact the kids, make them walk away feeling that they had grown, were better human beings and had had the most amazing experience,"[17] commented Marc Kay, the Specialty supervisor who dreamed up the elaborate graduation theme. Originally, it was a whim he

1990s FOOD

In 1992, campers began to eat together in an open-air, covered pavilion located on the water-front. Food was trucked in and it was a horribly inefficient system. Harvey Finkelberg pushed for a modern, kosher dining facility that would be able to feed 1,200 – 1,500 people at a time. The Mahler Dining Hall opened in 1999. Three times a day, the entire camp gathers around the *degel,* the flagpole, to exchange greetings and messages, say a Ha-Motzi and eat. Food favorites include pizza, grilled cheese, macaroni and cheese and potato knish.

THE RACHELS
Specialty campers 1995: (l to r) Carly Leipsitz, Rachel Williams, Rachel Margolis and Rachel Horowitz celebrate the conclusion of their Specialty trip at Mackinac Island.

had back in 1986, but it turned out to be a lasting tradition.

There is a prom, a senior skip day, parades with floats and a graduation. "One year graduation was at the beach,"[18] recalled Jill Bruss, a 1998 Specialty supervisor. "We put candles on floating boards, the campers got to make a wish and float their candles off into the red water of Lake Phipps." They said goodbye to their days as campers at main camp and eagerly anticipated the following summer when they would hop onto a big coach bus and travel on the Alaska or Western teen trip or head to camps Kennedy or Agree.

A Jewish Camp For Jewish Kids

In 1990, the Council of Jewish Federations published a demographic survey. The results validated what many intuitively knew. Before 1965, according to the survey, the intermarriage rate was nine percent. Between 1985 and 1990, it had increased to a whopping 52 percent.[19] The effect was that families, children in particular, were less and less exposed to Judaic culture and education. For many children, summer camp was the only Jewish component of their lives.

The confines of summer camp presented a rare opportunity for Jewish educators to dramatically impact and influence children and

THE ADVENTURE CENTER

The idea was to build a camp in the city, or rather a camp in the mall. Tel-12 Mall to be exact. "Bob Lipsitz had the idea," credited Allan Nachman, board president in 1980. "It was in the center of our population...a sales tool." Patrons paid an admission and spent the afternoon climbing the Jungle Jim or maneuvering around a ropes course. There was a nature center and crafts area and an indoor amphitheater. It operated only one year, from February to June. In these six months, over 4,000 people visited.

SHIFFMAN BUNK I
SESSION 4 1999
Jenny Farber (center) was counselor to a bunk full of wonderful young girls who loved to swim, stay up late and dress alike. One of the season's favorite nights was a Hawaiian pool party with Applebaum boys. They decorated the pool and ate a poolside dinner. Farber is flanked by co-counselors Jimmy Sams and Jenny Parkes.

counselors. One-third of Tamarack's campers were not affiliated with any synagogue while another third attended on scholarships. The board, staff and community realized it was time to pay attention to Jewish programming.

The best way to learn Judaism was to live Judaism. By 1990, it had become routine for campers to participate in formal rituals like Oneg and Kabballat Shabbat, celebrate Tish B'Av and Purim and experience informal education with Jewish songs and dance. The beautiful Judaic sculptures around the campsite lent an important visual aspect to the programming.

For many years, Judaic programming was left to the imagination of Gail Gales, who implemented a variety of creative programs. "Camp gave you an opportunity to participate in Judaism in a way you couldn't anywhere else," she explained. In 1993, she hired her first assistant, Dina Shtull-Leber, a Jewish educator and administrator. A year later, Gales stepped aside and Shtull-Leber took over. With a staff of 10, Jewish programming has become part of the fabric of camp.

Licking her lips, Alana Nedelman, a 2000 Fishman camper remembered a chocolate seder. "Instead of wine we drank chocolate milk, instead of bread we had chocolate covered matzah. Chocolate syrup was the salt water and you dipped pretzels, which was the parsley, into the salt water." Not much of the suffering of the Jews, but the campers enjoyed and learned from the exercise.

Every village adopts a Jewish theme. Younger campers learn about Tikunn Olam, the repair of the earth, while older Berman and Hermelin campers find out about Jewish survival.

"One night in Berman, we were told to make a play of having Shabbat dinner. We had 15 minutes to prepare,"[20] remembered Ashley Schwartz, a 2000 Berman camper. Each bunk assigned someone to play the mother, father, grandfather, children, etc. About five minutes into the role-play, the doors swung open and there stood the counselors dressed as Nazis. "We were put in the back of a Tamarack truck, packed in, no room, like people were in the Holocaust. We were taken to Berman field and divided up by age and sex. They passed out yellow felt Jewish stars."

The re-enactment continued, the counselors playing their roles true to character. "We were tied together, blind-folded and taken away, thinking we were going somewhere terrible, but really we were being helped," continued Schwartz. "We had to go on canoes blindfolded and row across the lake to the senior side, which was Israel." When they landed, the game ended and a valuable lesson had been gained.

ZIP LINE

Climb up a 60-foot white pine tree in Berman Village, hook into a trolley and, if you weigh more than 100 pounds, off you go, 90 feet in the air, 1,200 feet across Lake Radin. "The zip line is one of the most dramatic in the world," brags David Brassfield, whose Challenge Initiative course staff mans the mid-air thrill built in 1999. "Once the bugs were worked out and the 100 pound weight limit was set, no one has gotten stuck," he assured.

"You hear this over and over from campers, that the program they remember is the one that touched them emotionally. It really impacted their memories,"[21] said Shtull-Leber. "We are not religious, but we are strengthening Jewish identity, culture and values."

Kabballat Shabbat and Havdallah

The rituals and memories of the Sabbath observances are among the most precious souvenirs campers carry home.

The Kabballat tradition is almost as old as camp itself. In the waning hours of Friday afternoon, campers and staff freshen up, don clean clothes and eagerly march to the Zaks Amphitheater. The bleacher seats fill and the din becomes a roar, few ever noticing that for the only time that week, Radin Lake (Phipps Lake) is quiet and still. The song leaders take their place on the floating stage and the evening's hosts, perhaps DeRoy Village or the Arts and Crafts staff, set up their *schtick*, play or skit. Finally, the strum of a guitar and a booming voice on the microphone says, "Shabbat Shalom." The Sabbath has begun.

It begins with singing. "Song leading is what camp is about," said Rick Goren. "When you looked back and saw 300 staff members and all the campers singing, it was incredible." The songs are loud and joyous, the candle lighting solemn, and the highly anticipated Shabbat feast -- roasted chicken,

INVENTORY

In 1980, there were approximately 135 buildings on camp property. Twenty years later, over 200 buildings stood. Many of the old cabins had been updated, 50 new ones had been built and all of the village washrooms were updated. New buildings included the kitchen and dining hall, multi-use gymnasium and covered pool, camp office, laundry facility and nature center for the junior side.

Never let it be said there is nothing to do at camp:

1992: Slides added to each beach.
1993: Kayaking and windsurfing added to program.
1995: Gymnastics program added.
1996: Blob added to each beach.
1997: Log added to each beach.
1998: Rave added to each beach.
1999: Driving range, second climbing tower and challenge course added

PEAS IN A POD
(l to r) Jordan Silver, Simon Levinson and Jake Bayer don't seem to be bothered by the legendary Agree black flies. These three 1996 Pioneer campers spent a week at Agree and years together as campers.
(photo courtesy of the Levinson family)

potato knish and apple turnovers – is delicious. Afterward each village hosts their own activity centered around a Judaic theme.

The following day is subdued; campers sleep later, breakfasting on Entenmann cakes in the lodge and attending morning services. Sports and swimming fill the rest of their day. As the sun begins to set, the ending of the Sabbath and the start of the Havdallah service arrives.

"Havdallah is what being Jewish is all about. That little service is what kids remember," said Finkelberg.

Unlike long-standing Friday night Shabbat services, the more sedate Havdallah ritual began in the early 1990s when a committed team consisting of Marc Kay, Gail Gales, Elliott Sorkin, Marv Berman and Warren Cohen, the then program director, began to intensify Jewish programming.

"The villages were supposed to be doing Havdallah but they were not," remembered Kay. He and Gales decided to hold a unified service to help counselors become comfortable with the routine. They brought camp together at the Friedman Auditorium. It was meant to be a one-time affair, but the experience was so profound it became one of camp's most treasured events.

"Absolutely one of my most favorite parts of camp is the Havdallah service,"[22] said Jennifer Farber, a 1990s camper and Shiffman Village supervisor in 2001. "As staff, I never took off a Saturday night so I wouldn't miss Havdallah. It was a time to reflect on the past week and think about what is ahead. You sit there and realize, 'Wow I'm here and having these amazing experiences.'"

Havdallah is a spiritual ceremony that separates Shabbat from the rest of the week, explains Shtull-Leber. "It helps us end one week and get ready for the busy and exciting week to come." Song leaders and village supervisors lead the service, gathering on the stage with wine, spices and lit braided candles. There are songs and stories

LEAVIN' ON A TAMARACK BUS
As their mothers stood behind the cameras crying, thoughts of clandestine raids and bonfires race through these 1999 campers minds. (l to r): Ben Lesnick, Adam Forman, Scott Schwartz, Jordan Rosenbaum and Maxx Lesnick.
(photo courtesy of Wendy Schwartz)

and prayers. When the service concludes, the supervisors dip their candles into a glass of grape juice. At that moment, the only two sounds heard are the crickets beginning their nightly chirp and the sweet hiss of the candles being extinguished.

The Circle Of Life

Five cousins, all between the ages of nine and 13, sat together on a Saturday evening thinking of camp. After rousing reviews of Foxfire, Color Wars and their village activities, the conversation turned to their beaded bracelets. "You get a bracelet the first day of camp," began Alana Nedelman, age 11. "You get beads for certain activities and you go around camp showing everyone your beads. It makes you proud that you did all that. It stands for something you did really well."

Her cousin Lindsay Canvassser, age 12, chimed in. "You get a separate bracelet for horseback riding. You wear these bracelets all through camp and never take them off."

Taking a break from talking about her white water rafting trip as a Berman 8 camper in 2001, the eldest of the group, Erica Nedelman, boasts for a moment about her five years at Tamarack. "I have all my bracelets from camp. Last year I got my five-year jacket. You work your way through camp, you make friends and you keep in touch with them." She and her cousins have befriended kids from all across the nation and as close as the next community. They talk online and email each other constantly.

"We are building memories, friendships, confidence and relationships; things you can't build anywhere else because of the intensity that camp provides," said Finkelberg. "All of the things we do, the water skiing, the drama, the sailing, give kids opportunities to excel and learn new skills. They are the tools we use to teach kids independence, socialization and self-esteem. And, we are molding children's lives in a Jewish environment and there is no greater good than that."

Children and teenagers leave camp with autographs, hand-painted canoe paddles, beaded bracelets, dirty clothes, mosquito bites, paper

SISTERS
For many campers, having an older sister or brother at camp is a comforting feeling. Alana Nedelman not only has her older sister Erica, but a bunch of cousins at camp, too. "I like Shabbat because I get to see my sister and cousins, and at Saturday lunch you can sit with whoever you want," said Alana.

plate awards, achievement awards and memories galore. But camp
does something that none of its competitors – and by 2000 camp had
plenty – can do. Matthew Roth, a 1980s camper who became staff in
the 1990s, understood.

"Camp was my everything. All of my best
friends are from camp. When I was in college,
my friends went off to internships in the summer.
For me it was never an issue. I always came to
camp," said the assistant district attorney. "They
say that a trip to Israel is the thing that makes a
young Jewish individual feel close to Judaism. I
went to Israel, I didn't feel any more Jewish. I
feel very close to Judaism because of camp."

As the first 100 years of Fresh Air came to
an end, the trails of camp bore the markings
of campers that have come and gone, and await
those yet to come. For the Detroit Jewish community, once a small enclave of immigrants and
first-generation pioneers, camp has come to embody
all that living in a community is about….a circle of
life where seeds are planted for future generations and
foundations are laid to honor the past. Times change,
people change, but the essence of Fresh Air Camp – to provide a
healthy respite from city life – remains much the same.

DEBBIE FRIEDMAN

This nationally beloved
Jewish song writer and
singer was invited to camp's
1999 annual meeting to perform for the dedication of
the Stephen and Nancy
Grand Multi-Use Indoor
Facility. She was so over-
whelmed with the camp,
campers and response to
her program that she made
the unprecedented request
of returning to camp
for the 100th
Anniversary.

DIRTY AND LOVIN' IT
Tracey Graham and Debbie Bienstock (Fishman)
relish their dirty bodies and faces after a mud
fight outside of the arts and crafts cabin in 1991.

SMOOTH MOVES
Every afternoon, executive director Harvey Finkelberg
has a date. He heads to the basketball courts to play
a little basketball with campers and staff.

HEROES

CAMP LEADERS WHO HAVE LEFT INDELIBLE MARKS ON CAMP:

Joe Bender, Ortonville Baker

He was the baker who baked 'til dawn, and oh, what a baker he was. "You could visit him at night when he was baking and, if he liked you, he'd slip you a bag of cookies. That was the best," salivated Eli Greenbaum, a counselor from the mid-1960s. Bender, described as a gentle giant of a man, was a commercial foods instructor at Chadsey High school in Detroit. He spent his first of 14 summers at camp in 1961. When not baking, Bender would collect any or all of his six kids and together they would fish, swim or putter in the arts and crafts cabin. His cookies and hot Bender Buns became a warm, sweet memory for a generation of Tamarack campers. Joe Bender died just days after his wife, Isabelle, in November 1988.

Marvin Berman
Counselor, Resident Director, Assistant Executive Director

Over a 32-year camp career that began in 1955, this easy going, soft-spoken Ph.D. nurtured Fresh Air's growth in many ways. He did practically everything there was to do at camp, counselor, program director, resident director, tripping director, outdoor education director and assistant executive director. His warm smile highlighted his kind demeanor and subtle sense of humor. "Once you got to know him, you could see he had a great sense of humor. He was the best people person and best manager of people I've ever encountered in my life," fondly remembered Howard Davis, one of the many who grew and matured under Berman's tenure.

Rick Goren, Counselor, Development Director

Some knew him as "Snoopy," the kind and gentle mannered camper, counselor, waterfront supervisor, tripper and, later, Development Director of Tamarack Camps. One of the first children to attend Family Camp in the 1970s, Goren became the first of that generation to become a Tamarack staff member in 1989. In 1997, Goren's first duty as Development Director was to spearhead the $2.7 million capital campaign. Aided by a strong committee, $4.1 million was raised in six months. In 2000, Goren married his camp sweetheart, Katie, at camp and shortly afterward moved to a new career.

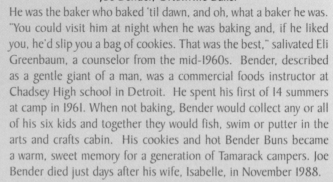

Gordie and Vera Levenson, Camp Kennedy Supervisors

The Levenson's, a sweet couple in love with kids and the outdoors, touched the hearts and souls of the hundreds who came to stay at their summer retreat, Camp Kennedy. Twice a summer beginning in 1965 the Levenson family, "Welcomed campers into our summer home. We lived our lives with an extended family, it was just a matter of having an extra 24 children," remembered Gordy, who together with Vera, relished watching young campers mature into skilled and confident young men and women. They retired from Kennedy in 1974. Vera passed away in 2000.

Mort Levitsky, Brighton Director

Levitsky first came to Fresh Air Camp as athletic director in 1944. After two years, he went off to other camps pursuing his career as a physical education teacher, and later became a Detroit elementary school principal. In 1951, he returned to Brighton, spending five years as waterfront director, then becoming resident director in 1956, a position he held until he retired in 1966. It is said he ran camp like a tight ship, with detailed organization and strict rules, but he always remained devoted to the children. He loved to get involved in everything at camp, especially showing off his canoeing capabilities.

Bob Lipsitz, Mio and Kennedy Supervisor, Outdoor Education Director, Associate Executive Director

Like so many other camp couples, Bob and Joan Lipsitz share a common passion: the outdoors. Bob, a camper through his youth, was about to become a Good Humor man when he was recruited as a 1971 Western Trip leader. A year later, while supervising the Mio base camp, he met tripper-in-training, Joan Rottenberg. By the time they married in 1979, the couple had established themselves as important camp leaders. Over an 18-year span of time, Bob immersed himself in camp, supervising Camp Kennedy, Ortonville, the ROPES courses, Outdoor Education and Butzel Conference Center. In 1983, Bob became interim executive director and left camp in 1988 to open the Double JJ Resort in Western Michigan.

Bob Luby, Counselor, Brighton Director

Throughout his life, Bob Luby had a love affair with athletics and camping. Brighton's director and Irwin Shaw's assistant until 1955, Luby came to Fresh Air in 1947, after his tour of service with the U.S. Air Force. He had many rewarding experiences at camp, including helping to launch the first overnight canoe trips. Luby left camp in 1956, beginning a long career with the Interlochen Arts Academy.

The Maintenance Men

Maintenance Team, 2001

"They all had one syllable names," noticed one previous staff member. Chuck Bumstead, Floyd Young, Chuck Bayer, Ed Nettleton, Bill Bradley, Joe Bolton, Dick Haas, Ike Simmons, Tappan Thomas, James Cooper, Marc Guindon, and Kirk Faulds. But what they lacked in letters, they more than made up for in punctuation. "The one reason Tamarack was able to grow," insisted Sam Marcus, "is because the men were able to build so much with so little money." They were fun, too. Counselor Joe Lash remembered Chuck Bayer's brilliance and fondness for telling jokes. "He carried a little joke book and in it were key words to his jokes. He'd say pick a number, he'd look up the number and there would be key words like horse and rabbi, and then rattle off his joke."

Lenny Newman, Brighton Director

The pied piper of Brighton began as a Brighton waiter in 1964. Once he became director of Brighton, it was never the same again. He brought a magic to the camp that many tried to emulate, but could never quite match. Perhaps this M.S.W., who loved to wear bright socks, was really just a big kid in a goatee. Everyday, Newman would sing the menu to his campers, meet them around the flagpole and be there when they went to sleep. He resigned from camp in 1985. Newman initiated the Jamboree, the winter recruiting fair, established Block time and helped launch the Brighton Renovation Project.

Beth Sonne, Agree Outpost Supervisor,
Director Family Camps and Grand Resort

She calls herself Ambassador of Fun, and when correctly pronounced, her befitting last name is sunny. A late-blooming camper, Sonne began her camping career in 1975 in Specialty one session and Agree the next. Little did she know that her love of the outdoors would prove to be her lifelong career. Breaking only for another camp assignment, Sonne has run the Charles N. Agree Outpost camp since 1983, lending her own sense of poetry, spirituality and brawn to the area. In 1999, Sonne added the position of Family Camp and Grand Resort director to her responsibilities.

Jody Winkelman, Camp Kennedy Supervisor

For 11 summers, Maverick, a black Labrador, has accompanied his master, Jody Winkelman to Camp Kennedy. She first set foot in the northern haven in 1979 as a camper. She returned as a counselor in 1982 and '83, became supervisor in 1987 and hasn't left since. During the off-season, she teaches health, biology and outdoor leadership at Lake Orion High School, although she never strays too far from the camp she's grown to call home.

Susie Zaks
Assistant Camp Director

A long line of Zaks have spent their summers at camp, lending their fervor, passions and ideas to make it a better place. Susie Zaks began her camp career as a seven-year-old, staying on until she became a counselor in the 1950s. After marrying Dr. Jeffrey Zaks, she returned to help him in the clinic and then, in 1987, Susie came back as a supervisor and has been with camp ever since. Spending countless hours recruiting and training counselors and organizing camp events, she always has a warm smile for those who meet her. It is worth every sleepless night, she says. "We work very hard and we are exhausted at the end of the summer, but you know you made a difference."

"*Once camp is in your blood, it is hard to get out.*" Harvey Finkelberg

"*Just a magical place.*" Donna Bloom

"*I am convinced that there is no other camp like Tamarack.*" Kelby Shaw

"*Camp was more than something to do in the summer.*" Jeffrey Appel

"*I always thought of school as the time between camp.*" Joe Lash

"*As I recall, we were always just dirty at camp.*" Kim Lifton

"I learned to be an I-can person. If you will it, there is a way." Jenifer Rosenwasser (Adler)

"There was always someone who I could talk to, someone who would listen." Brian Kepes

"Camp was a way for us to give back to the community and be a part of the community." Harriet Berg

WELCOME BUNK 2 TULIP

"As a camper, I couldn't imagine having more fun... until I was a counselor." Amy Guggenheim

PART II

THE GEMS OF CAMP

THE OTHER SIDE OF CAMP

*"The returned camper will be different. A momentous event
has taken place. The child has met a challenge and has found
his or her own way of coping with the unknown and the strange,
something no one could tell the child how to do.
But few, if any, children can put into so many words how
they managed or how they feel about it all.
It will take a lot of listening to find out."*

**Margaret Mead, "How Summer Camp Changes a Child,"
Redbook Magazine, August 1971**

In 2001, the 99th summer of the Fresh Air Society, 2,000 campers *schlepped* their duffle bags to Camp Maas; an additional 160 went on teen travel trips and 55 spent a session at Camps Kennedy and Agree. By all measures, it was a record year that would have made Blanche Hart proud.

Campers are the bread and butter of Tamarack, yet just a fraction of the thousands who stroll its 1,500 acres. Those others, some 30,000 in all, are the other side of camp. They are of the side that welcomes people of different ages, abilities and religions to enjoy its forested splendor, plentiful facilities and rustic lodges; the side that is as much a part of the soul and spirit of camp as the devotion that built it and the love that has sustained it.

Silverman Village

In 1962, the first "caseworkers" (social workers) came to live at camp and assist children with emotional difficulties. Three years later, Sam Marcus began meetings with Dr. David Faigenbaum, a Children's Hospital psychologist, and Gerald Levin, director of Children's Orchards Services, a children's treatment home operated by the National Council of Jewish Women. They met to establish a residential camping program for children with special needs.

Eighteen boys between the ages of eight and 12 came to Brighton for two weeks in 1969, the first participants in what was referred to as the "special camping program conducted by the Orchards."[1]

SILVERMAN
FISHERMEN
Just before they toss
this small mouth bass
back into the lake,
these two 1991
Silverman campers,
proudly show off
their fishing ability.
Fishing has always
been a favorite way
to while away part of
a hot summer
afternoon in
Silverman Village.

SHY NO MORE
Chuck Mays launched his camp career shy and unsure in 1997, but within a year was a veteran Silverman camper. He is pictured here in 2000 with counselor Erin Bennis. *(photo courtesy of Connie Mays)*

Often highly intelligent, children with emotional problems, such as ADHD and other behavior disorders, are prone to disruptive outbursts preventing them from functioning normally within a group. They need close supervision, clear guidelines and a structured environment. The close quarters of Brighton were hardly ideal. Marcus made it a priority to find the Orchards program a new home. The dream came to fruition when the children of devoted camp benefactors, Nathan and Esther Silverman, provided funding for the construction of a new village. Ortonville's Silverman Village opened in 1974 with 60 boys and 26 staff. Girls were accepted two years later.

Silverman ran under the direction of Levin until 1976. Two years later an associate, Barbara Vedder, a school psychologist and educator, became director. In the 22 years since, Silverman Village has flourished, filling to capacity three times a summer. There is almost always a waiting list. Located on the opposite side of Phipps Lake, the village offers privacy but is close enough to allow campers full access to all camp activities, such as go-carting, water skiing, kayaking and nature lessons. A two-to-one camper to staff ratio provides the support Silverman campers often need to be successful.

"We all deserve to have a special time when everything is perfect,"[2] said Vedder. "Our primary goal is to have the kids feel good about themselves and their experience."

"The children didn't have to fight for anybody's attention,"[3] remarked Ronnie Capling, mother of three Silverman campers. Her oldest, Jeff Freeman, became a counselor in 2001. "There was always someone available for them. They could be a shining star. This was a place where they could go and grow and learn."

Like every camper, Silverman kids begin their camping experience timidly and uncertainly. By the end of their session, they are true alumni, eager to return the following year.

SILVERMAN VILLAGE 1978

Barbara Vedder, Ed.D., supervisor of Silverman Village, obtained funding from the Skillman Foundation to build a high- and low-ropes and obstacle course at Silverman Village. The course helped older campers learn responsible group behavior and develop skills that enabled them to go on out-of-camp wilderness trips.

Wearing black rubber boots on the wrong feet, a frightened five-year-old Chuck Mays first boarded the camp bus in 1997. Five years later, this confident soccer player couldn't get to camp fast enough.

"I like being in the wilderness. We swim every day and I like the hiking, the ropes course and go-carting … I flipped twice," Chuck bragged. In 2000, a most unusual honor was bestowed upon him. "I had the most awards, about 35. I got the swimming and fishing award and the frog award." The latter given to him for persistence in the face of a very froggy event. "One kid bragged that he had a frog in his mouth for five minutes. I said, 'Oh yea? I'm going to get four frogs in my mouth for a long time.' And I did it! Everyone in the entire camp was proud of me." The frogs survived the episode, and Chuck brought home an award and a memory he'll never forget.

DANCE

In 1962, Harriet Berg, at the time an aspiring young dancer, hosted a dance weekend at Butzel Conference Center with Julliard dance instructor and choreographer, Ruth Currier. Twenty-eight junior high and high school girls participated over the Thanksgiving holiday weekend singing, eating, exploring and learning Israeli dances.

The thrill of accomplishing something unique and special is a milestone every camper – regardless of their abilities or disabilities – cherishes; indelible moments that become immortal camp memories.

Nachman Horizons and Horizons Avodah

Josh Levinson was talking with a counselor one 2000 summer afternoon about the upcoming Sadie Hawkins party. His mother, Elise, the camp doctor's wife, happened to overhear the conversation. "The counselor was talking about who is going to marry who, and

WESTWARD HO! Nachman Horizons camper Josh Levinson (l) went on the Western Trip in 1997. Standing with two of his all-time favorite counselors, Josh Jacobs and Tracey Roth, Josh's Western trip marked his last year as a camper. He went on to become one of the first Nachman Horizons Avodah staff. *(photo courtesy of the Levinson family)*

Josh sat down and started deciding who should dance with whom. It was very cute. But, most importantly, at that moment, I saw he was an equal,"[4] she said.

Josh has Williams Syndrome, a physical developmental disability. In 1993, he became an inaugural member of the Nachman Horizons program. In contrast to Silverman, Nachman Horizons children are integrated into main camp, living in the same bunks with children their own age and participating in the full range of camp activities. The program is the brainchild of Harvey Finkelberg, camp's executive director and former social worker. "I believe every child, regardless of his or her special needs, should be able to go to camp," said Finkelberg.

The Horizons program has a simple premise, but its impact is profound. Kids with developmental disabilities – who normally would be excluded from a residential camping program – are integrated into a bunk with a shadow, their own personal counselor, who stays with them throughout the day.

BUTZEL 1983

A small fire at Butzel was caused by wood joists in the attic being too close to the kitchen exhaust system. The damage was minimal and the whole building was examined for further hazards.

"Just think, there is a Jewish kid out there who wants to come to camp. He shouldn't have to go to New York. He shouldn't have to go to a place with only special needs kids, he can come to Tamarack," said Finkelberg.

"This is as close to being like everybody else as it gets for people like Josh," said Dr. Marty Levinson, Josh's father. "Other people treat him as one of them. The campers also benefit. As important as this program is for Josh, that's how important I see this for other kids who don't have exposure to people with special needs."

Avodat ha let means work of the heart. Seeing the Horizons campers flourish, Finkelberg took the program one step further and created Horizons Avodah. "We had these kids who graduated from Horizons. They couldn't be counselors, but wanted to stay with us. Now, we include them as part of our staff in Specialty areas (horseback riding, arts and crafts, etc.)." In 2001, 34 Horizons children, brought as much joy to their bunkmates as their own accomplishments brought to their families.

CHALLENGE INITIATIVES COURSE

General Motors constructed their own ropes course at camp in the 1980s that was later destroyed by a storm. "Lightning struck a tree, traveled along the cable, taking out two trees and two of three obstacles," remembered Rhonda Sandweiss. The course was rebuilt and by 2001, Camp Maas had three, state-of-art high-ropes challenge courses and one low-ropes course. In addition, the initiatives course includes two 30-foot-high climbing walls.

Butzel Conference Center

As the Ortonville property was being designed in the early 1950s, an area on the west side of Phipps Lake, near where the Butzel Conference Center would eventually stand, was designated as the Jewish Community Center day camp area for senior citizens. A newly built shelter and beach provided a nice daytime retreat. Beginning in 1962 with 75 older adults, the JCC began to host weekend winter camps in the villages.

Lacking was a special "senior village," an area designed with the needs of the elderly in mind. In 1966, Justice Henry M. Butzel gifted $150,000 toward such a village. Four years later, the Justice Henry M. Butzel Senior Citizens Village and Conference Center opened, featuring 10,000 square feet and three guest houses, each with eight semi-private rooms and private baths. It quickly became a favored destination.

OUTDOOR EDUCATION

In the late 1970s, the Pioneer Skills Center was constructed. School children helped "peel the logs that helped build the first cabin."

Whenever the seniors were not using Butzel, corporations were. As a corporate retreat center, Buztel was in high demand, especially for General Motors, who booked the center for about one half of the year.

Elliott Sorkin was running Butzel Conference Center in 1992 when GM's contract ended. Suddenly Butzel was empty. "We knew we had to make it profitable. We began direct marketing to businesses, non-profit agencies and synagogues. We overcame the loss quickly,"[5] he said.

BUTZEL 1983
As family camping continued to grow in popularity, the need for a chapel became significant. In 1981, the Morris B. Adler Foundation provided a gift to the Fresh Air Society enabling the construction of the Rabbi Morris B. Adler Chapel. Michael Zaks began the project and dedicated the chapel in 1983, a few months before his death. He is pictured here with Evelyn Kasle, wife of the late Robert Kasle, board president.

THE SPIDER WEB
One of the favorite group obstacles along the Challenge Initiatives Course is the Spider Web. The goal is to get each group member through the web without getting caught by an imaginary spider. Of course, there are a few obstacles: each time a member passes through one of the openings, that opening is closed to other members. Each time a member brushes up against an opening, they have to begin again knowing that the passage they just used is also closed. As fewer openings become available, the team realizes the importance of planning, collaboration and communication. *(Photo courtesy of David Brassfield)*

Quickly is an understatement. By 2001, Butzel was booked solid. Seven days a week, retreats, family camp, reunions, conferences, weddings, b'nai mitzvot and Elderhostel groups filled the 24-bedroom hotel. Now, to book a weekend, guests must plan early. Weekends fill up four years in advance.

The Outdoor Education Program

Inspecting swamp water samples under a microscope, studying leaf formations and identifying edible berries are just a few of the science-based lessons students undertake when they come to Tamarack Camps' Outdoor Education program. Originally managed by the Tamarack Hills Authority, the committee that acted as landlord of the Ortonville property, teachers and students began spending week-long spring and fall educational adventures at camp in the early 1960s. In January 1966, 8th grade students from Royal Oak's Adams Junior High School were the first to come during the winter months. Since then, hardly a month has gone by when some school, youth or adult group hasn't walked the trails of camp. During the 1976/1977 school year, nearly 9,000 people from 138 different groups attended some off-season activity at camp.[6] By the end of the century, over 22,000 school children participated in the outdoor education program yearly.

Schools bring their own chaperones and teaching staff, while Tamarack's out-

OUTDOOR EDUCATION 1979

Toboggan slides were updated and cross-country skiing and snowshoeing were introduced as activities for school-aged campers.

door naturalists act as guides. Many students are experiencing their first overnight camp adventure. Bonfires and s'mores and games of flashlight tag are common, but the real rewards are the small victories. Tamarack's Outdoor Education director, Pat Sharpe adores watching these students. "The best part of my job is to watch the child who is not an academic superstar come to camp and really shine. Just the other day, a little girl came up to me all misty-eyed and said, 'I just caught my first fish ever.' This happens all the time and those moments tug at your heart."[7]

1990

Outdoor Education suffered a dramatic blow when executive director, Sam Fisher, decided to close the program in 1990. Dozens of school reservations had to be cancelled. During the nearly two-year hiatus, a few weekend groups came to participate on the ropes challenge course and a handful of schools came in the spring and fall. Harvey Finkelberg quickly reinstated the program when he became executive director in 1992.

Challenge Initiatives Courses

In the middle of the Tamarack woods, a bewildered group of students stands with their eyes pointed upward looking at a giant Spider Web constructed of thick ropes between two trees. They are pondering the puzzle: how will each of them get across the web without falling to the ground? But, points out their guide, it is their work as a team that will get each member across. And, that is the whole point of the exercise.

Although she never overcame her fear of heights, Alana Zaks got across the Spider Web. "When you are young, you are scared. By the time you are older and you go across, you know you are really team building. You know you can do it."[8]

The Challenge Initiative Courses at Camp Maas – three high-ropes courses and one low-ropes course spread across hundreds of wooded acres – are among the most elaborate in the nation, according to the program's manager, David Brassfield, who has held the position since the early 1990s.

"Challenge Course programming is a good way to break down

HIGH ROPES
With two ropes to hang on to and a cable below, this element of the New High Ropes Course, built in 1997, is called the Cakewalk. David Brassfield, course director explained, "We wanted an easy beginning to the course." The Balance Beam, located to the right of the Cakewalk, is a little tougher. Participants are cabled in from above, with nothing to hold onto, but their vanishing fears. *(Photo courtesy of David Brassfield)*

barriers, bring people together and get them to take a fresh look at one another,"[9] commented Brassfield. "Especially the group initiatives. It allows a forming group to come together quickly and allows an existing group to start fresh with one another."

The ropes courses are one of camp's biggest attractions. Each year, thousands of Outdoor Education students, Butzel guests, Silverman Village and Camp Maas campers test their skills and build confidence on the challenge courses. The thrill of swinging from a rope attached to a tree limb high above the ground and landing on a platform hundreds of feet away is totally invigorating no matter what the age of the participant. Deeply immersed in the exercises, the adventurers hardly realize the communication and self-confidence skills they are acquiring.

An agile and fearless pair of tree climbers, Bob Lipsitz, then director of Outdoor Education, and Barney Brown, a trip supervisor, built the first ropes course at camp in the late 1970s. Their course was modeled after a federally-funded program called Project BACSTOP (an acronym for Better Acquisition of Cognitive Skills Through Outdoor Programming).

"The Pontiac Schools were part of our Outdoor Education program and were having racial problems,"[10] recalled Lipsitz. "The school was looking for ways to build connections between students. We wrote a grant request to integrate black and white kids and received the funding to build the ropes course. I remember climbing trees with Barney trying to build that thing, thinking we were out of our minds."

Instantly, the ropes course became central to the outdoor education and camping experience. "The schools recognize how the challenge course helps children learn to interact with each other and plants seeds of team concepts very early in their experience," added

THE STORY KING Marvin Berman, camp's resident director, was a frequent family camp visitor who loved sharing stories with the children. *(photo courtesy of Marvin Berman)*

THE CREW Summer family camps began in 1975. By 1979, these one-week summer vacations had become as traditional as fireworks on the 4th of July. Gathered together are five families: the Gorens, Zaks, Kash-Zorns, Leichtmans and Ornsteins. *(photo courtesy of Aaron and Sherry Goren)*

JEFFREY ZAKS FAMILY
The brother of camp director, Michael, Dr. Jeffrey and his family became regular family camp participants. Lisa Zaks, the oldest of the two girls, remembered, "We thought we owned the camp. We weren't the type of family that went on a lot of vacations to Florida, we went to family camp." (l to r) Jason, Lisa, Jeffrey and Alana. *(photo courtesy of Zaks family)*

Pat Sharpe, Outdoor Education Director. For campers it is the same. "The challenge courses build self-esteem and teach kids to challenge themselves both mentally and physically,"[11] added Rhonda Sandweiss, a 2001 course supervisor. "The experience reinforces basic concepts like helping ourselves, and teaches us how to get along with one another."

Family Camp

It wasn't the first in the state, nor is it the largest, but for the Jewish community, it is certainly the finest. Tamarack Camps' Michael and Donna Maddin Family Camp program has grown from simple week-long and weekend camp experiences into a year-round program with two locations hosting hundreds of families each year.

In an era when families spend too little time forming close bonds, family camping has become a booming part of the camp business. "We know that one of the problems with families is they don't have enough time together as a nuclear group,"[12] said Michael Maddin, who together with his wife, Donna, endowed the program in 1997.

From the moment the family Suburban pulls into Camp Maas' gates, every member of the family becomes a camper – bunkmates – and begins a bonding experience designed to cement Judaic images and rituals into the fabric of family life. Even more so, said Ruth Grey, one of the early family camp regulars, "It is *hamescha*. Family camp is being together. It was like going to the cottage but even more wonderful."

Family camp's humble beginnings can be traced back to 1973 when Maddin, a Fresh Air Society board member and a member of the United Jewish Appeal Young Leadership Cabinet, was searching for a family-friendly facility to conduct a UJA retreat. The Butzel Conference Center seemed ideal, but at the time it was only used for senior citizen

FAMILY CAMP

The first week-long summer family camp was held in 1979. Five families participated.

camping and corporate retreats. Children had never roamed its halls. "We told the Board that we would take full responsibility for our children," remembered Maddin. "And, by golly, it worked!"

That weekend retreat compelled Michael Zaks, Lenny Newman and a group of devoted alumni to bring family camp to Tamarack.

"I had gone to Michigania. It was very popular but the parents and kids were doing everything separately,"[13] remembered Aaron Goren, an alumni who attended the first Tamarack family camp. "I talked to Michael (Zaks) and suggested we plan our family camp with activities for parents and children together."

In December 1975, eight families gathered in Sheruth Village for a Chanukah family camp. "It was a vacation, a time when we bonded as a family and with other families," remembered Goren. "There was sand in the pillows, though, which in the winter seemed intolerable." The next year they moved to Butzel and made it a gala New Year's celebration. Those New Year family camps continue to this day.

GRAND TIMES
The first summer of family camp at the Grand Resort on Mullet Lake was spectacular in many ways. For two young campers, Justin and Alexandra Sherman, they had the pleasure of palling around with counselor, Simon Levinson.
(photo courtesy of the Levinson family)

In short time, New Year's weekends were just one of several family camp options. Winter weekends and week-long summer family vacations were among the most popular. The Gorens were regulars and their two children, Lisa and Rick, went on to become Tamarack campers. Rick discovered his allergy to pea soup and Lisa uncovered her spectacular sense of humor at family camp, but they gained something far more valuable.

"Family camp was our vacation. It seemed like an environment where parents loved each other and their kids more than anything. I had no idea what divorce was then. We arrived with our own families and then quickly melded into one big family for the weekend," remembered Lisa.

Learning and living Judaism and forming community connections in a non-threatening way was the ultimate goal of family camp. In 1984, 547 participants experienced the program, yet the Fresh Air Society had barely tapped the surface. Spreading the word and increasing participation became its greatest challenge. In 1986, the Jewish Experiences for Families (JEFF) project got underway. With Jewish Federation funding, JEFF partnered with congregations and other Federation agencies to host family camp weekends. Suddenly, thousands of families were attending.

Only the best Tamarack supervisors and staff were asked to

A NEW TRADITION
The first ever Bubbie Zadie Kinder camp at Butzel was held in March 1988. "There was an unbelievable response to the idea," remembers Carol Parven Hutter, one of the first supervisors of the program. By the end of the 1990s, there were seven Bubbie Zadie camp weekends per year.
(photo courtesy of Carol Parven Hutter)

work family camp, bringing with them all of their favorite camp games, rituals and antics. Smiling brightly as he holds his own future camper, former family camp supervisor and new father, Rob Bienstock, remembered his many family camp weeks and weekends throughout the 90s. "The goal was to pour on the fun and energy and never let it stop. Never let them see you yawn. I always told my staff to keep it safe, but offer as many fun activities as we can. Smile, clap and sing the whole way."[14]

Just like at main camp, singing was a family camp constant. Taps at nighttime, flagpole in the morning and the Booberator became long, time-honored camp traditions. Solving the Booberator riddle remained, even after 30 years, one of family camp's most anticipated rituals.

"Good morning everybody, Bokar Tov to you
Time for the 1st Booberator clue.
It's smaller than a house and bigger than a shoe
Be sure to tell Helayne in time for lunch."[15]

"It was such a big deal, but the funny thing was all they won was the chance to be the back-up (doing the shoo waps and bops) for the rhyme," remembered Helayne Shaw, family camp director in the late 1980s.

Family camp harkens back to the time when families packed the station wagon and went up to Lake Huron for waterside vacations in small white cottages. And, beginning in 2000, families actually loaded up minivans and headed to the Grand Resort at Mullett Lake.

In 1999, businessman Stephen Grand and his wife Nancy, long-time Fresh Air Society supporters, sold their automotive business.

Not included in the sale was an 18-acre northern Michigan resort, operated by the Grands for the purpose of providing an affordable vacation spot for employees. The couple decided to donate the property and all of its buildings to the Jewish Federation of Metropolitan Detroit for use as a family camp, with Tamarack Camps as the operating agency.

The 13 two and three-bedroom cabins overlooking the lake were booked the moment the resort opened in 2000. The Shulman family was grateful they got in.

2001

22,000 school children participated in the Outdoor Education program.
2,600 Bubbies, Zadies, sisters, brothers, mothers and fathers attended Family Camp weekends.
120 families spent a week at the Grand Resort.
257 room nights were booked at Butzel by non-profit agencies, corporations, youth groups, bar and bat mitzvah and wedding guests.
100 children with learning disabilities enjoyed a two-week camp experience in Silverman Village.

"If you were to describe the perfect family to go up there, it would have been us. We have young kids, grandparents who want to go, kosher food is served and the facility is on a great lake,"[16] contentedly commented Sanford, a camper from the 1970s who was only too happy to come back.

"Everything is there," he said with two children at his feet. "The camp could have been in Walled Lake, anywhere. But the people make it special because most have some Tamarack history and they bring that spirit with them."

Bubbie and Zadie Camp

At the end of every family camp week or weekend, tears are often shed. In a matter of hours, incredible bonds have formed between staff and campers, and no one wants it to end. It is the Tamarack magic, explained Carol Parven Hutter, a long-time family camp counselor and supervisor. "It is the staff and the spirit, and when you have a really strong staff, you have a really strong program."

So, why should parents have all the fun? Why not the Bubbie and Zadie?

That question was posed by Jeff Metz and Jeannette Tilchin in 1988. Jeannette was camp's registrar for many years and, by that time, a grandmother. Jeff was directing both Brighton and family camp. "We had an unbelievable response to the idea," said Hutter, a Bubbie Zadie counselor that first year.

"You can be with the kids every minute!"[17] exclaimed a very happy and proud Zadie, Dr. George Blum. He and his wife, Joyce, have attended Bubbie Zadie Camp three times. "It is such a wonderful experience," remarked Joyce. "Each time we take two of our grandchildren. We rotate them." The Blums, who have ten grand-children, are no strangers to Tamarack. Dr. Blum was one of the many devoted camp doctors during the 1960s. Gushing, Blum claims camp was better the second time around. At Bubbie Zadie Camp, he doesn't have to work.

Kids and their grandparents, brothers and sisters, friends and strangers. The roots of Tamarack reach deep into the Detroit Jewish community. Most families, like the Blums, retain strong memories of their summer camp experiences. Their lives and the community are all richer because of the passion that camp leaders have for inclusion, for acceptance and adherence to the principal that no child should ever be denied a camp experience.

BUBBIE ZADIE
Dr. George and Joyce Blum love coming to Bubbie Zadie Camp. A camp doctor from the 1960s, Blum used to come to Brighton each summer with his five children. At ages 70 and 65, the Blums have 10 grandchildren. Madeline Blum and Henry Moss came to Bubbie Zadie Camp in 2000.

Romance
Love and Kisses; Cookies and Milk

From as far back as anyone can recall summer camp romances have been as much a part of camp as cookies and milk… sweet, irresistible and unforgettable.

To fall in love at camp – whether it is the first time or the only time – is to be guaranteed memories more timeless than camp itself. Unforgettable moments like the swooning of a first kiss, the tingle of a warm embrace and the feeling of falling head over heals in love.

"Camp is like Shangrila," described Leslye Landau, a 1970s romantic. "You are doing something adventurous, being outdoors and you are with the opposite sex. What greater situation can there be?"

There is no official record of the first Fresh Air Camp romance nor any tally of how many Fresh Air alumni became husband and wife. Surely it is in the hundreds and dates back to at least 1917 when Harry Brown, the brother of camp's director Gussie Brown, and Sadie Keidan, a weekly chaperone, fell in love.

Jenifer & Mitch Rosenwasser

Met 1984, Married 1995

"Family legend has it," remarked Judy Cantor, a descendant of Harry and Sadie, "that Sadie was a high spirited, sassy woman who loved to tease and make jokes. She, like many others, came to camp to volunteer her time and chaperone the children." Harry's visits in his classy, Pierce Arrow automobile became much more frequent after he met Ms. Keidan. She was not an easy catch, though. Finally, seven years after he began courting her, the two exchanged wedding vows.

The Gensers moved a little faster. In 1940, dramatics counselor Lillian Mellen met a chap named Oscar Genser. "I was standing at the flagpole with my best friend, Leada Miller (Teicher). Oscar started walking toward us. He looked terrible, wearing an old, torn sweater." That first image was all it took. They married in 1942, shortly after he went into the Army.

Camp romances are as individual as the couples whose lives unite. How they met, where they met, who introduced them, when they got together, where they got together vary greatly. The process, though, does have a pattern. It begins the moment counselors arrive at camp.

"Each session, the waiters would size up the senior girls. To see who was hot and who was not," remembered Howard Steinmetz, a 1951 waiter. That summer he noticed a long braid down the center of one girl's back. "She turned around and I fell in love," he crooned. Her name was Barbara Bandler. Steinmetz worked hard to impress her. He tossed a rope up above the rafters in the recreation hall and climbed it with his bare hands. "I noticed him," smiled his wife. They were married in 1956.

Many a bachelor mastered the art of courting. Allan Warnick met his bride, Liz Borger, in 1957. He was a Brighton counselor and she a CIT. "We all knew each other and one thing led to another and we were paired off at the end," she recalled. To impress the young maiden, Allan would go out to the lake and catch the largest bullfrog he could find. "At lunch time, I would come in and put it next to Liz," he recalled. Such a gift of love.

Chivalry is not a required precursor to romance. Howard Rankin, a 1988 trip supervisor, was leading Berman campers on their canoe trip up the AuSable when he first met counselor Jodi Klein. "Every calamity that could happen to him, happened to him," Mrs. Rankin recalled. "While building a fire, he singed every hair on his arm. He caught his shoelace in a pile of canoes and fell face forward. He was stung by bees," she laughed. Of course, she was no Grace Kelly herself. "I

Ruth & Jim Grey
Met 1965, Married 1968

Rob & Debbie Bienstock
Met 1992, Married 1995

got really, really sunburned. I had to sleep in a tent with Howard, another tripper and counselor. I woke up in the morning and my lips were so swollen, I looked like Mick Jagger. I was mortified."

No matter. The two fell in love and were married in 1995.

To fall in love at camp is to fall in love with the real person. Sunburned, ratty hair, no make up, unshaven. There are no facades. Donna Bloom, a counselor from Montreal, met her husband, Kelby Shaw, a counselor from Great Britain, at camp in 1994. "I got to see the way he interacted with the kids, and it was irresistible," she said. Their 1998 marriage reception was held at camp.

Together all day, every day, relationships at camp become intense in a short amount of time. Some come to camp hoping to find romance, others happen upon it. Rob Bienstock had been a camper, a counselor and was a supervisor in 1991. Romance was the last thing on his mind. "I wasn't planning to fall in love," he mused. "When it happened, it just happened." He romanced Deborah Fishman that summer and married her four years later.

To fall in love at camp is to find a soul mate, someone who shares the same love of the outdoors and is from a shared background. It is also a great place to meet a nice Jewish boy or girl. "We saved the price of matchmaking by going to Fresh Air Camp," chuckled Irving Lash. His sons, Steve and Myles, met their wives at camp, as did his grandson, Joe. "Thank God for camp. In this family, it made happy marriages," the 87-year-old Fresh Air alumnus declared.

"It was an honor to be picked as staff for family camp." Helayne Shaw

"Camp is a nurturing environment, a great environment for families and campers." Aaron Goren

"Camp gives strength and character." Gail Gales

"There is never a better smile on his face than when he is at camp." Dr. Marty Levinson

TEEN TRAVEL

EAST, WEST, NORTH
AND POINTS IN BETWEEN

*"It was the first time most of us had ever seen mountains.
Imagine, waking up in the middle of a basin surrounded by
snow-capped mountains. Mountains, everywhere, as far as you
could see. At that moment, I knew, without a doubt, that someday
I would bring kids back here. And I did, three times."*

Sari Berman, life-long camper and assistant camp director 2001

Oone summer day in 1992, a bus load of Kennedy campers was driving along Highway 28, near the western edge of the Upper Peninsula, when they came to a corner with four gas stations. "At one gas station was the Western trip heading to the Porcupine Mountains, at the other was the Alaska trip heading to Kennedy and us, we were on our way to the Boundary Waters,"[1] marveled Jody Winkelman, Camp Kennedy's perennial camp supervisor and fearless trip leader. "It turned into a great staff reunion."

Logging over 100,000 miles each year, Tamarack Camps' campers, counselors and trippers dot the hemisphere. Agree campers portage the frigid waters of Lake Superior near Wawa, Ontario, while Western Trip teen travelers hike through the Grand Tetons of Wyoming. Alaska teen trippers gaze in awe at Mt. McKinley's peak just as Berman campers, thousands of miles away, navigate rapids along the AuSable River. In Ontario, Hermelin campers watch Shakespearean actors perform at the Shaw Festival and, in Ortonville, Camp Maas' youngest campers anxiously prepare for a simple overnight to the Pine Forest, located just a few paces away from main camp.

ENGLAND
In 1977, nine campers and two counselors boarded a jumbo jet and headed to England. It was the first time camp had sent a group overseas. The group hiked and camped, slept in youth hostels and spent a Shabbat weekend with host families. The highlights of the trip, remembered Jodi Wolfe (Kasmer), were seeing Windsor Castle, going to Wales, living on a houseboat for five days and being one of the last groups allowed to walk up to Stonehenge. Pictured here is the group's tour guide, British native and counselor, Jonathan Fingerhut and camper, Cindy Lax (Weiner).
(photo courtesy of Jodi Wolfe)

STAFF TRIPS

Through the 1970s, 80s and early 90s, village staff went on three-day canoeing trips up to Mio or Mesick. They traversed the same course as their own campers would weeks later and, more importantly, developed a strong sense of cohesiveness. In 1994 and 1998 camp supervisors and teen travel trip staff were taken to Israel to learn how to enrich camp and themselves Judaically. "It was an amazing, incredible trip," remembered Rick Goren, who was development director at the time. "We learned so much. We were able to bring a piece of Israel to camp. When we came back we did a lot more Jewish programming and did little things like giving the horses Jewish names."

One Canoe Makes Way For Thousands Of Trips

The first overnight expedition was in 1940 when a group of Brighton senior boys and their counselors put two, 18-foot canoes in the Huron River near what eventually would become Kensington Park.

Their trip whet an appetite that only Mother Nature could feed. Nine years later, while searching for a new Fresh Air Camp location, Irwin Shaw toured the newly opened Kensington Park and was shown the group camping facilities. Just nine miles from Brighton, Shaw realized it was the perfect place for an outpost camp.

At the time, Fresh Air owned none of the necessary camping equipment. The Sheruth League, a women's service organization dedicated to helping every child have a summer camp experience, came to the rescue with a $500 gift enabling camp to purchase tents, pots and cooking equipment at greatly reduced prices.[2]

A few years later, a second outpost was established, this

THE HONEYMOONERS Myles Lash married Linda Borger just three days before the two escorted a Western trip in 1968. They had met three years earlier at a camp Sadie Hawkins dance when Linda was a counselor and Myles worked in the kitchen. *(photo courtesy of Myles and Linda Lash)*

TRIPPING TIMELINE

1959: The Ortonville trip center is built.

1960: Teen travel trips originate. The first trip headed to Wisconsin and finished at Mackinac.

1961: Two Eastern trips were made.

1961: Eight-day canoe trips to Algonquin Park begin.

1962: First Western trip.

1963: Camp Kennedy, near Munising is acquired through a gift of Edward C. and Pauline Levy.

1966: Canadian Wilderness trips begin. Starting in Minnesota campers went on a 14-day, co-ed excursion, exploring Lake Superior Park.

1969: Charles N. Agree Outpost near Wawa, Ontario acquired.

1970: Mollie M. Burtman Campgrounds acquired near Mio for use as a base camp.

1971: Mesick site acquired for use as a base camp.

1977: Nine high school seniors travel to England with trip leader and Britain native, Jonathan Fingerhut. The group stayed with Jewish families in the Manchester/London area on Shabbat. The cost: $700 including airfare.

1978: First Israel trip, a five-week tour of Israel that included climbing Mt. Sinai, visiting Haifa and Biriya to plant trees.

1982: First Alaska trip.

1985: Eastern Trip is renamed Atlantic Seaboard Adventure and includes spelunking, rafting and rock climbing through the Smoky and Blue Ridge Mountains. Stops also included the Grand Old Opry, Williamsburg and Cape Hatteras, North Carolina.

time within the woods of the new Ortonville site. In 1959, the Ortonville trip center opened. By then, camp owned its own truck and
canoe trailers and was taking senior Ortonville campers, selected
for their leadership potential, on three-day canoe trips down the
AuSable River. "It was a huge undertaking," remembered Marvin
Berman, at the time the tripping supervisor. "We spent days preparing the kids and the truck. It was just the start of the trips up
north."[3]

A week by the Lake Michigan waterside was an extravagance
enjoyed by relatively few families in the 1950s. A trip out West was
rare. For many kids, camp was their vacation and the overnight
trip the extent of their travel. As they reached their teenage years,
the early baby boomers were bored, although they didn't know it.
There were no camp programs and, as leaders within the Detroit
Jewish community realized, no teen summer
recreation programs at all. The youth of the
day had little more to do than spend their
summer crooning over Elvis Presley at the local
drive-in. A joint committee comprised of the
United Hebrew Schools, the Jewish Community Center and the Fresh Air Society
tackled the task of creating teen summer
recreation programs. It was a new market
for Fresh Air, a market that had endless
possibilities.

Eastern and Western trips, bike trips,
expanded hiking and canoe expeditions and

TRIP LOG ISRAEL

"We've walked in 120-degree
desert heat, showered in 40-foot
waterfalls, climbed mountains, visited
historical sights...leaped tall buildings
in a single bound... We'll remember
this trip the rest of our lives. We all
think of Israel as our home and know
that we'll return someday. We say
shalom and lehitraot."
**Robert Bick, Bob Murav and
the entire 1978 Tamarack
Israel camping trip.**

ISRAEL
"The two most
emotional moments
were visiting Yad
Vashem and planting
the trees," recalled
1978 Israel teen
tripper, Jodi Wolfe
(Kasmer). "You
picked your tree, dug
the hole and planted
it. I planted one in
memory of my
grandfather and one
in honor of my par-
ents for letting me
go to Israel."
*(photo courtesy
of Jodi Wolfe)*

the first Pioneer villages were all outgrowths of this period of programming. By 1968, 40 canoe trips with over 600 children were organized by Fresh Air. Extended trips to Canada's Algonquin Park were offered to Pioneer campers, and the beautiful Camp Kennedy had been acquired allowing young teens to live in and explore Michigan's Upper Peninsula. One year later, in 1969, the rustic wilder-

EASTERN 1975 Selecting lobsters for a lobster bake and sleeping in a laundromat are two of the most memorable moments from this 1975 Eastern trip. Pictured: top row (l to r) Sue Gottlieb, Andi Feig, Jaqi Green. Front row (l to r) Julie Herzback, Lee Fivenson, Linda Singer and Marni (last name unknown). *(photo courtesy of Jodi Wolfe)*

ness on the north side of Lake Superior in Canada became home to Tamarack's Camp Agree.

EXPO '67

Eastern trippers in 1967 headed to Montreal, Canada for a five-day stay at Expo '67. Elise Levinson (Chapin) vividly remembered the trip. "We stayed on campus at McGill University. The most fun was waiting in line, like at the Israeli pavilion. It was so popular we had to wait for hours. We sang songs and met lots of people. We were just little *pishers*, going into 10th grade."

The Mio and Mesick outpost base camps were up and running by 1971. By that time, stacks of trip logs and notes detailed a myriad of trails and rivers, and camp had plenty of green buses gassed up for even greater expeditions. In 1978, the first group of Tamarack campers toured Israel and in 1982, Barb Feldman and Phil Jacobs escorted 16 young adventurers, aged 15 and 16 to Alaska. The Tamarack life cycle had evolved and travel trips, especially for the 90s generation, became a routine part of the experience.

The Western and Eastern Trips

The first teen travel trip took off in 1960 with 12 kids and three adults loaded into two green station wagons and a trailer truck. There was much ado and excitement in preparing for the trip. "Tripsters" were required to have a complete set of Salk polio shots, an extra pair of glasses, four handkerchiefs, two dungarees, one pair of low-cut Keds and $10 in pocket change.[4] The trip included visits to the state capital, Wisconsin's Camp Chi, Mackinac Island and the Stratford Festival in Canada where campers saw Romeo and Juliet. It was a huge success.

One year later, gas tanks full, the caravan took off again, this time headed East. For 17 days campers trekked through Vermont, New Hampshire and New York. They saw a concert in the Berkshires and gazed at Niagara Falls. The cost for the trip was $160, and eight of those who went participated at scholarship rates.

EASTERN 1974 Bus driver Harold Friedman (l) and counselor Jonathan Licht steal a moment to take in the view at Acadia National Park, Maine. "From there, we put the bus on an ocean ferry and went to Yarmouth, Nova Scotia," remembered Friedman. "It was quite a trip, beautiful scenery." *(photo courtesy of Roz Blanck)*

A yearning for longer, more adventurous expeditions led to the Western trips that launched in 1962. One could safely assume that most of those early Western teen travelers had never seen Old Faithful, set foot in the Rocky Mountains or canoed rivers in the Dakotas. The trips sold out in record time and finding staff was never a problem. A few couples even combined their honeymoon with the pleasure of traveling in a bus full of young teenagers. Arnie Collens wanted to lead a Western trip with his girlfriend Dorothy, but Sam Marcus would not hear of it. So, they got married and spent their 1966 honeymoon with 26 teenagers. Myles Lash worked in the Ortonville kitchen. In 1968, three days after he married his sweetheart Linda Borger, a well-regarded counselor, they boarded the green bus with "15, 16-year-olds chaperoning us,"[5] he fondly recalled. They pitched tents in a new location every night, marveled at the scenery and watched the girls flirt with the boys. Everyone was well-behaved, swore Lash except perhaps he and his new wife.

WESTERN TRIP 1998 (l to r) Adam Jacobs, Liz Hauser, David Lipson and Erin Lowen are pictured in Arches National Park. *(photo courtesy of Erin Lowen)*

HERE COMES THE
BRIDE (NOT)
In 1978, Joanne Rowe
(Korn), center, and
Mike Wiener were
the Eastern trip
counselors. The
campers decided that
the two ought to
get married. They
planned an entire
wedding affair
complete with a
bridal veil, bouquet,
bridesmaids and a
caterer (trip
supervisor, Barb
Philka [Feldman]).
The wedding took
place on a Friday
night, nicely
coordinated with the
Shabbat service.
*(photo courtesy of
Joanne Rowe)*

"One night a windy storm blew in. It blew our tent away and we realized that a bunch of teens were standing there watching us."

Once rolling, the infamous green Tamarack busses never stopped. A more rugged 30-day Western trip was established in 1969, traveling through Banff and Lake Louise, Canada, then Montana, Wyoming, Minnesota and finally home to Michigan. The beauty and splendor of the trip was, as camper after camper would note in logs and letters, remarkable. "Before us laid Banff and the Canadian Rockies,"[6] wrote Jay Kehoe, in 1973. After a stop at the Dairy Queen, "Canadian DQ's are the best" he noted, the group continued toward their campsite. "We came up through Kootenay National Park which had the most beautiful scenery I've ever seen."

By 1975, there were three Western and one Eastern trips each summer. Western trips varied by degrees of difficulty, campers could choose from more and less rugged hiking experiences. The Eastern trip, for kids entering 10th and 11th grades, began its route in the Finger Lakes region of New York, then traveled up through Maine, Montreal and Quebec City. In the White Mountains of New Hampshire, campers climbed Mt. Lafayette, 5,200 feet above sea level with

WESTERN TRIP LOG 1965

"Whenever a person or a group travels anywhere there is always one stop, one place, that stands out as the highlight...For us the most memorable moments were spent at Miller, Kansas...we were even made honorary members of Miller Rural Fire Department with a vehicle sticker placed on the bus windshield...The teenagers of Miller entertained us with a demonstration of Western dancing and our trippers reciprocated with Hebrew folk songs and dances." **Neil Cote, Supervisor**

snow covered trails in the middle of summer and boulders half the size of the Tamarack bus. "The scenery was absolutely gorgeous,"[7] wrote Mimi Spiwak in 1980. "Waterfalls poured with the clearest sparkling water, so pure that we drank right from the stream. The climb was hard and treacherous, because the majority of it was climbing straight up on boulders."

Low enrollment for the Eastern trip prompted camp staff in 1985 to re-route and re-name the trip the Atlantic Seaboard Adventure. It ventured through the Smoky Mountains, stopped at the Grand Ole' Opry and Cape Hatteras. The change revived the trip for a while, but by the late 1990s, it was no longer offered.

Not so for the Western trips. The route became strictly within U.S. borders and varied slightly each year depending on the trip supervisors, who were given a certain amount of leeway in choosing stopovers. In 1979, for example, Barbara Feldman took her West-

LAS VEGAS
Five weeks seeing some of the most beautiful scenery in America was more than 2000 Western trip counselor, Simon Horne, could have ever imagined. The British counselor said, "being offered the chance to supervise a Western trip was unbelievable. I can also tell you that it was unforgettable!!!!" As far as Las Vegas, this unplanned stop turned out to be a bonus. "It seemed like WE were the tourist attraction - imagine seeing 25 crazy kids walking down the Strip at midnight!"
(photo courtesy of Simon Horne)

ern teen travelers to Zion National Park in Utah. High water levels prevented them from the planned two-day hike to Narrows Canyon, so instead they hiked up Orderville Canyon. "It was fantastic,"[8] she wrote. "Probably the campers' favorite hike of the trip."

Seeing amazing sights was only part of the travel experience. Learning group responsibility was equally transforming. "Everyone had a certain job. If you didn't do it, it was bad for the group. You learn how important it is for everyone to contribute,"[9] remarked Andrew Landau, a 2000 Western tripper. He and his best friends, most of whom he met at camp, had the time of their lives on the Western trip. "All of us are good hikers. We like to push ourselves to the max. We give it our all so we can go as far as possible and see the best view."

In 1979, Lisa Elconin (Buckfire) went on the Western II Trip. "My job was to wash the bus windows. I was very glad I didn't have

WESTERN III TRIP LOG 1980

"This is our first morning in the desert land of Zion National Park. The temperature is hot and the color of the land is red with the mineral iron... We hiked to the Emerald Lower, Middle and Upper pools. At Lower pool, we showered in a small fall and ran through the pool... We hiked up to Upper pool for a beautiful swim and some rock climbing."
Sara Diem

WET AND WILD

In 1976, Western campers drove through one heck of a rainstorm to get to Estes Park, Colorado. What they didn't know was, as they arrived, the road they had just traveled had flooded and washed out. Dozens were injured. It was a catastrophe that made national news. Before cellular phones, even though camp had an itinerary of the trip, administrators were at the mercy of counselors to phone in and report their whereabouts every once in awhile. Parents were panicked, remembered Beth Stone (Katz), who is pictured happily standing on the right. It wasn't until two or three days later, in Denver, before Stone called her mother who, although she knew the bus had been spotted, felt much relieved to hear her daughter's voice. Stone is pictured with Marla Kushner.
(photo courtesy of Beth Stone)

the job of wiping the greasy salamis that were hanging in the back of the bus. I loved the Western trip. We were only 16-years-old and got to set up our own tents, cook our own food, make our own campfires. We grew so much."[10]

Every trip had three things in common… good food, great memories and at least one memorable bus breakdown misadventure. Elconin's trip was spared. Not to be denied the experience, however, the group faked their own breakdown. With a rope tied to the front bumper, one of the counselors "pulled" the bus into the JCC parking lot.

That scene, whether real or staged, became a dreaded icon of the travel experience. Executive director Harvey Finkelberg put an end to it in the early 1990s when he retired the green Tamarack buses for the long road trips, retaining them for shorter distances. Western and Alaska travelers began riding aboard coach buses complete with bathrooms. Instead of $10 in pocket change and Salk polio shots, the 2000 teen traveler carried a credit card and a digital camera.

WESTERN TRIP LOG 1996

"We're having a contest with us guys to see who can kill the most mosquitoes. Josh I. is probably in the lead. We also are having other contests, but I won't go into detail. All I have to say is there are 10 teenage guys together for two nights without any of the beautiful women of Western II… Use your imagination."
Jay Mentzel

Timeless though were the memories. Jason Zaks went on the 1988 Western trip. Like so many others, he swears the trip changed his life. "It was a spectacular month away. Growing up, learning about other people, learning to be tolerant of other people's differences. That is the underlying thing that happens on a trip. Everyday you are going around seeing different things, but on these trips, you are learning about people."[11] Zaks never forgot the night he slept atop one of the arches at Arches National Park. "Where do you get to do that?" he marveled.

The memories become a part of each traveler's fabric, precious morsels they carry forever: a snowball fight on a mountaintop in July, a midnight shopping excursion, reaching the summit of a mountain after a treacherous climb, or a late night dinner around a campfire with stars above and buffalo roaming nearby. After experiencing these wonders, campers know they will never be the same again.

"We'd all made a pact to stay awake until we got home, and at around 5 a.m. we pulled over into a rest stop, got off the bus as the day was dawning, and huddled for a final circle,"[12] reminisced Simon Horne, Western 1 Trip supervisor in 2000. "We lit a candle and everyone said a few words about their summer. It was at this point that it hit me hard – what an amazing time we'd had and the impact the group members had made on one another. Tears flowed from both staff and campers… We truly had lived through a great experience which I can guarantee nobody on the trip will EVER forget."

FRIENDS
A camper since age 12, Aric Melder could barely contain his excitement at being chosen to lead the Western trip in 1993. It got even better when he found out two of his best friends were coming along as fellow counselors. (l to r): Rick Goren, bus driver Rodger "The Dodger," Andrea Wolff, Aric Melder and Mike Levy. *(photo courtesy of Aric Melder)*

Alaska The Beautiful

In 1973, Bob Lipsitz, at the time the supervisor in charge of the Mio base camp, asked his friend, Barbara Philka (Feldman), if she would be interested in coming up to Mio as a tripper. She had never been a Tamarack camper, nor had even heard of Mio, but she had certainly been a camper. So, at the age of 21, Philka headed to Mio as the base camp's first female resident tripper. The all male staff anointed her "Ma," a nickname that stuck for many years. After a few summers in Mio, Ma boarded the ole green school bus and began supervising Western and Eastern trips, caving, rafting and exploring some of the country's most beautiful sites.

But it was in 1982 that this high school math teacher's greatest adventure began, when she was asked to plan and escort a camper

GIRLS' DAY OUT
"The water at String Lake was crystal clear. It was such a beautiful day and area, we decided to skip our second day of hiking and just relax on the beach instead," remembered Katie Cohen (left), Western I 2000 tripper. After their leisurely day, Cohen and Rachel Mansfield packed up their backpacks and finished the backcountry hike through the Grand Tetons. *(photo courtesy of Katie Cohen)*

trip to Alaska. The year before, Marvin Berman visited his twin brother who lived in the 50th state. He came back and told Michael Zaks about the area and its incredible beauty. Zaks, remembered Berman, said, "Let's do it!" and recruited Philka and Phil Jacobs, another experienced trip leader and bus driver. Neither had ever been to Alaska and relied primarily on maps to plan the 42-day extravaganza.

"We traveled on a shoe string,"[13] remembered Philka. The trip cost each participant $1,500, a low fee thanks to Alaska's free camping facilities and philanthropists Jack and Aviva Robinson, founders of Perry Drug Stores, who underwrote the trip's major costs. The real hero of the trip was the green bus. It was cheap to operate and, more importantly, said Philka, set the tone of the trip. "The bus gave us a lot of validity. It defined the trip. It symbolized where we were going, not just how we were getting there. We ran into people all over the place that recognized the green bus. They would chase after it. We also found that people were more likely to help a bunch of students on a school bus."

Philka escorted trippers to Alaska for three years. A camper named Howard Rankin rode along on her last trip. "We were a bunch of kids from West Bloomfield who were totally ill prepared," he remembered. "My parents and I had never been out west or to the mountains. They bought me all this stuff from the Army Navy Surplus. Then, they throw you in Alaska. We were hiking in a total wipe out blizzard. People were just a wreck, but I thought it was the

FERRY TO ALASKA
"I would have never water skied, backpacked or gone to Alaska if it wasn't for camp," said Alana Zaks, pictured among the cubby creatures aboard the ferry to Alaska in 1997.
(photo courtesy of Alana Zaks)

coolest thing in the world."[14]

It was a trip that changed his life. "Every chance I got in college and law school I went out West backpacking. I love the mountains and I love the terrible weather," Rankin continued. He also loved that green bus. "We only had five or six showers the whole trip. It was only after a shower, that you realized how smelly the bus was."

The Alaska trip included a ferry ride that departed from Prince Rupert, BC and landed, two and a half days later, in Skagway, Alaska. Campers hiked in the midnight sun to the Yukon Territory, following the famous Chilkoot Pass, the same trail used by gold miners in the late 1800s. They camped at Denali Park, at the foot of Mt. McKinley where, on a rare clear day the very top of the continent's highest mountain might be visible. In 1997, David Zaks, Michael Zaks' son, witnessed one of those exceptional glimpses. "It was amazing," he recalled. "The most beautiful place I've ever been."[15] Recording his feelings in the trip log, he wrote, "This year, being my last year as a camper and being on a trip my father began, I knew that from the beginning it would be special to me. This year I pushed myself harder both mentally and physically. I did it both in honor and in memory of my father."

Imagine 24 hours of sunlight every day for 42 days. That is one

ALASKA 1989
Trip leaders, (l to r) Joe Lash, Jody Winkelman and Mitch Rosenwasser escorted 16 campers to Alaska in 1989. One year earlier, 14 of those campers and all three counselors had been together at Camp Kennedy. *(photo courtesy of Jody Winkelman)*

GREAT HAIR DAY
Pictured is Melissa Meyers showing off her amazingly stiff hair in 1990. Her friend Rachel Grey observed, "You don't shower for so long, your hair can do anything."
(photo courtesy of Rachel Grey)

ALASKA TRIP LOG 1990

"Some Indian guy asked Carin for her hand in marriage. Sadly, she said no. Rachel Nobel fell in love with the hot (clean) guys in a hot (clean) car. But she realized she wasn't clean and got very depressed." **Melissa Beth Slaim**

aspect of the Alaskan trip. Mitch Rosenwasser couldn't get enough. He went in 1987 as a camper, and three times as a trip leader. Memories of the incredible scenery and tremendous challenges of the trip brought a radiant glow to his eyes. Then, he remembered one of the Alaskan Shabbats. "Being on the trail made Shabbat hard because it never actually got dark, it just sort of got dim. We always packed things for Shabbat, though…we packed grape juice for wine in our packs. We wrote our own service. I remember one year a deer joined us for prayers."[16]

"Alaska is just…Alaska. Unbelievable," uttered Simon Levinson who went in 1999. Intense hiking trips and a four-day sea kayak expedition along Alaska's coast were his best souvenirs. "I was with my

PHILIP A. HART
MICHIGAN

United States Senate
WASHINGTON, D.C. 20510

COMMITTEES:
COMMERCE
JUDICIARY

August 11, 1972

Mr. Camp Tamarack
18100 Meyers
Detroit, Michigan

Dear Mr. Tamarack:

When I got back to the office the other day I found the card telling me of your visit. I certainly am sorry not to have had the chance to visit with you, and I hope the staff did all they could to make your Washington visit a pleasant one. Don't hesitate to let me know if there is anything I can do for you.

With best wishes,

Sincerely,

Philip A. Hart

MR. TAMARACK
Eastern teen travelers often stopped in Washington DC to see the sites of the capital and shake hands with lawmakers. In 1972, Senator Philip Hart missed his chance to visit with the group, but penned this note of thanks instead.

ALASKA 1992
"If you live in a
bus for six weeks,
you better get
comfy," remembered
Lisa Zaks, Alaska
teen tripper 1992.
"Alaska was all the
more amazing, the
scenery, the whales.
It was hard to
describe what it was
like to be out there,
to be free, to be
with your friends,
doing things as a
unit and learning
about group decision
making." Pictured is
Lisa Zaks on top of
a heap of duffles,
flanked by an equally
lucky traveler,
Carrie Atlas.
*(photo courtesy
of Lisa Zaks)*

best friend. It was really not that difficult, it was just beautiful. You're sitting out on the ocean and all of a sudden it'll get difficult with the waves, then you start to relax again and all of a sudden a seal will pop up and follow you for a while," remembered the high school senior who became a camp counselor in 2000.

As any Alaska traveler will attest, nothing in the Great Lakes State compares to Alaska's great, untamed wilderness. "It was depressing coming back to flat Michigan," said Levinson. "It was tough coming back and realizing that the trip went by so fast."

He'll go again, he swears, and so will many others.

BEAR ATTACK 1990
Upon entering Denali Park, campers are taught
how to fend off any errant bear that may wander
onto a campsite. Demonstrating the technique
are (l to r) Stacey Weinberg, Rachel Grey,
Melissa Slaim and, seated, Carin Rockind.
(photo courtesy of Rachel Grey)

TRANSPORTATION TROUBLES

As McDonald's has its golden arches, Tamarack has its green school buses. From coast to coast they traveled, from town to town they were welcomed and from road to road they broke down. It seemed for years, every trip had its share of misadventures – a broken down bus, missing keys, flat tire or some other mishap. Rhonda Sandweiss, 1992 tripping supervisor, tallied a total of 47 bus breakdowns. By 1993, camp administrators had enough and chose comfort and safety over idealism. Chartered tour buses began loading up long distance teen travelers. The tales of bus mishaps were memorable, however.

Trip Journal Entry, Western Trip 1972

En route to Anaconda Park in Montana, campers pulled off at a roadside campground for the night. Anxious to get underway, they boarded the bus only to discover that the bus driver, Tom, didn't have any keys. Journal writer, Harriet Fortgang recorded the incident. "The keys to the bus were in his raincoat, his raincoat was in the car and Elise had the car. Judy came on the bus and said she had another set of keys, but…" she had given them to Elise. The car and the bus finally hooked up, when to the further dismay of the group, the car ran out of gas.

Trip Journal Entry, Eastern Trip, August 1980, Day 2

"After stopping for a terrific breakfast of cereal with the company of a truck full of piggies, we kind of had trouble with the transmission—we took the bus to a gas station at 12:00, ate lunch and sat by a dock on the Erie Canal until 5:00. During these five hours we all grew even closer to each other so it wasn't such a waste of time after all."
Laura Robinson

1994 Mio

"We had one bus that you couldn't turn off," remembered Rhonda Sandweiss, tripping supervisor. "It was an old diesel bus we called the 'dial-a-ride.' When you would turn it off, because the wires would overheat, it would take about 5 or 6 hours for it to be cool enough to start it back up. This one trip, we were having problems with weather and we weren't sure whether or not we'd have to pick up the kids or not, so we kept that thing running for four days. We never turned it off because we were scared that we couldn't get it back on," continued Sandweiss.

1998 Western

While traveling through Iowa, the bus broke down and the driver dropped the group at a park to get the bus repaired. They set up camp when suddenly, the sky darkened and a tornado siren blared. The travelers found shelter in the basement of a nearby home. "We stayed down there soaking wet, freezing cold. The tornado had touched down in two spots where we had been in the park," remembered Erin Lowen. After the all-clear, the campers stayed behind to help the family pick up their wind-strewn yard.

CAMP recipes

Anyone can make a grilled cheese sandwich,
but how many of us can cook a scrumptious dessert
over an open flame or a warm Shabbat dinner for 1,200?
While some love to hate it, in the caverns of their tummies,
every camper cherishes camp cooking.

During WWII, campers brought their own ration coupons to camp.
The combined purchasing power of a camp full of kids and their coupons,
meant meals far better than at home.

Pioneer recipes (1964)

Wild Tea

Use leaves from wild strawberries, sassafras or wintergreen. Add one teaspoon fresh leaves, or ½ teaspoon dried, to a cup of boiling water. Strain leaves from tea with a strainer and enjoy.

Apple Delight

12 large apples
¾ C biscuit mix
3 T cinnamon
4 t sugar
½ C raisins
½ C water

Core and chop apples in large pieces.
Mix sugar, raisins and cinnamon with biscuit mix. Stir into apple, add water. Wrap single serving size portions in pieces of greased aluminum foil, leaving enough space for steam. Cook in embers approximately 30 minutes.

Camp Agree recipe:

Minda Tilchin, Agree's first female head counselor, cooked her way into the hearts of many hungry Agree campers. Thirty years later, her Challah recipe still hangs on the wall. "This recipe makes two loaves so we would triple or quadruple it to make enough. One lesson we learned," warned Tilchin, "is never fully multiply the amount of salt or you'll be very unhappy with the results."

Challah
1 pkg Fleischman's yeast
4½ to 5½ C flour
3 T sugar
1½ t salt
1/3 C pareve margarine (soft, room temperature)
1 C very warm water
4 eggs (room temperature)
1 t cold water
¼ poppy or sesame seeds

1. In small bowl, stir 1 package of yeast in 1 cup of warm tap water with a pinch of sugar. Let stand 5 minutes until frothy.
2. Mix together 2 cups flour, sugar and salt.
3. Gradually stir in yeast/water mixture and margarine.
4. Stir in 3 eggs and 1 egg white, 1 at a time, mixing well after each.
5. Add ½ cup flour and mix. Continue adding flour in ½ cup increments until you have a soft dough.
6. Turn out and knead on floured board for 8 to 10 minutes until smooth and elastic. Form into large ball.
7. Place in greased bowl, turning to grease the entire ball. Cover with clean dishcloth and let rise until double in bulk (approx. 1 hour).
8. Punch dough down, turn onto floured board and divide in half. Divide each half into 2 pieces, one about 1/3 of the dough and one about 2/3 of the dough. Each of these pieces will also be divided into thirds. The larger thirds should be rolled out into three 12-inch ropes and braided together. Seal the ends. The three smaller thirds should be rolled out into 10 inch ropes and braided together. Seal the ends and place the smaller loaf on top of the larger loaf and seal ends of both braids together.
9. Place on greased baking sheet, cover and let rise for 1 hour, until doubled.
10. Brush loaves gently with mixture of remaining egg yolk and 1 tsp cold water. Sprinkle with poppy or sesame seed.
11. Place in a pre-heated 400 degree oven. Bake 20 to 25 minutes or until done. Cool on wire rack.

At Camps Agree and Kennedy, wild berries are plentiful throughout the summer. It is no wonder that campers and staff crave homemade pies and jams. "We had many campers who had never seen a pie baked from scratch," remembered Tilchin. "It was a wonderful treat for them to eat a homemade pie with berries picked in the wild."

Blueberry Raspberry Pie

Crust	Filling
2 C flour	3 C blueberries
I t salt	4 T flour or 2½ T cornstarch
1/3 C shortening	½ t cinnamon
1/3 C cold butter	¾ sugar
	3 C raspberries
	I T butter or margarine

Sift together flour and salt. Cut shortening into flour with a pastry blender until the mixture resembles cornmeal. Cut cold butter into the dough until the crumbs are pea sized. Sprinkle dough with 4 tablespoons cold water and blend lightly. Add a little bit more water to hold ingredients together and gather into a ball. Divide in half. Chill while making filling.

Combine blueberries with flour or cornstarch, cinnamon and sugar. Gently mix in raspberries. Taste and correct seasoning.

Preheat oven to 450 degrees. Roll out half the crust on a floured board. Roll it over the rolling pin and drape it into a deep 9" pie dish. Pour the fruit filling into the crust. Dot with margarine. Roll out the other half of the dough and drape that over the top of the filling. Seal the edges by tucking the top crust under the bottom crust and crimp the sealed edge. Make three or four vents in the crust with a sharp knife.

Bake for 15 minutes then turn oven down to 350 degrees and bake for another 40 to 50 minutes until crust is golden and fruit filling is bubbling out of the vents. Cool completely on a wire rack before serving.

With the nearest bagel joint hundreds of miles away, freshly baked bagels are a Camp Kennedy treat. Working together with campers, Jody Winkelman, Camp Kennedy's supervisor, has the process mastered. "We make the dough the night before, letting it rise overnight. First thing in the morning, we cook them. They are fantastic, better than anything you could buy in a store."

Kennedy Bagels

Makes 24
2 C water
2 tablespoon yeast (2 packets)
1/4 C honey
I T salt
6 to 7 C of all-purpose flour

Dissolve yeast in water, mix gently and let stand until bubbles form. Mix in honey. Add salt and slowly add the flour until a soft, elastic dough is formed. Place on floured board and knead 15 minutes. Place in bowl, cover and let rise until doubled in bulk.

Punch down and knead again on floured board. If you are adding any additional ingredients (cinnamon, raisins, garlic, etc), mix them into the dough at this time. Tear off chunks of dough and shape into balls. Create holes in the middle (Lacking fancy utensils, Winkelman uses a spice jar lid as her hole cutter). Place on lightly greased cookie sheets. Cover and let rise for 20 minutes.

Bring a large pot of water to a boil. Drop bagels into boiling water, a few at a time, and let boil for 20 seconds each. Remove and place on lightly greased cookie sheets. Sprinkle with coarse Kosher salt, if desired. Bake at 400 degrees for 20 minutes.

As he looks across the vast Mahler Dining Hall, Hayden Andrews, Camp Maas' director of food service, thinks about the task he has come to love, feeding 1,600 campers and staff three times daily. Together with his wife, Sophie, the team, who first came to camp in 1993, cook meals that nourish the children's tummies, and their hearts. "Sometimes, kids need something that reminds them of home. Food like their mother would make. I always say medicine doesn't just come from the clinic," comforted Hayden.

Greek Chicken Wraps

Serves 2

Chicken:

1 lb chicken or turkey breast
1 T garlic power or 1 clove crushed garlic
2 T fresh squeezed lemon juice or bottled
2 T mustard
1 t parsley
1 t oregano

Sauce:

1 8 oz. jar of mayonnaise or plain yogurt
2 T powdered garlic or 2 crushed garlic cloves
¼ cup lemon juice
1 cucumber, peeled, grated, excess liquid squeezed out
1 package pita bread
Chopped salad tossed with Greek dressing
2 medium tomatoes
1 small can of black or green olives

Chicken prep: Cut chicken breast into small cubes and place in bowl. Add crushed garlic or garlic powder, lemon juice, mustard, parsley, oregano and salt and pepper. Toss together in bowl and refrigerate at least one hour before cooking.

Sauce prep: Empty mayonnaise or plain yogurt into small bowl and add garlic. Add grated cucumber into mayonnaise mixture. Add lemon juice or vinegar and salt and pepper to taste. Mix and place in cooler to chill.

When ready to serve: Cook chicken in frying pan or bake until golden brown. Dampen pita bread with water and oil and cook in frying pan until soft. Place cooked chicken on pita bread slices. Top with the cucumber-white sauce, Greek salad, tomatoes and black or green olives. Roll pita into wrap with baking paper or tin foil and serve.

For 14 warm summers, Joe Bender's baking nourished the souls of Ortonville and Brighton campers. He'd fire up the ovens every night at 6:30 and bake countless cookies, breads and rolls. By 10 p.m., the kitchen was filled with raiders, camp staff craving an early sample of the next day's delights.

Joe Bender's Spritz Cookies

Yield 6 dozen

1 C soft butter
2/3 C sugar
3 egg yolks
1 tsp. Almond or vanilla flavoring
¼ C ground almonds
2 ½ C flour

Beat butter and sugar until smooth, add egg yolks and flavorings. Add flour and almonds and work into a dough with hands. Force dough through cookie press onto ungreased baking sheets in "S's," rosettes, bars or other desired shapes. Bake at 400 degrees until set, but not brown, about 7 to 10 minutes.

"Absolutely a phenomenal experience."
Jason Zaks

Camp Tamarack "RODEO" Western Trip

"I remember sneaking around Aspen trying to find a phone to call home." Lisa Elconin (Buckfire)

"As staff, I couldn't believe that camp was paying me to do this!" Joe Lash

ROSEBUD INDIAN RESERVATION

"We went to the bottom of the Grand Canyon just to do it." David Blume

"Everyday of our lives we live by the clock. It is nice not to have to worry about it."

"The group living experience was as important as what we saw." Barbara Philka (Feldman)

TRIPPING AND OUTPOSTS

*"You take kids and throw them out for seven to ten days into
a real wilderness area, with nothing but some footpaths as a
reminder that anybody has been there before.
It is a life-changing experience. An experience that is
so intense and wonderful, that it transformed us.
It is no wonder that it was all we wanted to do."*

**Howard Davis,
tripper and base camp supervisor, 1965-1972**

"When Jacob came home from his first year at camp," recalled Leslye Landau, mother of eight-year-old Jacob Gardner, "I gave him a hug and he smelled like camp, the exact precise smell I remember from camp. It was the combination of campfire smoke, sweat, old clothes, dirt and forest. I never expected to start sniffing him when he got off the bus."[1]

As a diploma symbolizes graduation, varying degrees of camp dirtiness are badges of honor every camper loves to bring home. Given the opportunity, a child will brag for hours about the liberating feeling of tramping through the yucky muck of Brighton's Dinoland or Ortonville's Swamp Walk. Out-of-control food fights are cathartic freedoms sure to be remembered around the dinner table on more than one occasion. But, for an adolescent, the dirt of tripping…of being in the woods and mountains and on the rivers and roads for days at a time with no cares in the world – and no shower – is the best dirt. It is the ultimate declaration of independence.

THE OJIBWAY

Ojibway Indians inhabit the land around Wawa, Ontario, home of Camp Agree on Lake Kabenung. Wawa means goose in Ojibway. Kabenung is the Ojibway word for maze.

PIONEER PROJECTS Conservation projects – clearing trees, making teepees, or even a lodge – were an integral part of the Pioneer experience. In the 60s, one Pioneer group decided to make a frog pond. "We scooped out the area. It was fantastic. We never planned for drainage, however. The first rain it became all muddy," recalled Dave Eason, a Pioneer counselor in 1960.

Pioneer Villages

The eagerness of Tamarack campers to live natural and free of the binds of urban life can be traced back to the creation of the first Pioneer village, for girls only, in 1959. The first boys unit came a year later.

In many ways, Pioneer units were early versions of the Outward Bound movement. Located on the backside of Phipps Lake, away from the rest of camp, Pioneer campers lived in a rugged environment where the success of the unit depended upon the interactions of the group. Yet, recalls Larry Gussin, an early 60s Pioneer who proudly turned hippie by the end of the decade, "Pioneer also grew out of a strong identification with Israel. It was really modeled on a kibbutz. We'd cook our own meals and do a conservation project for three hours a day."[2]

Jim Grey, a mid-60s Pioneer counselor, remembers sleeping on jungle hammocks, taking arduous hikes and the pride his group felt upon constructing an eating shelter, made from nothing more than large branches and leaves. They were a world away from the rest of camp and wouldn't have had it any other way. "Because we were in no man's land, nobody cared to see us even in the daytime, let alone the nighttime,"[3]

THE LODGE
They built it with
their own hands and
they hung out in
it in rain or shine:
The Pioneer Lodge,
circa 1966. Music
and bugs were always
present, remembered
Jim Grey, Pioneer
counselor.
*(photo courtesy
of Jim Grey)*

he laughingly recalled. "The roads were not passable so the directors never came to Pioneer." Two things were always present he added, "music and bugs."

Every Pioneer group participated in a conservation and building project. Beth Swartz (Robinson) remembered being a Pioneer counselor in 1978, the same year the village adopted the name *Chalutzim* (pioneer in Hebrew). "That summer the girls tried to dam up the lake in the back of the village to make it a private swimming area, but we couldn't get it to work,"[4] she remembered. So, they joined the boys and constructed a shelter. Among them, was a counselor named Steve Swartz. Twenty-five years later that shelter still stands and

Steve and Beth are the proud parents of two children, both Tamarack campers. "Pioneer is a very different kind of program," reflected Steve. "By the time you get to be that age, you've been through most of the activities at camp. Pioneer is the first program that really encourages campers to become self-sufficient, yet instills the value of working together as a unit."

Hiking and canoeing dominate the Pioneer experience, but beginning in the 1990s, the 8th and 9th graders began taking exhilarating rafting trips along the mighty Pennsylvanian Youghiogheny River. Never

MISSINAIBI TRIP 1976

"It is so relaxing to be lying on a rock where everything around is the way it is because it hasn't been developed yet. I wish I could have that feeling everywhere but I guess if we could, then it wouldn't be special." **Sue Weiner**

MISSINAIBI
For 18 days and 360
miles this crew of
nine campers and two
counselors portaged
and canoed up to the
Hudson Bay. (l to
r) Jan Baron, Leslye
Landau, Wendy
Burger, Mike Savin,
Susie Weiner
(bottom), Steve Katz
(top), Kathy Rissman,
Lou Weckstein,
Michael Sosin, Harvey
Weiner. Not pic-
tured, Robin Frisch,
who took the photo.

imagining that she'd become a professional tripper for Tamarack Camps, Lisa Wolfe was eager to try white water rafting but unsure about what to expect. "I was an awkward kid, made fun of and teased. I was definitely not cool,"[5] she mused. When she came to Pioneer in 1992, she felt nervous about fitting in. "It was amazing. Suddenly I had friends, I was functioning as part of the group, something I rarely did. And, I found that I had this great aptitude for camping."

It was an aptitude realized in a single moment, the moment she climbed Camp Maas' giant 30-foot climbing tower. "I got on the tower and couldn't do it. I freaked out, cried and got down off the wall. My counselor talked to me. He said, 'Everybody is different and everybody has different challenges. For one person it may be a challenge to just get on the tower, for another it might be to get to the top. People are built different and that is why we are all human.' Then he said, 'Why don't you give it one more try?' So, I tried it again and I made it all the way to the top. I felt great. It gave me so much self-confidence." Ten years later, at age 22, Wolfe trains trippers for Tamarack Camps.

PIONEER

By 1963, boy Pioneers were taking eight-day canoe trips to Algonquin Provincial Park. "We thought we were the kings of the universe," recalled Larry Gussin. "Going to Algonquin was such an eye opener to see that there was something out there other than Northland Mall." Girls were excluded, but all that changed in 1969, just one year after women's liberation groups protested the Miss America Beauty pageant in Atlantic City. Girl Pioneers proved themselves more than able to handle the longer canoeing and hiking trips.

The Gods of the Forest, The Trippers

The Huron River canoe trips that began in the 1940s soon became lackluster compared to the glamour and excitement that Michigan's other 36,300 miles of rivers and streams beheld.[6] Campers wanted greater challenges, and camp sought to quench their thirst. By the early-1960s, each week several groups were readying for a trip up to

WIPE OUT SHELTER In the early 1970s, the dock at Ortonville's Rodecker Beach was dismantled. Allan Brown transported the wood to the Mesick base camp where it was used to build a storm shelter that became known as the Wipe Out Shelter. Pictured is one of the architects of the building, tripper Jeff Applebaum.

the AuSable, the Manistee or even into Canada's Lake Superior Provincial Park. Then, in 1964, a waterfront supervisor named David Fisher approached Sam Marcus and Allan Brown with an idea.

"David Fisher saw that trips were being sent out lacking proper supervision," remembered Howard Davis, who, together with Fisher and John Shaw, comprised the first Tripper staff. "He urged Sam and Mr. Brown to use qualified staff with camping and canoeing skills, good judgment and the ability to work with kids."[7] The trio launched the Tripper program in 1965. Fisher and Shaw took the trips out, while Davis, a camper who had been through the Wilderness program, stayed behind. As the in-camp tripper, Davis taught campers basic camping skills and how to paddle, get in and out of canoes.

Thus began the tripper mystique. "I remember being a camper and viewing the trippers as...as absolute gods of the forest," recalled Leslye Landau, who became a god herself in 1977. "You were a little bit afraid of them, a lot in awe of them and you did whatever they told you to. Your life depended on them."

The trippers – wild-looking, confident and worldly – could carry canoes where no man (or woman) had carried them before, could face any challenge, overcome any obstacle, forge any river, climb any mountain. "Because we were out of camp a lot, that added to the mystique," blushed a mild-mannered Davis, who was quite a legend himself. "One group would come back from a trip and talk to the next. So, the legend grew." Laura Berman, one of camp's first female trippers recalled the awe. "I remember after one trip, a guy saying, 'Laura, she's not a girl, she's ... she's a man!' That was the biggest compliment."[8]

Trippers were also cocky.

MISSINABI TRIP LOG

"As I climbed into bed, I realized that it was an experience the likes of which I may never have again."
Lou Weckstein 1976

SIMPLE PLEASURES
Overnight trips to Isle Royale held endless wonders for campers. Sometimes, it was the simplest things that made for memorable moments. Here, Joanne Rowe (Korn), a 1970 Kennedy camper sits on the upside of a homemade teeter-totter with Debbie Cohen. "We took what was out there and made a good time out of it," remembered Rowe.
(photo courtesy of Joanne Rowe)

BURTMAN
BASE CAMP 1974
The crew…
Bottom
(l to r): Paul Harr,
Nancy Sklar.
Middle: Al Langnas,
Anita Boles,
Felicia Koblinksy,
Bob Lipsitz.
Top: Denise Landau,
Joan Rottenberg,
Barb Feldman,
Phil Jacobs,
Rick Adler.
Not pictured,
Rob Morrison.
*(Photo courtesy
of Denise Landau)*

Fueled by their own passion for the outdoors, trippers thrived on providing campers with daring challenges and the opportunity to succeed. "We wanted them to fall in love with the outdoors as much as we did,"[9] commented Brian Kepes, an early 1980s tripper. "One year we planned a trip, and when we got to this creek it had run dry. Unfortunately, it resulted in a very long portage. It was hard to keep the kids calm." Kepes, who became a real estate manager and vice president of the Fresh Air Society Board, reflected on that camp experience. "It was a safe place to try new things and grow at the same time."

The Mio and Mesick Base Camps

By the end of the 1960s, trips were running in and out of Ortonville and Brighton almost on a daily basis. Struggling to find an efficient way to drop off one group and pick up the next without returning home, Allan Brown suggested the creation of base camps: rustic meeting places with nothing more than a small lodge, a bathroom, some cleared land for tents and the back of a semi-trailer truck that doubled as an office and storage area. The camps were a shelter during foul weather and, in the days before cellular and wireless, a place with a telephone.

In 1970, camp began using two pieces of property: a 35-acre site in Mio and another in Cadillac. Mio's Mollie M. Burtman campground became the stopover for younger Ortonville campers while Cadillac housed the older ones. Getting the Mio camp ready was an experience shared by a team of seasoned camp staff including Allan Brown and Jeffrey Zaks. "We set up the camp and literally drilled

CANADIAN
WILDERNESS 1989
These are the faces
of happy Puckasawa
hikers: (l to r) Katie
Gorell, Emily Grey,
Lauren Steinhart,
Jennifer Franklin and
Sari Berman.
*(photo courtesy
of Emily Grey)*

the well for water. I lived in a trailer that smelled as if the old farmer who used to live there had stored salamis in it," laughed Zaks. A cardiologist, Zaks remembered how the trips were planned to the last 'molecule.' "The kids thought it was all spontaneous," he said.

It turned out that the Cadillac property, very rugged and centrally located, was not for sale, so camp went real estate shopping about 20 miles down the road, purchasing property in a small town called Mesick. The first crew of resident trippers came to Mesick in 1971. Jeff Applebaum ran the camp. He remembers building the bathroom the first year and the lodge the second. "It was literally just woods. Kids and staff slept in platform tents and under tarps," remembered Applebaum. "One year, a neighbor came over with his bulldozer and we made a volleyball court."

In designing the base camps, Allan Brown had one very clear vision. "Someone always had to be within earshot of the phone. Immediately …seven days a week, 24 hours a day," said Applebaum. "If any trip had a problem, the trip leader could get a hold of you." Sometimes, it wasn't so easy to remain tethered to the phone.

MIO

Inside of the main lodge at Mio sits a red couch. It arrived sometime in the 1970s and was still there 30 years later. Many pairs of trippers spent "quality time on that red couch," remembered one such person who wishes to remain anonymous.

Bob Lipsitz ran the Mio base camp from 1972 until 1976. Cunningly, he remembers the summer a group of campers arrived for their hiking trip with no trippers available to escort them. So, Lipsitz became their escort.

"We took a three-day hiking trip and never left the property. The kids never knew it," he chuckled. "We kept coming across the same high voltage power line, which should have been a dead giveaway that we were walking around in circles."

Fifteen to 20 trippers lived at the base camps each

summer. By 1976, camp found it more eco-
nomical to run Mesick without resident staff
and the camp was largely abandoned. One
day in 1990, Applebaum received a phone call from
the Tamarack office. It was Bob Lipsitz.

"He asked me if there had been a lodge at
Mesick. I said, 'Yea, I built it!' Then he said,
'Well, it isn't there anymore.'" Applebaum
thought Lipsitz must have forgotten its exact
location, so later that summer he drove to the
campsite himself. "The whole thing was gone,
not a trace of it was left." A new lodge was built
in 1994 as larger numbers of outpost campers
started to once again use the site.

Even though the base camp population is tran-
sient, the outpost experience is fodder for memorable
bonding and maturing experiences. Rhonda Sandweiss,
tripping supervisor in 2000, recalled the havoc a huge
rainstorm played on what normally is a rather sane operation.

GORDY LEVENSON

"One of my
favorite things
was to get up early and
take anyone who wanted go
trout fishing for a real
fisherman's breakfast,"
Gordy recalled. Carrying
potatoes ready to be fried,
Gordy and his sleepy-eyed
eaglets, headed down to a
stream, caught some fish
and "cooked it right there
on the spot in a frying
pan with lots
of butter."

THE KENNEDY
BUS 1998
Every year Kennedy
campers paint up the
ole' Tamarack bus and
head to Munising's
4th of July parade.
The 10,000
spectators anticipate
the green machine's
appearance, adorned
by Tamarack's finest,
paddling their way
through the parade
and throwing penny
candy to the kids.
*(photo courtesy of
Jody Winkelman)*

THE LEVENSONS
Gordy and Vera Levenson directed Camp Kennedy for
nearly 10 years and considered the historic retreat their
summer home and the 24 campers who joined them each
summer a part of their extended family. They are pictured
here with 1970 staff. (l to r) top row: Lon Kelly, Bill
Barnett, Mark Levenson, Gordy Levenson (standing), Bert
Levenson, Tim Levenson. Bottom row (l to r) Vickie
Sedman, Becky Levenson and Vera Levenson.
(photo courtesy of Joanne Rowe)

"There must have been six trips at base camp, each with around 15 people,"[10] she said. All the furniture was shoved to a little bedroom. A carpet of campers covered the main room of the small lodge. "It had rained for two days straight, the wind was blowing and it had dropped to 50 degrees," said Sandweiss. "Everyone was wet and freezing. The staff was trying to cook, keep everybody warm and happy. It was crazy." Yet, ask any camper and they'll laughingly remember hot chocolate by the gallon and lots of late night giggles.

Camp Kennedy

Not far from Munising, in Michigan's Upper Peninsula, is Adams Trail, the road leading to Camp Kennedy. It is about 25 miles long, a bumpy, narrow, endlessly winding, logging road. As the road goes on, all traces of civilization vanish and what is left are just forests. The stillness leaves newcomers speechless. A half-mile, narrow dirt driveway ends in the peninsula of the Camp Kennedy compound. Campers catch their first glimpse of the ancient barn, a few of the outbuildings and the lodge. Beyond lies shimmering Lake Nevins.

Upon arrival all campers must first relinquish their watches, insists Jody Winkelman, Camp Kennedy's devoted leader and keeper. In this electricity-less northern haven, there are no hair dryers,

THE VIKING DINNER Although most choose to dress in a toga, the traditional Viking Dinner at Camp Kennedy is truly an evening of elegance. "We eat cave person style, no silverware, and no hands; and we always serve chili," explains Jody Winkelman. Pictured here are four Vikings without their togas: (l to r): Alana Zaks, Carly Block, Carly Efros and their counselor, Amy. *(photo courtesy of Alana Zaks)*

no televisions and no watches. No exceptions. "Every day of our lives, we live by the clock. It is wonderful to not have to worry about what time it is. It adds to the rustic experience,"[11] said Winkelman.

The removal of timepieces is one of many long-standing Kennedy traditions, like eating when you are hungry and sleeping when you are tired. The place was and is a rare gift. "Take one Ortonville village and put it in the middle of nowhere, on a peninsula surrounded on three sides by water, and woods as far as you can see, and that is Camp Kennedy," described Winkelman, Kennedy's enthusiastic leader since 1987.

Once the hunting lodge of Michigan Governor Fred W. Green (1927-30), Camp Kennedy was given to the Fresh Air Society in 1964 by Edward C. Levy, a pioneering Detroit industrialist and philanthropist. Green built the rustic retreat in 1922 and every fall hosted extravagant hunting get-aways. Levy was a frequent guest. The men would "hunt, play cards and drink, hunt, play cards and drink,"[12] explained Edward Levy, Jr., Edward C.'s son. "A Catholic priest named Edward Kennedy was always present," he continued. A rugged and handsome man of faith, Kennedy loved to roam the area enjoying its wildlife and wilderness. Although he played cards and drank with the men, his presence served as a reminder to temper their behavior. After the Governor passed away, Levy bought the property from Green's widow in 1938 and began to carry on some of those same traditions. But as the years went by, Levy found himself spending less time at the property. Donating the land, its buildings and all of its rich history to Fresh Air was one way to preserve its heritage. Many of Governor Green's original artifacts remain, including

KENNEDY 1999

After numerous complaints that the sessions were too short, Camp Kennedy became a one-session, six-week outpost, giving everyone plenty of time for sea kayaking, horseback riding, snorkeling, hiking, canoeing and partying.

MOVING THE OUT-HOUSE 1982
In the old days, before cement holding tanks, every five or six years the hole underneath the outhouse would fill up and campers would roll up their sleeves to help move the outhouses to a fresh location. The outhouse pictured here is now a storage shed on the beach at Camp Kennedy.
(photo courtesy of Jody Winkelman)

the wicker furniture, the Model-T engine that powered the generator, the old card table, and hundreds of pictures of Green, his friends, the beloved Father Kennedy and Tamarack campers.

Arnie Collens, Kennedy's first supervisor, traveled with Sam Marcus, Allan and Barney Brown to preview the property in May 1964. Edward C. Levy acted as their guide. As kerosene lamps cast a golden light across the gigantic stone hearth in the lodge's main room, the men talked until 2:30 a.m. drinking in the lore and history of the camp.

Later that summer, Collens returned with 11 boys, the first Camp Kennedy campers. "We marveled at the color and stone formations on the boat ride from Munising along the Pictured Rocks,"[13] remembered Collens some 35 years later. "Yet the highlight of our stay was our close-up view of the Kennedy property. We walked across the meadow and headed into the deep woods, smelled the fresh forest air, identified birds. We saw deer and evidence of beaver dams, identified wild flowers and plants and ate wild berries."

But, there was more to see. Much, much more. Located just five hours and one ferry ride away from Isle Royale, trips from Kennedy to the island quickly became a standard. For 10 days, campers would canoe and portage around the island, exploring its rivers and bays. Gordy and Vera Levenson, who followed Collens as Kennedy's supervisors, guided them. Lisa Gleicher, a 1968 Kennedy camper, recalled their patient mentoring and invaluable lessons on geology, biology and science. "The Levensons were teachers and we would learn about the ecology, about the population of the wolves and deer. They were very ahead of their time,"[14] she recalled.

In 1975, Bob Lipsitz became resident director. With him came a tripper named Joan Rottenberg. The two fell in love at Kennedy and without knowing it, became mother and father to campers, just as the Levensons had. "Kennedy was a wonderful place. To be with no phones, no schedule, no time restraints and 28 kids was a fantastic experience for the kids and for us," remembered Bob. The Lipsitz's continued the long out-of-camp canoe trips, only they headed farther west to the Boundary Waters of Northern Minnesota. Campers hiked, canoed and portaged through the almost virgin wilderness of rivers, lakes and swamps.

"I remember just crying carrying a canoe on my shoulders in a swamp up to my waist,"[15] moaned Stacey Lash (Cohen). Despite hours of pain and agony, and gobs of mosquito bites, Lash survived. "In the end, I thought, yea! I did it. No one would ever believe that I did it. I was 85 pounds at the time carrying a canoe that weighed

KENNEDY

Homemade pizza, berry jam and bread.... Northern lights... mud football.... muck fights ... snorkeling in Lake Superior ... the dark room and the three-seater outhouse... ice cream in Grand Marais ... 12 Mile Beach.... bus rides.... Viking dinner.... taking a shower outside .... Miner's Castle ... Chapel Rock ... Jake the Snake from across the Lake ... Junk Band ... log slide ... finding a new home away from home.

BENNY AND THE BRIDGE
Benny Schonttenfels stands ready to assist Michelle Efros to construct a new bridge at Camp Kennedy. Benny is also the record holder in the annual Kennedy hot dog eating contest, devouring 13 of them in 1999.
(photo courtesy of Jody Winkelman)

as much as I did."

In 1993, Winkelman broke with tradition and began taking Kennedy campers to Canada's Algonquin Park. The Boundary Waters had become too populated. An 11-hour bus ride, the Algonquin journey is totally worth the effort, said Winkelman. "I was looking for (a place with) pristine wilderness, with lake and river canoeing, not a lot of people and access out within a day, if we needed it." The park held endless wonders for campers, and as an unexpected bonus there were far fewer portages required along the eight-day route.

Like her predecessors, Winkelman is mother duck to hundreds of baby chicks. The camp supervisors tenderly teach, mentor and share their vast knowledge of and love for outdoor experiences and foster young people to become confident and independent.

TEEN TRIPPERS Each year, five to 10 high school seniors are chosen to participate in the Teen Tripper program. The class of 1995 built this Jewish star on the Agree lodge. It has since become a favorite photo spot. Pictured here are: (top l to r) Paul Fagen, Amy Opperer, Andrew Hall. (bottom l to r) Yaneev Golumbeck, Mike Cohen, Brian Ruttenberg, Jamie Farr, Lisa Wolfe. *(photo courtesy of Lisa Wolfe)*

Although she is describing the Levensons, Joanne Rowe, a 1975 camper, could really be talking about any of the Kennedy supervisors. "Kennedy was magical, because of the way Gordy and Vera saw the world. They really believed in who you were. I once climbed a tree and asked Vera to help me get down. She said you got yourself up there, now you get yourself down. I remember how shocked I was, but I did it. I figured it out for myself."

Swearing hers was the greatest Kennedy summer, Lisa Goren, a 1990 Kennedy alumni, talked about the unique bonds that form at Kennedy. "It was a special group the year I was there, ask anyone. Within five hours of arriving, we were all playing volleyball in our underwear," she remembered. "We all got very close. That year, we went on a lot of backcountry trips. I remember I saw a huge moose and thought it was a horse with antlers stapled to his head."

The vision of a mother moose and its baby is one of Jon London's most vivid Kennedy memories. He chose Kennedy in 1999 because he wanted to experience outpost camping. "Kennedy was the best of all my summers at Tamarack,"[16] insisted this lanky, long-time camper. He hiked the Porcupine Mountains and Pictured Rocks and canoed through Algonquin. "Algonquin was the best of all the trips. It was so beautiful, so clean." That was where he saw the pair of moose. "They just stood there, blocking us. We had to wait for them to finally move." Maybe, mused London, the animals were urging them to stay.

Decision-making, responsibility and team-build-

KENNEDY

In 1969 Kennedy, still without any electricity, took a mechanical leap into modern times. The camp acquired a ski boat providing countless hours of fun for campers in years to come.

AGREE'S
OUTHOUSES
Melvin and Matilda
are oases of privacy,
but everyone has to
follow the rules:
• Check that the seat
is in proper position
before sitting
or aiming.
• Save batteries -
learn to aim
in the dark.
• Do not waste paper
- use both sides.
• We suggest you
whistle or sing to
obliterate
inappropriate noises
- song books.
available at no charge
• If flooding occurs
keep calm, life vest
under seat.
Tread water until
help arrives.
• Avoid crowds -
max. capacity in this
room is 16 persons.

ing are all inherent to the Kennedy experience. London credited his Kennedy summer for helping him mature into a young adult. "They know you don't need to be watched all the time. You are given a lot more privileges. Not everything was planned out and if it was, you planned it out."

Beaming, Winkelman thinks of how campers mature over the six short weeks they are in her care. They come together as strangers and leave as confident, independent young adults. They have learned to live together as community. "One of my favorite annual parties is the Unbirthday," explained Winkelman. "We invite all the neighbors, Jake the Snake from Across The Lake, his eight kids and 24 grand-kids. We make huge sheetcakes and celebrate everyone's birthday," she said. Each camper draws a name from a hat and makes a birthday gift for that person. "Sometimes someone will pick somebody they don't really like or get along with. They get into the project and do a phenomenal job and get past all of that. It is a mile-stone that impacts these kids forever."

WAWA GOOSE
When Ontario's Highway 17 was completed in 1965, the eastern portion met the western portion in the small town of Wawa. To celebrate, the townspeople erected this giant goose. Whenever an Agree trip leaves Wawa, which means goose in the native Ojibway language, campers utter a special blessing: First, everyone on the bus warms up their lips. Then they chant: "Nabisco eats Domino Sugar" (honk bus horn) (yell) "Yea Goose!" Pictured here are Ultimate Agree 1993 campers. *(photo courtesy of Beth Sonne)*

Charles N. Agree Outpost

The legend of Agree begins with Allan Brown. One late 1968 summer day, while having a cup of coffee in the small town of Wawa, Ontario, camp's maintenance supervisor and his son Barney heard about a newly built campsite that had been abandoned on the northwest side of Kabenung Lake. Obsessed with the growth of the tripping program, Brown put down his cup and went to see the site. "The brush was so overgrown,"[17] recalled Minda Tilchin, who married Barney a few years later, "that it took them more than an hour to find the first building."

Tripping was flourishing and desperately in need of an outpost camp and Wawa had already become a routine destination on the Tamarack trail. In 1969, Charles N. Agree agreed to underwrite the $10,000 acquisition and repair costs, and the Jewish Federation approved the deal. Within a short time, a bulldozer loaded into the back of a truck and a crew of camp veterans headed

AGREE: 1969

Before the first summer was over, staff and campers had built a traditional Finnish sauna just 20 feet from the lake, a sun deck and dock.

north. "We made the road that leads into Agree, dug holes for the outhouses and built the radio tower with Mr. Brown," remembered Mike Bossin, one of those very "politically active"(code word for hippie) 1960s and 70s counselors.

That summer, Agree officially opened for business. Black flies by the thousands welcomed the boys to the north; no women were yet invited.

A decade earlier, the absence of females would not have been an issue, but this was the 70s, the age of feminism and liberation. A camper all her life, Laura Berman assumed she'd naturally progress to the position of tripper trainee. She was astounded when she learned

BAG HEADS 1984 Advanced Agree, 1984 is the group credited with beginning the long Agree tradition of wearing a plastic bread bag while packing food for a trip.

women were excluded. "We had all this experience, but they didn't have a program for girls. We felt a sense of outrage that they had trained us and then dumped us," said Berman. She penned a letter to camp director, Marv Berman (no relation) in 1969. Three years later, he offered Laura the first female junior counselor position at Agree.

Berman was teamed up with the new Agree head counselor, Minda Tilchin. The two women walked into a totally male culture. "It was a real macho place. Hairy men, out in the wild with dirty socks," laughed Berman 30 years later as she sat with her longtime friend Tilchin.

Quickly, the weaker sex proved that hardiness is gender blind. In the rugged, natural environment of Agree, what really counts is ability and attitude. "It was a place where the group was the most important," explained Berman.

"Almost immediately, all the things that dictated whether you were in or out in high school – what you wore, how cute you were, the things that you had – went by the wayside. If you were somebody who would pitch in, work without complaining and was reliable, then your status was elevated," said Tilchin, who can still portage a canoe at age 46.

"All Agree is, is nine buildings and a waterfront," said Beth Sonne (pronounced sunny), Agree's director since 1985. "The thing about Agree is everything is a success. There are no failures. We call it 'you did it your best.' The kids come away with self-confidence, leadership skills and incredible communication skills."

Agree is powered by campers who, along with a small group

of staff, cook all the meals, turn the compost piles, clean the out-house, partake in conservation projects and maintain or construct new buildings when nature gets the best of them. No one is excluded. During his tenure as board president in 1982, Allan Nachman visited the site. "I got there and had to put shingles on a new cabin,"[18] he said. When the job was complete, he participated in another camp ritual, a hot sauna followed by "a run into the lake. After 30-seconds you had to get out, it was too cold."

Shivering just thinking about it, Jon Medow, a 1999 Agree camper, remembered the thrill of a hot sauna after a long hike. "When you are inside the sauna no one talks at all – it is dark and totally silent and you just sit there and think. You go in after each trip and it takes about two hours to get clean."[19]

At Agree, trippers and campers are in a constant state of pre-paredness for trips to places that most people have never heard of, let alone pronounce. While Shikwamkwa, Lake Superior Provincial Park, Gargantua, and Pukaskwa Provincial Park are familiar terrain to the Agree staff, their wonder and magic are endlessly splendid, especially for campers.

"It was an 18-day, 360-mile canoe trip with no way out," remem-bered Leslye Landau one of nine campers who, in 1976, paddled and portaged their way up the Missinaibi River to St. James Bay in the Hudson Bay. Jan Baron and Lou Weckstein led the group. In the words of Weckstein, the trip was "an experience the likes of which I may never have again."[20] Fishing in the Missinaibi River and catching 17-inch pike, shooting endless rapids (some just for the fun of it), portaging through acres of mud and reading Jack London around the campfire were among the many highlights. For Landau,

SAUNA
Erma the sauna proudly stands behind this group of 1997 Teen Trippers. The original Agree Sauna was built in 1970 but burned down in 1986. It was rebuilt in 1987. *(photo courtesy of Beth Sonne)*

her favorite moment was the night before heading back to Agree. "All of the stars were out. There were shooting stars, northern lights and even, I think, lightning in the distance. It was the most glorious end to the trip."

The Missinaibi trip was later shortened to a 10-day adventure, but the effect was still the same. "Campers arrive on the first day, nervous about everything and don't know if they are going to make it. On the last day they are glowing," said Sonne. "You see kids who might have been quiet or shy or unsure of themselves, and watch them become outgoing people. They have truly sustained each other, and rarely again in your lifetime will you experience the connectedness that you feel at Agree."

Connected is not exactly what Agree campers feel when they experience their solo survival test. A confident Bethany Schaer, a 1998 Agree camper, explained, "When you go on the solo, you are given about a 10 minute notice. You wear everything you can, or that you will need, and carry a sleeping bag. They give you some twine, visqueen, a Nalgene bottle and a bug helmet."

Soloists are taken to a small nearby island. First campers make their shel-

AGREE 1997
Agree is really about being out of camp, touching and connecting with nature and discovering internal strengths. After a decade of attending camp with the same group of friends, Carly Leipsitz went to Agree in 1997 alone. "We bonded the minute we got on the bus," she recalled of the group. "I grew from the Agree experience, I appreciated things more and realized I can cook my own food, go 11 days without a shower and go on hard hikes."

ter, a task Schaer completed in just 45 minutes. For the rest of her day and night she combated mosquitoes and wrote an elaborate letter to her mother, Agree's first female supervisor, Minda Tilchin. "There was not a part of me that wasn't bit. They even got through my rain gear!" When she woke up the next morning – or afternoon – she awoke to a beautiful sound drifting across the lake…music. "At Agree, you loose sense of time. You eat dinner at midnight, lunch at four and you never really know it until you get back home. When I woke up, they were playing Melissa Etheridge. It was so amazing."

Seldom does a camper return from Agree untouched by the pristine beauty of the area or unchanged by the experience. "Agree is a magical place,"[21] remembered a still-awed Abby Robinson, a 1983 Agree counselor. "Starting a canoe trip from your front door was so amazing and seeing water so clean that you could drink it.

"Camp is why I live in Boulder, it shaped who I am today. I joke that I have an interfaith marriage; my husband's a conservative Jew, but he's not a camper!" Robinson also has a few gem stories. "I remember going to the grocery store in Wawa with a camper named David Levine. We stopped at a hotel in town to use the bathroom. David was in there for the longest time. When he came out he had this grin on his face and I asked him what took him so long. He said he was watching the toilet flush."

Agree is one of G-d's blessings, one of the last North American places left untouched by developers and modernization. Campers see owls and loons that dot a sky free from city lights, smog and stench. Caribou, black bear, moose and fox freely roam the terrain. Even the omnipresent, sadistic black flies and mosquitoes have earned their place in Agree history.

And, being a Jewish camp, there is the time on the Sabbath when campers stop and rest. It is a chance to ponder the experience and light candles with peers who have shared unbelievable times. Campers reflect upon the week past, consider the one ahead and understand that these will become unforgettable moments. Their Sabbath prayers are sincere and profound. One of Sonne's favorites is: "And G-d saw everything he had made, and found it good. And he said: This is a beautiful world I have given you. Take good care of it; do not ruin it." *Gates of Prayer*

SEA KAYAKS
Agree introduced sea kayaking in 1994. Each session Agree campers load up their kayaks and oars and venture to Parry Sound in the Georgian Bay or Lake Superior Provincial Park. Ultimate Agree 1996 campers are pictured here readying for a trip. *(photo courtesy of Beth Sonne)*

BIKE TRIPS   Dreams of campers cycling across the Upper Peninsula began in 1963, when camp administrators tried to find staff for a bike trip program. Unsuccessful, they settled instead for including a five-day bike trip across the U.P. for Advanced Girl Pioneers. Twelve years later, in 1975, Denise Landau sat down with Mike Zaks and Rob Morrison and planned a 400-mile, 14-day journey across the UP. One year later, a series of bike trips were conducted, a muscular Landau leading the way. The most arduous was a three-week adventure that began in Glen Falls, N.Y. and went up through Maine. "They were amazing trips, but with all of the cars and the responsibility of watching kids and keeping them together with as much as a 30 mile difference between the strongest and weakest bikers, it was too much," remembered Landau. Those were the last bike trips. "It's pretty amazing to think about. All the places we went... the Green Mountains in Vermont, riding across the whole U.P."

If you ask Jason Klein, a camper from the 1980s, his favorite camp memories, he'll tell you about playing Ultimate Frisbee, sneaking PopTarts into camp and Cepacol. "Anytime you were sick at all, you went to the clinic and regardless of what you had, you were given Cepacol."

Cepacol soothes sore throats, assures Kathi Moss, R.N., one of many nurses who routinely come to Tamarack each summer. "There are a lot of sore throats at camp. The kids get them from screaming too much and from sleeping in cold cabins." Moss has doled out plenty of little throat lozenges in the 20 years she's been attending sick — and homesick — campers. "The most common thing we see is homesickness and we just give them lots of T.L.C."

They are the silent warriors of camp. The nurses and doctors who come for a week or two or even more, standing ready to respond instantly to a sore tummy, twisted ankle, cut finger or sore throat.

"There were a lot of kvetches," remembered Lee Henkin, a Brighton nurse in the early 1950s and mid-1960s. She and her husband, Dr. Ray Henkin, were camp regulars. They have a medicine cabinet-full of memories about campers who dreamed up imaginative schemes to get a little extra attention. With fond laughter, Lee recalled, "One kid claimed he broke his arm. Ray says to him, 'lift your left arm.' So he raised his left arm, then Ray says, 'How did you raise your right arm before you broke it?' So, the kid raises his right arm and shows us!" Laughing together, the Henkins utter a joyful "Oy," as they briefly relived their wonderful Tamarack years.

TENDER LOVING CARE AND CEPACOL

From the onset, camp's mission was tied to children's health. Providing fresh air and nourishment for poor children was the primary reason the Fresh Air Society was organized. Children were routinely weighed at the beginning and end of their weekly stays, while volunteers proudly recorded their weight gains. Even to this day, children are given a general exam upon arriving at camp.

Dozens of children suffering from various heart diseases ranging from rheumatic fever to congenital heart disease came to camp between 1928 and the late 1930s. Labeled "cardiac" campers, they stayed all summer and had their temperatures and pulses checked twice daily. Twice each week the cardiac patients, many of whom were not Jewish, repetitively climbed up and down an outdoor staircase while doctors measured their lung capacity. When these kids arrived at camp their activity-level was completely restricted, but by the end most were allowed to take short swims in the lake.

Another interesting experiment was conducted in 1977 when Fresh Air teamed up with Children's Hospital and the Kidney Foundation to host 11 children on dialysis. The patients lived in regular bunks and participated in all the village activities. Twice each day the dialysis patients, escorted by their counselors and very often a few bunkmates, walked to a trailer stationed outside of Maas Clinic. Inside, three dialysis units stood ready to provide life-sustaining treatments.

Then and now, the doctors of camp are always present. As a young pediatrician, Dr. George Blum couldn't imagine a summer without a week at Brighton. He, his wife Joyce and their family, which grew by one baby every year for four years during the 1960s, slept in the small pair of rooms located adjacent to the infirmary. It was a little wooden building where every sound was amplified ten times, remembered Dr. Blum. "We never had any major injuries…a small fracture, strep throat, an occasional stitch." When not tending sick campers and staff, the Blum's enjoyed their summer vacation, swimming, participating in talent shows and playing baseball. One of their children is nurse Kathi Moss.

Ortonville's Maas Clinic was built off the main camp road, not too far from the main entrance. In the late 1980s, Little Josh Levinson patiently waited for the twice-daily medication check. "He'd sit on the porch waiting for the kids to come. He'd start jumping and shout, 'the sick kids are coming! The sick kids are coming!,'" smiled his mother, Elise, wife of pediatrician, Dr. Marty Levinson.

Religiously, the Levinson's have come every summer since 1982. "Camp is part of the community where we grew up, where we live and work," said a graying Dr. Levinson.

Levinson remembered the time when camp administrators called him at home with a perplexing problem. A counselor from Australia arrived for pre-camp with chicken pox. She needed someplace to stay where she wouldn't spread the germs. "We took her in," said Levinson. "Would I have done that for somebody else, this stranger coming into my house? No, but she was part of the Camp Tamarack family. That's why we offered to do it."

In the late 20th Century, camp doctors were plentiful. It wasn't always

jewell and lester morris medical facility

camp maas

SIEGAL/TUOMAALA ASSOCIATES
ARCHITECTS AND PLANNERS INC

In 2002, the Fresh Air Society will commemorate its 100th anniversary with the dedication of the 4,000 square-foot Jewell and Lester Morris Medical Facility. Replacing the original clinic building, built some 50 years earlier, the new heated and air-conditioned medical center will be home to the John Maas Memorial Clinic. Doctors will conduct medical examinations in one of four spacious rooms while ill feeling staff and campers can rest in one of five sleeping rooms. Medicines will be securely stored in the Dispensing Center, named after the children, grandchildren and sister of Lester Morris: Patrice and Eric Phillips, Jennifer and Rachel Phillips, Robert Prentice Morris and Beverly Prentice Wagner. The clinic's head nurse will make her home in a small set of rooms adjacent to the main building.

that way. Even though pediatricians were ideally suited for camp, sometimes other medical professionals had to fill in. Jeffrey Zaks, an adult cardiologist, helped for a few years back in the 1980s. "One kid came in with bumps all over him. I kept looking at the bumps trying to figure it out," he chuckled. "The kid looked at me and said, 'It's chicken pox, dummy.'"

Like the nurses, the doctors deal with homesickness in many forms. Zaks recalled the time a young boy strolled into the clinic, declared he was homesick and demanded to go home. Explaining that many kids get homesick and in a day or so, he'd feel better, Zaks was stupefied when "the kid pulled out a $20 bill from his pocket and said this is for you if you get me home."

"*We were all physically fit.*" Denise Landau

"*We set the pace, a pace of living that everyone enjoyed.*" Gordy Levenson

"*Being a counselor was cool, being a tripper was prestigious.*" Jeffrey Appel

"*There is no way I can explain what I now know.*" Minda Tilchin

"Camp is like Shangrila. When you are the happiest person, it is easy to feel beautiful." Leslye Landau

"If I can do this, I can do anything." Dave Shepard

"The black flies and mosquitos will pick you up and carry you away." Beth Sonne

CAMP PEOPLE:
THE COUNSELORS AND STAFF

1987 ORTONVILLE

"Being at camp is a comfort zone.
We grew up there.
I spent all my summers there, I learned so much there.
My best friends, the friends I am absolutely closest with,
are from camp."

Jill Bruss, a counselor during the late 1990s

"Camp people are a different kind of people. They have camp in their hearts. They want to work with kids and make a difference in their lives." As timeless as camp itself, these words could have been spoken 80 years ago or, as they were, in 2000 by Susie Zaks, Assistant Camp Director. They sum up all that camp is about.

Every summer, an army of over 400 counselors, supervisors, trippers, specialists, cooks, maintenance crew, bus drivers and administrators converge on Camp Maas in the first days of June. As they prepare the grounds for the coming onslaught of campers, and as they go through the two-week period of pre-camp rituals and training, this group of "camp people" begins a bonding experience nearly 100 years old. It is a time when new friendships are formed and old ones are re-established. A time when they learn how to create magic and comfort a frightened child, to make each other laugh and put safety over adventure. The veteran leads the novice, the American welcomes the Israeli and the expert teaches the beginner.

Three months later, as the summer wanes and the leaves on the trees are speckled with red and yellow, the group re-convenes. Their bodies are tanner and their hair is longer, their clothes are no longer neatly pressed and their blue jeans bear a few new proudly worn holes in the knees. The pent-up excitement that a season ago bubbled through the crowd is now more subdued and signs of exhaustion are apparent. They are a much-changed group.

For three months, these young men and women have acted as mothers and fathers, been awakened in the middle of the night, remained vigilant against looming dangers and disasters, cared for

1918

ABE AND HIS ASSISTANTS —
NO TRAINED COUNSELLORS.

the homesick and cured the sore throat. They've cooked and cleaned, lifted and lugged, carried packs heavier than expected and sat through one too many storm. But, they made it and, as Susie Zaks said, "They made an impact and we changed them (the kids and the staff) forever."

"There is no way to bond with someone the way you bond with someone at camp,"[1] said Gail Gales, counselor and Jewish program director during a 25-year period that began in the 1970s. "The relationships people form there are unlike the relationships you form with anyone else...the intensity, the experience, the living together; being there for one another. It is a 24-7 deal."

It has always been this way.

1930s

From Chaperones to College Grads

Without a great staff, camp is just a bunch of buildings in the woods. For that reason, "camp has always had two tracts,"[2] commented Aaron Goren, a counselor and supervisor from 1959 to 1963. "One a camper's tract and one a staff tract."

Initially, Blanche Hart's friends came to camp, two at a time, to "chaperone" the children. They stayed for a week, often arriving in the same streetcar as the campers. Hart also had a kitchen staff, first-generation immigrants who came with their families to spend the summer by the lake and cook nourishing meals for the children and Gussie Brown, the first camp supervisor.

It didn't take long for the system of weekly, unpaid chaperones to become insufficient. The first paid counselor was A.J. Levin, hired in 1916. Older campers helped lead games, teach swimming and raise and lower the flag. Soon afterward, a small budget was allocated for recruiting college students. But competition for young talent was heating up as more camps opened. Carolyn Eppstein, camp's director in the 1920s, persistently appealed to the Board for higher wages. Penny by penny the pay scale increased and by the time Brighton opened in 1927, the hiring of permanent paid summer counselors had become routine.

From his winter Florida home, Irv Rosen, a very popular 1930s counselor, remembered how he and his fellow counselors, most of whom remained friends throughout their lives, loved to enchant the kids. The charm they brought was immeasurable. "The night before a hike, we would go into the woods taking apples and oranges, a needle and string,"[3] recalled Rosen. From a tree, they hung the fruit and the next morning, "we told the kids that we would go on a hike and maybe they would get lucky and find a magic tree that grew apples and oranges." Of course, the children were amazed upon finding such a mystical tree, and ate the fruit without hesitation.

Hanging fruit from a tree, dressing up as an old rabbi from Europe and spinning fantastic tales around a campfire are the magic morsels that make camp such an unforgettable experience. The place, be it Brighton or Ortonville or Camp Kennedy or a Western trip, sets the stage. It is the people, however, who create the experience, who make the magic happen.

WAGES

Since the beginning of camp, administration has fought to increase counselor wages. Here is a sampling of salaries over time:

	low	high
1936:	$ 25	$ 50
1965:	$ 200	$ 500
1977:	$ 400	$ 700
1984:	$ 850	$1,250
2000:	$1,100	$2,000

Finding Staff

Henry Baskin still has the first contract he ever signed. In 1951, Baskin, then 18, was hired as a counselor. "The good part was you got $75 in cash at the end of the 10 weeks and you got all your room and board paid for,"[4] said Baskin.

In 1951 counselors were plentiful. The war had ended and young men and women were eager to work. Applicants merely needed "a natural love for youth, a zest for outdoor life, interest, good moral character and integrity, emotional maturity, health and ability to work."[5] If the counseling positions were filled or if one preferred not to work directly with the children, there was always a position as a waiter, cook, truck driver or specialist. As with the campers, all staff hailed from Detroit. There was no need to look elsewhere.

In the years leading up to the end of the war, however, recruitment hadn't been so easy. Opening Brighton drained the budget, so the Board reduced counselor pay and increased the ratio of children per counselor. In 1926, the ratio was a comfortable 12.5 children to one counselor. One year later, it jumped to 16.5 to one. Coun-

FRESH AIR CAMP   APPROX 1932-1933

BRIGHTON 1932

selors had no time off and were assisted by "aides," older campers who volunteered for the summer experience.   During the Depression, the problems became even worse. Qualified personnel were scurrying to other camps where better wages were available. On average, a full-time 1936 staff person was paid $20. The head counselor earned $50. The result, as Irwin Shaw wrote in 1936, was a staff "characterized by mediocrity and incompetence."[6]   Still, Shaw commended those counselors, who, despite pitiful pay, were enthusiastic, cooperative and hard working.

1930s

Irving Rosen and co-counselor Sylvia Grenadier (Schwartz), who had her pilot's license, arranged to get candy kisses from Sanders Confectionary. The two flew over camp and dropped magical treats from heaven above.

When the Depression ended camp enjoyed a brief respite from the counselor dearth. Then came World War II. The job pool of young adults was sapped and the average counselor age sunk from 20 to 17. Those with some experience took over as specialists while the novices essentially shuttled kids from one activity to another. Young teens were hired to help maintain the daily operations of camp. Thirteen-year-old Moishe Last was hired in 1943, to cut the lawn and set the tables. "I did things that were normally done by adults or older teens, but because of the war, the younger children had to step into these roles. They got me very cheap,"[7] he recalled. Last went on to have a fluid camp career, coming back later as a music specialist and artist-in-residence.

When the War years came to an end, so too did the counselor shortage. Although many came without camp experience, they eagerly learned counseling skills. For the first time, a program spe-

cialist was retained. It was this person's duty to bring a taste of
Israeli culture into camp, teaching campers Jewish songs and folk
dances.

Beginning in 1954, as Ortonville's villages began to spring to life
a new staffing problem emerged. The number of staff required to
run a decentralized camp spread across many acres was far more
than expected. Recruitment efforts had to be stepped up. Pay scales
increased and camp sessions were shortened by one day in order to
give counselors an extra day off. Married couples were recruited and
staff from Baltimore, Chicago, Buffalo and Springfield was hired.

Becoming a camp counselor was an attractive way to spend the
summer for young 1960s and 70s collegians. They came in droves.
Dizzy with delight, and often marijuana, the hippies came to
camp singing folk songs and preaching about
peace, love, equality and the environment. They
were a grungy, happy bunch that loved
to play naked basketball and "never
shaved or cut their hair, including
the women,"[8] remembered Eli
Greenbaum, who included himself as a member of this elite
group.

It was a particularly political
and defiant time, remembered Marvin
Berman. "They were smart, Jewish kids

WAITERS

Waiters were first hired in 1937.
Not too many summers later, the waiters
threatened to go on strike because of low pay.
Irwin Shaw called the group together and told
them if they weren't happy, they could board
a bus home the next morning. When the bus
arrived, no one boarded. A six-day work
week was later negotiated.

BRIGHTON 1958

caught up in this. We lived through some summers where we had out and out rebellions. One group got their kids to parade around with banners reading 'Hell no we won't go to bed.' And, they wouldn't."[9]

The young men of the day also lived with the fear of the Vietnam War draft. Merrill Gordon, a 1972 Boy Pioneer, vividly remembered his counselor, Bobby Michaelson, receiving his draft number at camp. It was a low number and Michaelson, realizing that he was sure to be called, went white. "He fell apart a little bit,"[10] said Gordon 30 years later. "It made you think, we're out there (at camp) doing whatever we're doing, and this was reality."

The war ended, the rebellions quieted down and the hippies started getting corporate jobs. Coming up through the ranks was the next generation of counselors. The up and coming yuppie generation dressed a lot neater, never protested bedtimes and were much more interested in career development than summers in the woods. Counselor recruitment became challenging because modern America began to ask more of its youth. Longer school years, summer graduate classes, internships and the want of money lured potential counselors away from camp. Finding Jewish males was twice as challenging as finding females. Parents urged their children to get *real* jobs.

PROMOTED

Sy Kalish, a 1930s camper, came back in 1942 as a waiter. That summer, he recalled, "Moishe Weiss (who later became the psychiatrist Morris Weiss, M.D.) held the lowly position of camp janitor. Before the summer was over, Moishe had attained such great skill at unplugging overflowing toilets that he was promoted to 'chief of sanitary engineering.' The promotion was in title only and not in remuneration."

ORTONVILLE 1959

Marc Kay doesn't blame his parents for feeling that their son was wasting his young adult life on a fruitless career. Their complaints had become old hat by the time he became a program director in 1991. "One year my dad finally came out for Shabbat dinner and saw me in action. He saw me working with the kids, running the program, telling the stories. He never said another word,"[11] said Kay, who eventually became an English and history teacher. Working at camp, Kay acquired valuable people skills, skills no internship could have provided.

"When I was in college, a lot of people were saying I should get a real job. I never wanted to,"[12] reflected Amy Guggenheim, a late 1970s camper. "What better job could there possibly be than to have fun as your whole goal for the summer. I also had the feeling that I really was learning about responsibility and about management and communication skills." Guggenheim became a counselor in 1984.

"The most incredible thing was to see the metamorphosis from little kids who got off the bus crying because they were so scared, to three weeks later when they are little independent people crying because they are getting back on the bus." Her experience was so profound she wrote about it in her entrance essay for Harvard Business School.

FRIENDSHIPS

"The connections I have made with people at camp have flowed through my life." Julie Steinmetz. Brighton counselor, 1975-77.

Competing with other camps and with corporate America for staff has made 21st Century recruitment an art. Over 400 staff positions must be filled each summer with the best possible candidates. Two times a year, senior Tamarack staff tours the Midwest visiting college campuses, vying for staff candidates. The recruitment fairs – packed with camp recruiters from around the country – are arduous, competitive and necessary. Considered one of the premier camps in the nation, Tamarack has an advantage. In addition, the man and woman-power of the international staff, recruited by camp personnel and by international recruitment organizations like Camp America, has become vital to the recruitment mix.

The future of counselor recruitment lies in the 2,400 children who attend Tamarack Camps each summer. Many will become the next counselors and specialists. In their hands, the Tamarack magic will carry on.

The Training Season

When Jeff Metz, Brighton's director from 1985-1989, was a 10-year-old camper, he went on a canoe trip. He sat in the bow while the counselor sat in the stern. Although there was another camper in the middle, Metz and the counselor did all of the paddling. When the trip was over, the counselor came up to him and whispered, "We would have never made it without you."[13] It was a moment Metz never forgot.

Some 15 years later, Metz told this story to his staff at pre-camp training. It demonstrated, he said, the monumental influence counselors have on kids. "We all knew how powerful our impact was with these kids. During pre-camp I would always tell this story. I would tell counselors that the most insignificant thing, every little thing you do or say, can be very significant to the kids."

Before meeting their campers, the counselors, specialists and supervisors first spend about two weeks in pre-camp. It is camp for young adults. They sleep a bit later, water ski, challenge themselves on the ropes courses, hike and even go on an overnight. This camp, however, has a very serious purpose. "Pre-camp was an extremely critical time for us. It really set the tone for the rest of the summer," said Marvin Berman. "Our goal was to develop a team that would function together over the next 10 weeks."

Training counselors to understand their responsibility and learn to be surrogate parents was always a priority. Irwin Shaw had counselors and supervisors attend a series of once-monthly training sessions. Before camp started, the candidates took an oral and written exam. If they scored below 90 percent, their camp position was in jeopardy. In the 1950s, Sam Marcus worked with Wayne State University to develop a course used to train and recruit staff called Practician in Education Psychology #6732. It was offered for about seven or eight years. In the mid-1960s camp developed a comprehensive

WATERFRONT

Within the many specialty areas of camp, no one was more exposed than the waterfront supervisors. Irving Berg ran the Brighton waterfront for a year or two in the 1940s. He invented his own little limerick that helped campers learn to row and he had a strict supervision style. Anyone caught goofing around would hear Berg's deep booming voice echoing from his megaphone, "get out of the water!" Fifty years later, a young Rick Goren worked on the Ortonville waterfront staff and partnered with a much elder Irving Berg to rebuild the waterfront buddy board. The two bridged the past and the future. "Working on the waterfront, you got to know every kid," said Goren. "It was like being the uncle. They thought you were the cool waterfront guy and wanted to hang around with you. We helped them achieve real milestones, though. Everyone remembers the day they learned to ski or got their white water ranking."

Until the mid-1990s, a waterfront staff of five or six specialists did everything from teaching swimming, sailing and water skiing to supervising general swim. In the new century, a team of 40 dynamic waterfront specialists runs the bustling instructional and recreational waterfront program. In addition to all of the "old" sports, these bathing-suited devotees help campers career across Radin Lake on tubes, jet skis, kayaks and wind surf boards.

ORTONVILLE 1966

counselor-in-training program that included spring workshops and additional in-service programs at camp. When Harvey Finkelberg became executive director in 1992, he began using a business-like approach to training. He set clear and attainable goals that every staff member had to achieve. "Our mantra is: pay attention to detail, leave nothing to chance, exceed expectations, achieve excellence, meet the individual needs of every camper, all in a Jewish atmosphere," said Finkelberg.

The real test, of course, comes when campers arrive. "Even with all the training,"[14] recalled Rob Bienstock, camper, counselor and supervisor through the 1990s, "when those kids piled out of the buses, I found it overwhelming. I felt the responsibility and thought, can I just get to dinner?"

CIT, TP, TSS and So On

Diane Klein (Yura) became a CIT in 1959. "For the first time in my life, I felt independent and a responsibility that I hadn't known before. I took my leadership position very seriously."[15] She remembers singing "Tom Dooley" and the "Fresh Air Goat" with her young campers; square dancing and relay races; and on rainy days, playing silly games and improvisational dramatics. In 1960, she became a junior counselor and was paid the handsome sum of $50 for the summer.

Fostering youth to become outgoing, confident leaders has always been a part of the camp experience. Irwin Shaw implemented the first Counselor-In-Training program in 1936. Back then, regular camp programs ended for kids once they reached age 13. The CIT program gave them summer recreation while alleviating some of the pressures on the counselors.

In 1957, a nearly 16-year-old Liz Warnick (Borger) became a Brighton CIT. "We lived behind Dorm One in a tent,"[16] she recalled. "There were four of us. The CITs were kind of gophers. If the counselor needed anything, we did it."

With the advent of the tripping program a new type of CIT was needed: tripper preps or "TPs" for short. The fastest path to becoming a TP was to first enroll in the Explorers, part of the boy Pioneer program. Explorers, remembered Howard Davis, trip program director throughout much of the 70s, "were affectionately referred to as the Ozone Rangers for they were neither campers nor staff." They did as their name suggested – explored outpost and base camp areas to develop hiking and canoeing routes. Jeffrey Applebaum was a 1970 Explorer. Many of the routes he created were still being used well into the new century.

Applebaum landed his Explorer gig one year after the Agree outpost was established. "There were no paths into camp, it was all overgrown with brush,"[17] remembered the father of two daughters who

ORTONVILLE 1971

both followed in his hiking bootsteps. "All we did first session was basically clear brush, build tables and chairs and explore Lake Kabenung." Applebaum became a TP the next year and spent three years as a tripper before becoming the director of the Agree outpost from 1975 to 1978.

The TPs became known as Tripper Trainees and in 1995, Teen Trippers. The CIT program was renamed Teen Service Staff or TSS in the 1980s thanks to the recession. Trying to minimize the effects of the economic downturn, camp was able to reduce costs by enlisting young teens into the maintenance department.

Twelve "lucky" high school seniors were selected each summer. Half their time was spent scrubbing toilets and cleaning the villages, the other half working with kids. For many, it was their first paid job. One eager beaver, Jody Rankin (Klein), excitedly entered her 1987 interview wearing a cute little yellow dress. "I never got the job. It was my outfit that screwed me up. I'm positive,"[18] she giggled. Her friend, Stacey Lash (Cohen) wore jeans and was hired. "Being TSS, you had the combination of being part of a village and a member of a small little team,"[19] recalled Lash. "I preferred cleaning because you were done by noon and you could lay on the beach all day and get tan."

TSS helped run Smokler Pioneer Skills Village, feed farm animals, had the honorary task of lighting the Shabbat menorah on the last night of the session and, each morning, dashed to their assigned village to unload the food truck. Joe Lash (who met Stacey Cohen in 1987 and married her in 1997) was TSS in 1986. "We were these Jewish kids from West Bloomfield thrown in as maintenance staff and working with these great guys, the maintenance men. We were pretty excited about being selected. It was a big deal." Lash remembered his morning ritual. "You could hear the food truck rumbling down the road, so we'd get on our bikes and race down to the village. You had to be there to get the food off the truck."

BUDDIES

"My best friends are from camp," said Mike Bossin. Once a radical, long-haired counselor, he became an energy consultant who maintained friendships with about 30 of his camp buddies.

BRIGHTON 1980

BRIGHTON 1981

Glancing out at the San Francisco Bay from her apartment window, Amy Guggenheim remembered her 1983 TSS summer. "When I was a camper, I couldn't imagine having more fun...until I became a counselor," she recalled. "I remember the first time I was TSS and got my little paycheck. Marv Berman gave it to me and I remember thinking, 'Well *thanks*, I would have done it for free anyway.' It was so not a job."

By the mid-1990s, about 40 TSS participated each year. Marc Kay helped direct the program. Oddly, cleaning the toilets, said Kay, was the best part of the experience. "The kids who did it had real pride in how clean their village was. You would think it would be the worst thing they did all summer, but so many said that was the best part of their summer."

IMPORTANT PEOPLE

"Both of my best men at my wedding were friends I met at camp. You could say, the three most important people in my life who are not my family members are people I met at camp," said Matthew Roth. Camper and staff member, 1980s through 1995, who met his wife, Sarah, at camp.

Times change, and cleaning toilets lost its luster. Harvey Finkelberg removed the "refuse" part of the job and implemented a true counselor-in-training program in 1999. TSS enrollments soared. Erin Lowen began her camp career in 1992 as a camper. In 2000, she was one of nearly 100 TSS. After a week of sprucing up camp and orientation, Lowen spent the next nine weeks working in different specialty and village areas. The 10th week was hers to choose. "I asked if I could do my last 10 days at Fishman," she said. "I loved working with the little girls. I became really close to them. I would play with their hair, they loved all of my friends and they wanted my boyfriend to give them piggy back rides."[20]

Lowen is on track to become the ideal counselor. Her counselors were her mentors and as she prepared to step into their shoes, she hoped that she would inspire others to do the same. Nearly 80 percent of the TSS class of 2000 returned the following year as counselors. "They are the future of our camp," said Finkelberg.

International Staff

In 1967 Marvin Berman attended a camp directors conference in Israel. It was there that the concept of bringing Israeli counselors to American Jewish camps to introduce Israeli customs and culture first surfaced. Tamarack welcomed four Israeli staff members in 1968.

Ayanna Livney, a 21-year-old student, touched down in Detroit in 1972. She was one of 250 Israelis coming to the U.S. for the summer and one of 10 heading to Tamarack. For one memorable season she was a Fishman counselor. Thirty years later, speaking from her home south of Tel Aviv, the memories still warmed her heart. "They wanted someone with deep Israeli roots. I knew the Israeli songs, the dance. I was studying the Bible and Hebrew linguistics."[21] Ayanna found she fit right in and grew, both socially and emotionally, from her experience. "They called me the alien," she laughed. "I didn't know what that word was. I was different from the others, telling different stories. I didn't feel different. As an Israeli, it was good to see Jewish life in America."

What began as a novelty in the late 1960s, quickly became an important aspect of camp. By the end of the 1990s, nearly 100 international staff from Israel, S. Africa, the United Kingdom and Australia arrived each summer adding an important cultural mix to camp. For the international staff the experience was equally rewarding.

"I got a letter from Camp America saying that I had been placed at a camp called Tamarack in Brighton, Michigan. Try searching for that on a map,"[22] reminisced a witty Kelby Shaw, who came to camp from Britain in 1991 and returned for eight more summers. His first summer was an eye-opener. "We Brits are somewhat reserved, so yelling out camp songs and playing snaps was completely new to me. All the Americans were playing softball and us five Brits were playing soccer. We felt a little left out until everybody got to know us and invited us to play." He then added, "and Americans think cricket is boring!"

MEMORIES

"My fondest memories are the friendships. We are all turning 40 now, and here we are still talking about who liked who back then, what we did in our bunk. These are the ties that bind," said Julie Yolles (Smith). Yolles, a 1970s camper, grew up to be a professional actress and she and her husband Ron endowed the Camp Tamarack drama program.

Shaw found camp to be more than he ever imagined. He discovered that he loved working with children and made it his profession. He fell in love at camp, meeting Donna Bloom who became his wife, and he discovered his Jewish identity. "The Jewishness of camp felt strange to me especially during Saturday services. People would be praying in baseball caps and jeans, far more relaxed than in Manchester. The sole reason for me going to camp was to meet the needs of the campers ... and to strengthen my Jewish identity... This could only happen at Tamarack."

Clare Stephens, also from Britain, was a Fishman supervisor in 2000 and 1999. Nothing in her life matched the Tamarack experience. "You get addicted so fast, there's something that draws you in,"[23] she exclaimed. "You think about all of the friends you made. No one believes how magical a place this is until it is time to say goodbye." She came to camp for five years and was able to watch small campers grow into young adults. "The girls become more like women. When they started they were this big, now they rule the camp, they run the camp."

What Is With The Cross Dressing?

A.J. Levin, the foresighted 1917 counselor, knew that children laughed the hardest when "the female counselors and the older boys and I would cook up some hilarious stunts for which we would dress as the opposite sex." Cross-dressing, known during the Vaudeville era as camp, is definitely camp.

The number of reported cross dressers at camp is in the hundreds, too many to mention. It seems to be more of a "guy thing" and goes on just about anywhere and everywhere. For a camp talent show, Chuck Wolfe, an engaging 1960s counselor, wrapped himself in a bath towel, stuck a rose in his mouth and, as Maria from West Side Story, sang 'I'm So Pretty.' His imitation was so memorable that Aaron Goren, Wolfe's co-counselor, never forgot it. "I still remember that Chuck brought the house down. Only Chuck could pull it off."

Self described as quiet and reserved, Marvin Berman donned any number of costumes on every possible occasion. "It brought out the ham in me," he said. So, when he transformed himself into a Japanese geisha complete with kimono and clogs or squeezed into a tutu for the Nutcracker, no one was too alarmed. Then

FRIENDSHIPS

"I loved the *ruach*, the spirit, the singing, the songs and Shabbat. And, meeting your friends, people I am still friends with. Now, I am going to their children's weddings," said Susie Zaks. She was a camper in 1966, a counselor in the 1970s, a camp doc's wife in the 80s, a supervisor in the 90s, and then became Assistant Director.

there was the time Mike Zaks, the often-too-serious camp director, dressed as a woman for a camp talent show and no one could figure out who he was.

Rick Goren fondly remembered when he was waterfront supervisor in 1991 and, for the talent show, dressed as Sandy from 'Grease' and sang 'Summer Lovin'. In 1994, supervisor Rob Bienstock, borrowed a mini skirt from Deborah Fishman, the arts and crafts counselor, for a gag. The kids loved it and so did she. Three years later, in 1995, the two tied the knot. Did any 1984 Levison camper forget the lunchtime lectures on camp life and hygiene delivered by the well-appointed Russian man-woman Lynn Bashevitz – also known as counselor Dave Brown?

The phenomena isn't limited to staff, although it is nearly certain that at every Second Night Show or Talent Show there will be at least one counselor or supervisor who laboriously adorns himself in a sexy outfit and struts across the stage. The camper population is also stricken. Beth Schwartz was a Berman counselor in 1999. That summer her village got together with Hermelin 8th grade boys and put on a fashion show. The task of dressing the boys was put to the girls. "It was the funniest thing I've ever seen,"[24] laughed Schwartz. "It was so much fun to see these little boys dressed in girls clothes and make up. The girls even styled the boys hair. It was crazy." Crazy? No, just camp.

CAMP MAAS STAFF 1983

ORTONVILLE 1983

In The End, It Comes Down To This...

"Camp is where you find out it is o.k. to be on your own,"[25] said Julie Steinmetz Shaffer, who brought those memories with her when she became a counselor in 1975. "You learn that you can become part of another community. It gives you a lot of confidence to know that you are doing fine without your mom and dad. That's a huge thing for a kid. A really good counselor enables this to happen."

What is a really good counselor? Defining that is as complex as defining what makes a good parent or a good leader or a good teacher or a good friend. A counselor is all of those.

BRIGHTON 1991

BONDS

"Once you were a camp person, you were part of a group. There is an immediate bond when you meet someone from camp," said Jeffrey Appel. A counselor through the early 1970s and a Board member in the late 1990s.

"You really had to have a yearning to work with children. The good counselors *played* with their kids. They didn't plan activities and then sit back and watch them, they played with them,"[26] commented Ruth Grey, a camper and 1960s counselor who returned in 1984 and spent the next 10 years as an associate camp director. "For me, camp was about the kid that came with no friends, low self-esteem and found a place where they discovered they were amazing. That made me feel I was doing something wonderful."

In 100 years, counselors' roles have changed only slightly. During the first 50 years, counselors were entirely responsible for campers' entertainment. They did the programming, generated the ideas and worked with them on projects and crafts. Their creativity defined the experience. Modern programming inched the counselor away from being the hub of all activities. Instead a variety of people interact with campers throughout their stay. Yet, from the moment a child gets off the bus until the moment, one session later, when their mother and father embraces them, the counselor has been the center of that child's life.

"When you were a camper, you thought your counselor knew everything," remembered Jody Rankin (Klein), a camper who became a counselor in the late 1980s. "If you were lost in the middle of the woods, your counselor knew how to get you out. When I was a counselor, I had no clue how to get out of the woods, but you present yourself as though you do. It's like being a parent. My son thinks we know everything about life. But, you have no clue. You're just wingin' it."

Rankin knew that every summer at least one child who started out insecure, or who had a rough home life or just needed attention, got the love they needed to feel special at camp. "It was your job to see that they had so much fun, that they forgot everything. For that month, they were in your world," she said.

"We had the time for these kids. We lived with them," explained Henry Baskin. During the early 1950s, when he was a counselor, many of the children were immigrants who had escaped the Nazis. "These kids were telling us about their family problems, crying in our arms, trying to cope with this society because they were from another country. They were put on the bus and many felt they were being sent away. They got off the bus

THE MAGIC

"There is a magic about Tamarack that you can't understand unless you've been here. The smell you wake up to each morning, the people. It just becomes a part of you," said Julia Morianis, Drama Supervisor 2001.

ORTONVILLE 1992

and we just loved them."

Baskin also recalled the emotional story of two brothers and a sister whose father was in jail. The kids became special to the counselors, in particular Baskin. Later that year, while taking a criminal law class at Wayne State University, Baskin and a few fellow law students found themselves inside the very jail where the father was incarcerated. "We walked through one of the cabins where they house these guys, it was a minimum security place. And there, on the wall, was a picture of me with his son. It was the strangest thing. We talked to him and he cried a lot as we told him what great kids he had."

For many counselors, the greatest test of their effectiveness is at nighttime when all is quiet, the lights are out and the memories of home flood a child's emotions. "A good counselor,"[27] whispered Marshall Hersh, a 1961 Pioneer supervisor, "would go around and talk to the kids in a quiet, individual manner. It was one of the best times. You got to know the kids in the best way. There were no facades like when they were with other kids. They were really who they were at that particular time."

PEERS

"My peers are not from high school, they are not from the fraternity. They are from camp. Camp ties you together for life," said Bob Lipsitz, consummate camp supervisor and director for 18 years.

Campers relish the camp experience because they gain independence and maturity. Counselors gain something far greater. Lisa Zaks was practically born at camp. As one of three children born to Susie (camp administrator) and Jeffrey (camp doctor), Lisa was a staff kid, camper, counselor and supervisor. Above all else, she says, it was her counseling experiences that formed the person she became. "You grow as a person by taking care of kids. You are in charge of their safety and well-being. Answering their questions, being there 24 hours a day. You want these kids to get the same thing you got. You want to try to introduce them to all these new things, teach them new skills and just feel good

ORTONVILLE 1995

ORTONVILLE 2000

about themselves."[28]

For Zaks, who will finish medical school in 2002, the last day of the season impacted her the hardest. "You are sad it is over. You are tired. You have to enter back into the real world. You have to stop being a kid again." She smiled broadly and continued, "You get to be a kid all summer and you just love it! At the end of the summer you know you have made a difference in a child's life."

That sensation isn't limited to counselors. In 1937, Lillian Genser ran the camp store, the laundry and the library. She also taught dramatics for the evening programs. A young boy named Gabriel Slomovitz frequented her dramatics class. He was mentally impaired and, as Genser described, was always repeating the same phrase, "Miss Lillian, Miss Lillian," over and over. "I decided that when his parents came on visiting day, I would have him do something (in the play). I took him aside and taught him one action. It was a cowboy thing where he would remove a cowboy hat and say 'hi-ya folks' and that was it. I worked with that kid over and over and over again. On the day of the performance, his parents were in the audience, he was sweating; trying to focus on that one thing. He did it beautifully. His parents started to cry. We all did."[29]

At age 80, the noted professor and peace activist cried again. "In all the things that I've done, that was a good one."

How many alumni can say that? Probably, just about all of them.

FRIENDS

"When you have experiences like that and make lifetime friends...truly lifetime friends... you go back and see someone you haven't seen in 30 years and you don't have to play catch-up," said Moishe Last. 1930s camper, counselor, artist-in-residence and life-long camp friend.

Works of Wonder,
Works Of Art

Jonah And The Whale

Irving and Harriet Berg,
Artists-in-Residence,
1978-1999, 2000, 2001...

They are there to touch, to ponder and to inspire. Cast concrete, wood and welded steel sculptures not meant to be in any museum, but to lend a visual Jewish identity and different beauty to an already beautiful environment.

"Next time you go to camp, take a good view of what you see," expressed Moishe Last, a camper who once carved his name on Brighton dorm plaques and later became one of Tamarack's artists-in-residence. "If you ever woke up and looked at the lake in the morning, the trees, the scenery and serenity – you know. Art was a very natural way to commune with nature."

It really isn't something you expect...walking around camp's 1,500 forested acres and bumping into an eight-foot sculpture of Jonah and the Whale. Yet, it isn't out of place. It blends perfectly into the environment, just as the guitar player who strums and sings beside a campfire or the dance troupe that leaps across a stage set in a clearing so close to the woods that they can almost touch the trees. It is as if the performing and fine arts have always been at camp. The relationship is symbiotic: the arts were meant for this environment and the environment is there to inspire the visions and dreams of young artists.

Irving and Harriet Berg were young 50-year olds when they first came as artists-in-residence in 1978. In 2000, they were still there. She came to dance, he to sculpt. Both had once been young Fresh Air campers and were teaching, he in the Detroit Public Schools and she at the Jewish Community Center, when Michael Zaks invited them to Tamarack.

"I said build me a dance barn where I can teach," remembered the gracious dancer and choreographer, Harriet. Sam Marcus teamed up with his wife, Irma, a ballet dancer, and Sidney and Melba Winer. Together they designed the dance barn where Berg taught for the next 20 years. Irma added touches like an unfinished wooden dance floor, Melba chose the barn-style design and Berg led Tamarack Dance City, a four-week dance wonderland for campers to immerse themselves in jazz, ballet, Israeli and international dance styles. "I loved my time in the dance barn," said Berg. "Working with the kids, performing with them. Our performances were so beautiful, so inspiring, so exciting."

In the meantime, Irving began to sculpt. His first project was a menorah built

The Holocaust Memorial

above the bleachers at the Allen Amphitheater. The most ancient of all Jewish symbols, Berg holds the menorah in high regard. Over the years he created many more, but his first has special meaning. "Every kid at camp put in a screw, hammered in a nail, did something. It was one of my most exciting projects," *kvelled* Berg. The wooden candles were made from trees cut from the campground, milled at camp and carried to the site. Harriet's dancers dedicated the 12-foot-high sculpture with a special Sabbath dance.

Nearly deaf in both ears from the years of sawing and milling wood, Berg's work at camp – an outdoor gallery of structures filled with wit and wisdom – has helped him remain young at heart. Slowly flipping through the pages of his scrapbook, scanning his work and the people he has met, Berg credits the campers. "When I work with the kids, like on the Wall of Hope or a menorah, to me that is the most satisfying. I get to know the kids, and the fact that they have contributed means they will remember it."

Miriam And Her Drum

Harriet continues, "Our work is dedicated to teaching and inspiring campers and staff about Jewish values and history. My favorite sculpture of Irving's is the Holocaust memorial. We can teach while giving something significant to the community."

"Everybody should be exposed to the arts," urged Julie Yolles (Smith), who as a camper participated in every play she could and, later, returned to camp as "Julie Drama," the drama specialist in 1979. Her passion for the stage became her profession and, in 1997, she and her husband, Ron, became benefactors of camp's drama program. "We believe encouraging children to explore art and drama as a culture form is an important gift that Tamarack gives the community."

Ceramics, dance, sculpture, music, drama. "The fine arts at Tamarack is unusually strong because the Jewish community strongly has always revered the arts and supports it," reflected Paula Zaks, MFA, who supervised Tamarack's arts program for 15 years. "It started with Irwin Shaw, then Sam Marcus brought puppetry to camp and Moishe Last upgraded the ceramics programs." Zaks, who was married to executive director, Michael, introduced campers to batik, string art and silk screening.

More than the trinkets campers bring home, the arts at Tamarack is a lasting gift that comes in many forms: the smiles on the faces of senior citizens watching a play or dance, the quiet solitude found by a waterside Irving Berg sculpture, the pride of learning to play guitar or the small sculpture that rests on the family mantle. Small acts that imprint lasting impressions on young people's minds and help shape and form the people these campers become.

The Wall Of Hope

In 1998, the Teen Service Staff joined Berg to undertake an elaborate project. Box by box, they built a Wall Of Hope, reminiscent of the Western Wall. The piece was inspired by the work of artist Louise Nevelson. "Teams of four campers came to work on the Wall," proudly described Berg. "They each designed their own box and took a lot of pride in their work. That is why it is so good." Campers insert written messages, prayers and wishes into the wall's openings.

The Holocaust Memorial

In a quiet, wooded spot, just off the main camp road, the Holocaust Memorial rests. It is at once striking and wrenching. Berg began the memorial to the six million Jews in 1984 and completed it nearly a decade later. Its cast concrete figures reach out to the observer, their hands made of welded steel, begging you to remember the atrocities. The harsh fence, made by campers, and barbed with a shield of nails, pushes you back, reminding you to never forget.

Miriam and Her Drum

Located at the Lookout, a quiet, peaceful alcove overlooking Radin Lake, this life-size statue is dedicated to Sharyn Finkelberg, executive director Harvey Finkelberg's wife who passed away from cancer. "Her favorite place was the lookout. She used to go there

Eternal Flame

a lot to sit and read," remembered Finkelberg. Sharyn Finkelberg also loved music, convincing Irving Berg that a sculpture of Miriam, the sister of Moses who welcomed the children of Israel with song and dance, would be an appropriate memorial.

Eternal Flame

"I wanted to see how tall I could make something," said Berg. In all, this cast-concrete sculpture is 16 feet, 12 feet above ground and four feet underground. "The flame is slashed in-half as a symbol of the holocaust, just as the Nazi's tried to extinguish the flame of the Jewish people."

Dance Barn

"This place is so unique," said Harriet Berg, who taught dancers here for more than 20 years. "The setting, the building, the fact that it transforms from a studio into an outdoor amphitheatre in the woods."

Wall of Hope

Dance Barn

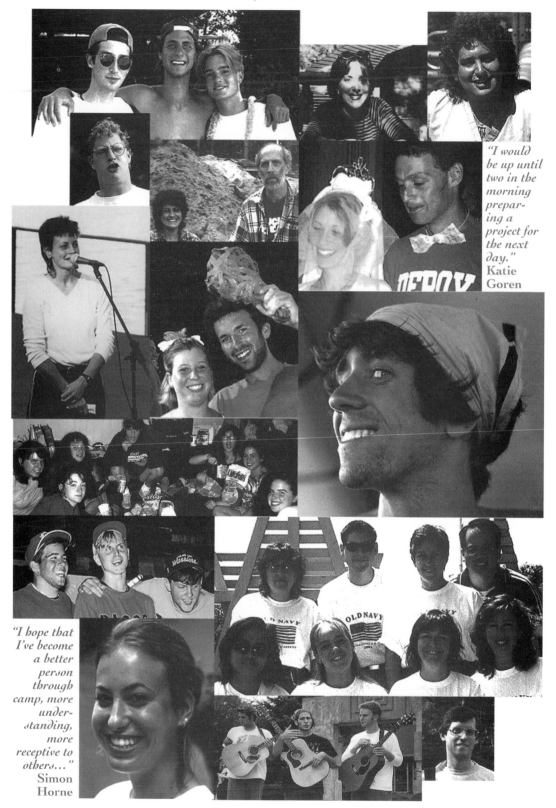

"I would be up until two in the morning preparing a project for the next day."
Katie Goren

"I hope that I've become a better person through camp, more understanding, more receptive to others..."
Simon Horne

"You wanted to give your campers the same experience your counselors gave you." Rick Goren

"I want to be a role model for my campers." Erin Lowen

"It was a paid summer vacation." Liz Warnick (Borger)

"I felt lucky, in fact honored, for being trusted for this position." Rob Bienstock

FRESH AIR SOCIETY PRESIDENTS

✤	Ida V. Kopple	1902-1912
✤	Josephine Van Noorden	1912-1916
✤	Edith Heavenrich	1916-1920, 1923-1931
✤	Gertrude Wineman	1920-1923
✤	Sarah Kaplan	1923
✤	Esther Rosenthal	1931-1937
✤	Sally Nirenberg	1937-1939
✤	Harry L. Jackson	1939-1941
✤	Alex Schreiber	1941-1944
✤	Harry Jacobson	1944-1946
✤	Charles N. Agree	1946-1947
✤	Barney Smith	1947-1950
✤	Milton M. Maddin	1950-1953
	Nathan L. Milstein	1953-1956
✤	Dr. Irving Posner	1956-1959
✤	Maxwell E. Katzen	1959-1962

	Dr. Peter G. Shifrin	1962-1965
	A. Arnold Agree	1965-1967
✤	Agnes Scott	1967-1970
	Sol G. Kurtzman	1970-1973
✤	Sidney J. Winer	1973-1975
✤	Robert Kasle	1975-1977
	Harvey Gordon	1977-1980
	Allan Nachman	1980-1983
	Michael W. Maddin	1983-1985
	Dr. Richard Krugel	1985-1988
	Richard Komer	1988-1991
	Jonathan Haber	1991-1994
	Edward Lumberg	1994-1997
	Dr. David Harold	1997-2000
	Henry Wineman, II	2000-2002

✤ *deceased*

PAST PRESIDENTS, 2001: (l to r top row) Richard Krugel, Arnold Agree, Edward Lumberg, Richard Komer, Allan Nachman, Nathan Milstein, Jonathan Haber, Harvey Gordon; (l to r bottom row) Henry Wineman II, David Harold, Michael Maddin

A FINAL NOTE
FROM THE 2001 BOARD OF DIRECTORS

In 1923, Gertrude Wineman completed her term as president of the Fresh Air Society Board of Directors. Back then, children came for two-week sessions, swam in Lake St. Clair, hiked, sang and played games around the flagpole. Campers paid no fees, the United Jewish Charities and the Detroit Community Union subsidized Fresh Air's entire budget. The all-female board often volunteered at camp and spent the rest of the year tending to the North End Clinic and the budget. As Wineman's presidency wound down, Fresh Air had $2,200 in the "Sinking Fund," a reserve, and $64 in the bank. Four years later, Wineman was among the first to welcome campers to camp's new Brighton location.

Nearly 80 years later, Gertrude's grandson, Henry Wineman II, began his term as the 31st president of the Fresh Air Society. Endowment funds had replaced the Sinking Fund and the budget had grown to $5 million. Our year-round meetings dealt with the Butzel Conference Center, Maddin Family Camping Program, Jewish identity, the budget, maintaining and upgrading facilities and Fresh Air's insignia, Camp Maas' camping programs.

Campers, no longer satisfied with hiking and swimming, beg to email typed messages home and insist on being physically challenged — on the water, in the air and on the land. Organized sports, biking, rock climbing and travel consume their interests. It has become a priority to ensure to continually enhance these programs to attract and retain these young people while strengthening their Jewish identity.

Our most fundamental task, however, is one that has existed since camp's beginning: ensuring that no child is *ever* denied a camping experience. Approximately one-third of our campers attend on a scholarship. But, as operating expenses increase, holding true to that promise becomes increasingly difficult. While the Jewish Federation of Metropolitan Detroit provides generous allocations, camp's future can only be secured by increasing our endowments. We believe that is our most important goal.

One hundred years after the first child experienced Fresh Air Camp, much has changed, yet much remains the same. Camp is where youngsters first realize they can live away from home — independently, happily and successfully — with other children and adults. Camp is where youth lives and learns Judaism and builds upon their heritage without opening a single book. Camp is where children gain immeasurable self-confidence and make friends that last a lifetime. And, camp is where we find ourselves connected as a community, a community that for 100 years has fed the fires of the Fresh Air Society and will do so for generations to come.

EXECUTIVE DIRECTORS

Miss Blanche Hart

Miss Augusta Brown (-1924)

Miss Carolyn Eppstein (1925-1936)

Irwin Shaw (1936-1942, 1946-1955)

Alvin Skelly (1942-1945)

Sam Marcus (1956-1980)

Michael Zaks (1980-1983)

Steve Makoff (1984-1986)

Sam Fisher (1987-1991)

Harvey Finkelberg (1992-)

2000-2001 FRESH AIR SOCIETY BOARD OF DIRECTORS

Executive Committee
Henry Wineman II, **President**
Ronald Sollish, **Vice President**
Brian Kepes, **Vice President**
Barbara Tronstein, **Treasurer**
Donna Maddin, **Secretary**
Tim R. Cohen
Frank Ellias
Darren Findling
Sharon Hart
Pamela Lippitt
Charles Schiff
Jeffrey Sternberg
David Harold, M.D., **Past President**

Lifetime Honorary Member
Jack A. Robinson

Board of Directors
Mark Adler
Jeffrey Appel
Fred Bartholomew, M.D.
Elise Bratley

Rabbi David Castiglione
Terri Cassels Cooper
Greig Davis
Jeffrey Devries, M.D.
Hi Dorfman
Susan Langnas Feber
Stuart Goldstein
Arnold Gross
Linda Kaplan
Barbara Kappy
David Kirsch
Mitchell Rosenwasser
Susan Roth
Todd Sachse
Robert Sher
Stan Singer
Vicki Solway, M.D.
Steven Swartz
Daniel Weberman
Lori Weberman
Julie Yolles
Esther Zalenko

CAMP DIRECTORS

Camp Tamarack at Brighton

Known until 1963 as Fresh Air Camp, Camp Tamarack at Brighton was
acquired in 1925, a gift of Mr. And Mrs. Edwin M. Rosenthal.

Carolyn Eppstein 1927-1936
Irwin Shaw 1936-1942, 1945-1949
Alvin Skelly 1942-1945
Robert Luby 1950-1954
Henry B. Stern 1955-1956
Mort Levitsky 1956-1966
Howard Green 1967
Bob Jaffe 1968
Robert C. Austin 1969-1977
Lenny Newman 1972-1977, 1982-1984
Marvin Berman 1978-1981
Jeffrey Metz 1985-1989
Susie Zaks 1990-1993

Camp Maas

When purchased in 1951, the 600-acre tree farm became known as Camp Tamarack.
In 1953, DeRoy Village welcomed campers.
One year later, three others opened and the expansion of camp hasn't stopped since.
In 1981, Camp Tamarack was renamed Camp Maas.
By 2001, over 2,400 campers annually accessed Camp Maas' 1,500 acres.

Resident Directors
Mary Lee Nicholson
Jack Baroff
Sam Skolnick
Carl Hartman
Marvin Berman
Marshall Hersh
Michael Zaks
Lew Hamburger
Harvey Finkelberg

Senior Staff 2001
Harvey Finkelberg, Executive Director
Susie Zaks, Assistant Director
Beth Sonne, Family Camp Director
Nancy Rothfeder, Chief Financial Officer
Gail Yaremchuk, Comptroller
Debbie Landau, Director of Development
Cheryl Miller, Director of Junior Side
Pat Sharpe, Director, Outdoor Education and Butzel Conference Center
Craig Charnas, Director of Specialty Areas
Jason Charnas, Director of Outside Groups
Sari Berman, Director of Teen Service Staff

CAMP TAMARACK MAP
CIRCA 1965

Ortonville, Michigan

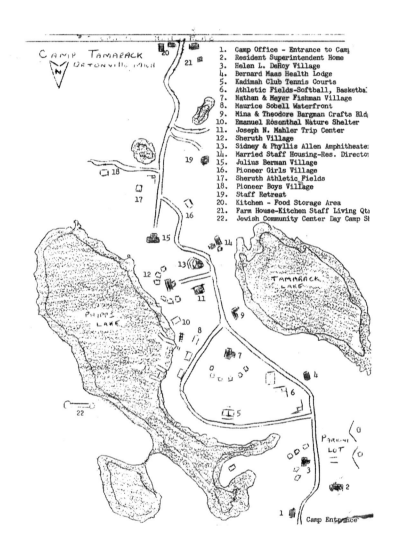

1. Camp Office - Entrance to Camp
2. Resident Superintendent Home
3. Helen L. DeRoy Village
4. Bernard Maas Health Lodge
5. Kadimah Club Tennis Courts
6. Athletic Fields-Softball, Basketball
7. Nathan & Meyer Fishman Village
8. Maurice Sobell Waterfront
9. Mina & Theodore Bargman Crafts Bldg
10. Emanuel Rosenthal Nature Shelter
11. Joseph N. Mahler Trip Center
12. Sheruth Village
13. Sidney & Phyllis Allen Amphitheater
14. Married Staff Housing-Res. Director
15. Julius Berman Village
16. Pioneer Girls Village
17. Sheruth Athletic Fields
18. Pioneer Boys Village
19. Staff Retreat
20. Kitchen - Food Storage Area
21. Farm House-Kitchen Staff Living Qts
22. Jewish Community Center Day Camp St

-Note the direction of North on this map

BENARD L. AND ROSALYN J. MAAS RECREATION AREA

Ortonville, Michigan

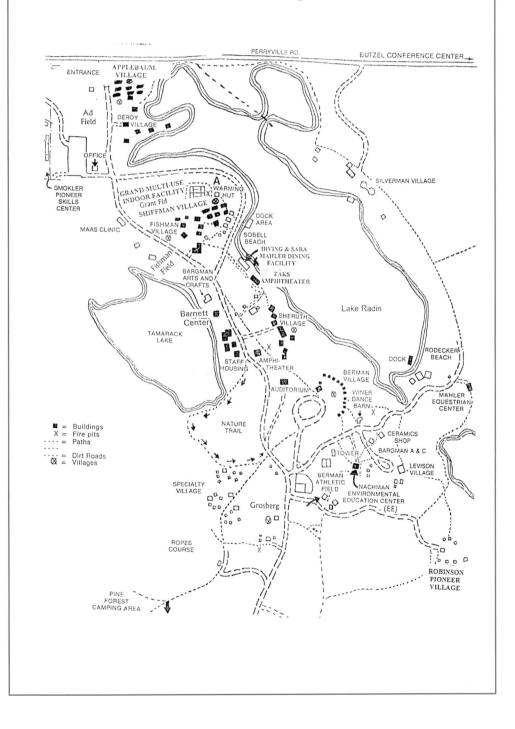

SOURCES

Rockaway, Robert A. The Jews of Detroit, From the Beginning 1762-1914. Detroit: Wayne State University Press 1986.

Anna W. Chapin, Fifty Years of Organized Jewish Charity; The History of the United Jewish Charities of Detroit from 1899-1949, The Story of The Jewish Welfare Federation of Detroit from 1926-1949. Written and compiled for the Jewish Welfare Federation, 1949.

Bolkosky, Sidney. Harmony & Dissonance, Voices of Jewish Identity in Detroit; Detroit: Wayne State University Press 1991.

Eells, Eleanor. History of Organized Camping, The First 100 Years; American Camping Association, 1986.

Kosmin, Barry A. Ph.D., et al. Highlights of the CJF 1990 National Jewish Population Survey. Council of Jewish Federations in association with The Mandell Berman Institute-North American Jewish Data Bank The Graduate School and University Center, CUNY. 1991.

Transcription of Abraham J. Levin interview, July 1997 by Melba Winer, Sidney Winer, Miriam Friedman.

Katz, Irving. The Fresh Air Society and Fresh Air Camp, Rabbi Leo M. Franklin Archives, Temple Beth El.

Katzen, Maxwell E.. Sixty Years of Youth, 1962, Rabbi Leo M. Franklin Archives, Temple Beth El.

Leonard N. Simons Jewish Community Archives, Jewish Federation of Metro Detroit. Part I. Boxes 47, 121, 133, 134, 135, 168, 189, 228, 382 Part II Boxes 529, 530.

The Value Of A Dollar, 1860- 1999; 1999 Grey House Publishing, Lakeville, CT.

Jewish News, January 19, 1996. Blazing Trails and Memories, by Julie Edgar. Page 74-75.

Jewish News various editions 1943, 1944.

Sy Kalish letter to Camp Tamarack, August 25, 1985. Fresh Air Society Collection.

Highlights in the History of Jewish Community Services, Irving I. Katz, 1959.

Harry C. Saltzstein, M.D. Sinai Hospital and the North End Clinic, Wayne State University Press, 1963.

Michael M. Maddin personal files.

Detroit: American Urban Renaissance, Arthur M. Woodford, 1979, Continental Heritage, Inc.

Detroit's 250th Birthday Festival, Inc. Historical Books 1 – 18. Burton Historical Collection.

The New York City Comic Book Museum.

The Comic Book in America, An Illustrated History, Mike Benton, 1989.

Jerry Acker, Attorney
Hayden Andrews, Food Service Director
Jeffery Appel, Attorney
Eugene Applebaum, CEO, Arbor Investment Group
Jeffrey Applebaum, Gold Star Products
Marc Applebaum, Gold Star Products
Henry Baskin, Attorney
Marcia Baum, Karmanos Cancer Institute
Joe Bender, Director, Patient Accounting, St. Joseph Mercy Hospital
Irving and Harriet Berg, Still Artists
Laura Berman, Journalist and Columnist
Marvin Berman, College Financial Coordinator Jewish Vocational Service
Sari Berman, Associate Camp Director, Tamarack Camps
Minnie Bernberg Cohen
Rob and Debbie Bienstock, Goodwill Printing Bindery/Goodwill Printing Management
Lisa Blanck, Student
Roz Blanck
Donna Bloom, Social Worker, Children's Aid Society, Ottawa
Dr. George and Joyce Blum, Physician
David Blume, Controller
Syd Bolkosky, Historian
Mike Bossin, Electrical Utility Industrial Consultant
David Brassfield, Founder, S.T.E.P.S.
Martha Brown White
Jill Bruss, Managing Editor of Beverage Industry Magazine
Lester Burton, Beverage Industry
"Kip" Cliff Cantor, Attorney and Rock Climber
Judy Cantor, Writer and Historian
Amanda, Elizabeth and Lindsay Canvassar, Students
Ronnie Capling
Amanda Chiat, Student
Ben Chinitz
Bertha Chomsky
Katie Cohen, Student
Arnie Collens, Janitorial and Industrial Supply Business Owner
Howard Davis, Gourmet Food Broker
David Eason, Attorney
Barbara Eisenberg (Hillman), Clinical Social Worker
Lisa Elconin, Internist
Jennifer Farber, Student, University of Michigan
Belle Freedman, Retired
Michael Freedman, V.P. Communications, George Washington University
Amy Friedman, Student
Harold Friedman, Cardiologist
Gail Gales, High School Teacher
Aaron Gellerman, Retired
Lillian and Oscar Genser, Former Director, Center for Peace and Conflict Studies Wayne State/Land Developer and Builder
Iris Gilbert, Dental Hygenist
Robin Gleason (Frisch), Teacher
Lisa Gleicher, Attorney
Brian Gordon, Commercial Real Estate
Merrill Gordon, Attorney
Aaron Goren, Attorney
Lisa Goren, Talent Agent
Rick and Katie Goren, Assistant Director, Major and Planned Gifts, University of Michigan Health System
Amy Gotliffe, Environmental Educator
Eli Greenbaum, Writer
Emily Grey, Special Education Teacher
Jeffrey Grey, Student
Jim and Ruth Grey, Accountant
Rachel Grey Ellis
Amy Guggenheim, Internet Advisor
Larry Gussin, Technical Writer
Jonathan Haber, Retired CPA
David Harold, Urologist
Ray and Lee Henkin, Physician/Registered Nurse
Marshall Hersh, Retired School Social Worker
Sue Hodess, Financial Advisor
Simon Horne, BBC Producer
Larry Jackier, Attorney
Alan Kandel, Historian
Mary Katz, Retired
Marc Kay, Associate Director of Education and Youth, Adat Shalom Synagogue
Brian Kepes, Commercial Real Estate
Sherri Ketai (Kay)

Jason Klein, Dir. Sales/Marketing, CLAIMSPRO Management Services
Diane Klein (Yura), Community Volunteer
Richard Komer, Vice President, Wineman and Komer
Lisa Kopelman-Fenberg, Special Education Teacher
Andy Krafsur, Attorney, Vice President Shoe Spring, Inc.
Iris Kramer
Richard Krugel, Orthopedic Surgeon
Alan Lado-Devesa, Teacher
Andrew Landau, Student
Denise Landau, Executive, International Association of Antarctic Tour Operators
Leslye Landau, Environmental Attorney (former)
Irving and Rose Lash, Retired
Joe and Stacey Lash, Attorney/Physical Therapist
Myles and Linda Lash, Health Care Consultant/Pre School Teacher
Steve and Carol (Stutz) Lash, Orthodontist
Moishe Last, Retired Teacher and Musician
Carly Leipsitz
Margaret Leipsitz, Corporate Investment Manager
Gordy Levenson, Retired
Marty and Elise (Chapin) Levinson, Pediatrician
Simon Levinson, Student
Charlotte Levitan
Dan Levitsky, Dentist
Ed Levy Jr., President, Edw. C. Levy Co.
Kim Lifton, Writer
Dan Lippit, Photographer
Bob and Joan (Rottenberg) Lipsitz, Owners of Double J Ranch
Marvin Littky, Attorney, P.A.
Ayanna Livney, Student
Jon London
Erin Lowen, Student, University of Michigan
Bob Luby, Development Assoc. for Special Projects Interlochen Center for the Arts
Ed Lumberg, Wholesale Jeweler
Michael Maddin, Attorney
Frances Malin
Sam Marcus, Retired
Connie and Chuck Mays
Jon Medow, Student
Aric Melder, Attorney
Jeff Metz, Executive Director, Jewish Community Center of Delaware
Julia Moinis, Student
Kathi Moss (Blum), Registered Nurse
Allan Nachman, Attorney
Erica and Alana Nedelman, Students
Rabbi David Nelson
Carol Parven Hutter, Executive Producer of Fun, Fun Factor, Inc.
Barbara Philka (Feldman), Teacher
Jodi and Howard Rankin, Attorney/Accessory Business Owner
Abby Robinson
Shelby Robinson, Jewlery and Clothing Designer
Lenore Rosa (Rhinestone)
Michelle Rose, Artist
Howard Rosen, Financial Advisor
Irving Rosen, Retired
Dr. Mark Rossenwasser, Corporate Physician
Mitch and Jenifer (Adler) Rossenwasser, Controller, Star Trax Events/Civics and Sociology Teacher
Matt and Sarah Roth, Assistant Prosecutor, Oakland County/Elementary Teacher
Joanne Rowe, Educator
Monica Sageman (Steinmetz)
Beverly Salasnek
Rhonda Sandweiss, Tripping Supervisor/Ropes Challenge Course Manager
Bethany Schaer, Student
Elaine Schonberger (Malin), Jewish Book Fair Director, JCC
Sanford Schulman, Criminal Defense Attorney
Ashley Schwartz, Student
Beth Schwartz, Student
Evan Schwartz, Student
Jeffrey Schwartz, Attorney
Wendy Schwartz, Registered Dietician
Bruce Shaffer, Attorney and Teacher
Pat Sharpe, Outdoor Education Director
Helayne Shaw, Program Director, Camp Chi/Early Childhood Director, Shaarey Zedek
Irwin Shaw, Retired, Still Volunteering
Kelby Shaw, Child and Youth Counselor, Children's Aid Society, Ottawa
Dave Shepard
Marc Shindler, Brody's Owner
Dina Shtull-Leber, Jewish Program Director, Tamarack Camps
Marilyn Shulte (Jonas), Teacher
Jill Silverstein, Student
Beth Sonne, Family Camp Director, Agree Outpost Director, Tamarack Camps
Elliot Sorkin, Executive Director, Beth Israel Congregation Ann Arbor
Howard and Barbara Steinmetz
Julie Steinmetz Shaffer, Consultant to Jewish Non-Profit Agencies
Clare Stephens, Elementary School Teacher
Beth Stone, Jewlery Designer
Holly Swartz, Student
Nathan Swartz, Student
Steve and Dr. Beth (Robinson) Swartz, Real Estate Developer/Pediatrician
Asher Tilchin, Retired Attorney
Minda Tilchin
Nancy Triest (Rosen)
Barbara Vedder, Silverman Village Director, Tamarack Camps
Alan and Liz Warnick (Borger), Dentist/Homemaker
Henry Wineman, Secretary/Treasurer Wineman and Komer
Melba and °Sidney Winer, Community Volunteer
Jody Winkelman, Supervisor, Camp Kennedy, Tamarack Camps
Chuck Wolfe
Eric Wolfe, Student
Jodi Wolfe (Kasmer), Health Club Membership Administrator
Lisa Wolfe, Teen Tripping Supervisor, Tamarack Camps
Arik and Erica Wolff Green, Architect/Attorney
Julie Yolles (Smith), Actress, Writer
David Zaks, Student, Michigan State University
Alana Zaks, Student, Emory University
Jason Zaks, Former Assistant Director, BBYO
Jeffrey Zaks, Cardiologist and V.P. Medical Affairs, Providence Hospital
Lisa Zaks, Medical Student, Wayne State University
Susie Zaks, Assistant Director, Tamarack Camps
Paula Zaks-Stein, Artist and Art Teacher

° Deceased

ENDNOTES

Chapter One
1 *Detroit's 250th Birthday Festival, Inc.* Historical Books 1–18. Detroit, Burton Historical Collection.
2 Robert A. Rockaway, The Jews of Detroit, (Detroit: Wayne State University Press 1986) 52
3 Rockaway 52
4 Rockaway 47
5 Board minutes, Fresh Air Society
6 Irwin Shaw "Administrative and Organizational Problems of a Co-Educational Children's Camp", Graduate Council of Wayne State University 1941, 10
7 Eve Dishell letter, "Once Upon A Time," Fresh Air Society
8 Abraham J. Levin. Interview with Melba Winer, Sidney Winer, Miriam Friedman. August 1976 A Very Simple Beginning

Chapter Two
1 Ellen Knoppow interview with Mary Katz. June 1999
2 Fresh Air Society director's report. August 1926. Fresh Air Society
3 Edith Heavenrich letter to Fresh Air Society board members. January 1925. Fresh Air Society
4 Fresh Air Society director's report and board meeting minutes 1928. Fresh Air Society
5 Interview Minnie Bernberg Cohen. August 2000
6 Interview Irving Lash. September 2000

Chapter Three
1 Interview Irving and Rose Lash. September 2000
2 Fresh Air Society Director's Reports. June, September 1930. Fresh Air Society
3 Report of Fresh Air Society to Board of Directors, Carolyn Eppstein. October 1933. Fresh Air Society
4 Interview Irwin Shaw. November 1999

Chapter Four
1 1985 letter to Tamarack Camps, Sy Kalish, Fresh Air Society
2 Interview Asher Tilchin, June 2000
3 Interview Irwin Shaw, February 2000
4 Interview Oscar and Lillian Genser, October 2000
5 Letter from Richard Haas to Fresh Air Society, Aug. 1993
6 Fresh Air Society Board Meeting minutes
7 Jewish Federation Collection, Archives of Labor & Urban Affairs, Wayne State University. Part I, Box 530
8 Eugene Applebaum interview, May 2000
9 *Proposal To Social Planning Committee For A Sub-committee On Camping*, December 1946, Irwin Shaw; Fresh Air Society

Chapter Five
1 Interview, Beverly Salasnek, December 2000
2 Interview Lenore Rosa, December 2000
3 Interview Henry Baskin, December 2000
4 Harmony & Dissonance, Voices of Jewish Identity in Detroit; Bolkosky, Sidney; 1991 United Jewish Charities
5 Barbara Steinmetz interview, October 2000
6 Moishe Last interview, November 2000
7 Sam Marcus interview, July 2000
8 Steve Lash interview, November 2000
9 Myles Lash interview, February 2001
10 Marshall Hersh interview, February 2001
11 Fresh Air Society board records, 1964
12 Gail Gales Interview, August 2001

Chapter Six
1 Interview Margaret Leipsitz. March 2001
2 Fresh Air Society. Comparative Statistics Report. August 1970
3 Interview Michelle Rose. January 2001
4 Interview Susie Zaks. June 1999
5 Interview Larry Gussin. March 2001
6 Interview Merrill Gordon. April 2001
7 Interview Harold Friedman. April 2001
8 *Tamaractivites*, Nov. 1969
9 Interview Monica Sageman. March 2001
10 Dena Raminick interview with Mark Rosenwasser. February 2001
11 Interview Marty and Elise Levinson. May 2001
12 Interview Cliff Cantor. February 2001
13 Interview Julie Steinmetz. November 2000.
14 Fresh Air Society board meeting minutes. June 6, 1974
15 Letter to camp parents, 1977. Fresh Air Society

Chapter Seven
1 Minutes of the Budget & Fees & Ad Hoc Committees, October 8, 1980. Fresh Air Society.
2 Interview Aric Melder. April 2001
3 Interview Rick Goren. February 2001
4 Interview David Harold. April 2001
5 Interview Harvey Finkelberg. May 2001
6 Interview Jonathan Haber. May 2001
7 Interview Andy Krafsur. May 2001
8 Interview Evan Schwartz. May 2001
9 Interview Jenna, Lisa, Roz Blanck. March 2001
10 Interview Donna Bloom. May 2001
11 Interview Helayne Shaw. March 2001.
12 Dena Raminick interview with Elaine Schonberger. February 2001
13 Interview Holly Swartz. May 2001
14 Interview Jason Zaks. March 2001.
15 Jeffrey Grey email correspondence. March 2001
16 Interview Evan Schwartz. May 2001
17 Interview Marc Kay. April 2001
18 Interview Jill Bruss. April 2001
19 Council of Jewish Federations. Kosmin, Barry A. Ph.D., et al. Highlights of the CJF 1990 National Jewish Population Survey. 1991. 13-14
20 Interview Ashley Schwartz. April 2001
21 Interview Dina Shtull-Leber. May 2001
22 Interview Jennifer Farber. June 2001

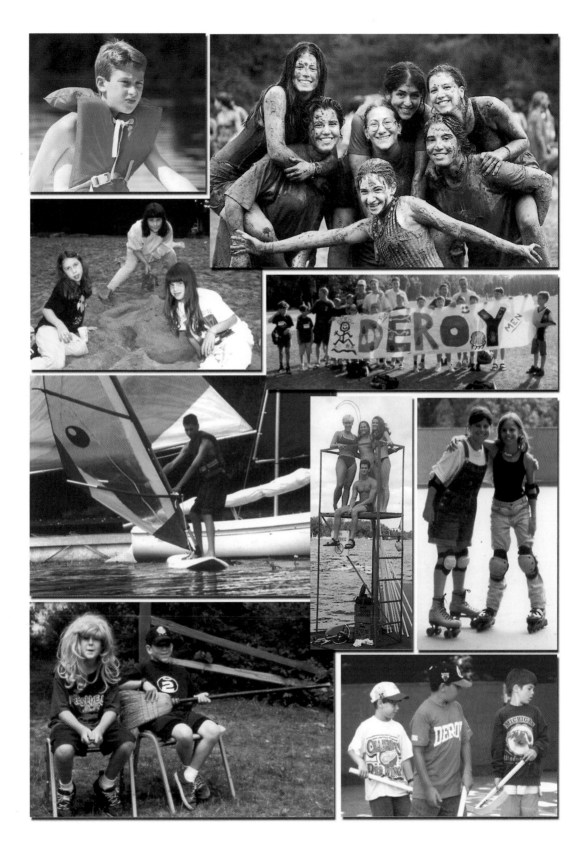

Chapter Eight
1   Minutes of the Special Projects Committee. Fresh Air Society. January 25, 1971. Fresh Air Society.
2   Interview Barbara Vedder. May 2001
3   Interview Bonnie Capling. May 2001
4   Interview Elise and Dr. Marty Levinson. May 2001
5   Interview Elliott Sorkin. September 2000
6   *The Detroit Jewish News*, January 28, 1977. Smokler, Marcus cited, p 39.
7   Interview Pat Sharpe. June 2001
8   Interview Alana Zaks. May 2001
9   Interview David Brassfield. May 2001
10   Interview Bob and Joan Lipsitz. March 2001
11   Interview Rhonda Sandweiss. May 2001
12   Interview Michael Maddin. June 2000
13   Interview Aaron Goren. January 2001
14   Interview Rob and Debbie Bienstock. April 2001
15   Interview Helayne Shaw. March 2001
16   Interview Sanford Shulman. June 2001
17   Interview Dr. George and Joyce Blum. April 2001
18   Memorandum. Tamarack Hills Authority to teachers of outdoor education. April, 1979. Fresh Air Society.

Chapter Nine
1   Interview Jody Winkelman. March 2001
2   Shaw, Irwin. "Report of the Establishment of the outpost camp," Board of Directors Meeting, August 31, 1949.
3   Interview Marvin Berman 2000
4   Dear Friends letter to parents of teen travelers by Sam Marcus. 1960. Fresh Air Society.
5   Interview Miles Lash. February 2001
6   Western Teen Trip Log. July 1973. Fresh Air Society.
7   Eastern Teen Trip log, August 4 – August 25, 1980. Fresh Air Society.
8   Trip Report, Western Trip I 1979 by Barbara Feldman. Fresh Air Society Field Reports 1979
9   Interview Andrew Landau. May 2001
10   Interview Lisa Elconin. May 2001
11   Interview Jason Zaks. March 2001
12   Horne, Simon. Email to author. March 2001
13   Barbara Philka. Interview with Dena Raminick. November 2000.
14   Interview Howard and Jody Rankin. April 2001
15   Interview David Zaks. March 2001
16   Mitch Rosenwasser. Interview with Dena Raminick. November 2000.

Chapter Ten
1   Interview Leslye Landau. February 2001
2   Interview Larry Gussin March 2001
3   Interview Jim and Ruth Grey. May 2000
4   Interview Beth Swartz. May 2001
5   Interview Lisa Wolfe. May 2001
6   Michigan Department of Natural Resources
7   Interview Howard Davis March 2001
8   Interview Laura Berman. February 2001
9   Interview Brian Kepes. March 2001
10   Interview Rhonda Sandweiss. May 2001
11   Interview Jody Winkelman March 2001
12   Interview Edward C. Levy, Jr. March 2001
13   Email correspondence to author. Arnie Collens. February 2001
14   Interview Lisa Gleicher. March 2001
15   Interview Joe and Stacey Lash March 2001
16   Interview Jon London. June 2001
17   Interview Minda Tilchin and Laura Berman. February 2001
18   Interview Allan Nachman. March 2001
19   Interview Jon Medow. June 2001
20   Missinaibi Trip Log. 1976. Entry by Lou Weckstein. Leslye Landau.
21   Interview Abby Robinson. June 2001

Chapter Eleven
1   Interview Gale Gales. August 2000
2   Interview Aaron Goren. January 2001
3   Interview Irving Rosen. January 2001
4   Henry Baskin interview. December 2000.
5   Fresh Air Society Board Meeting Minutes
6   Fresh Air Society. Irwin Shaw Director's Report 1936
7   Moishe Last interview. December 2000.
8   Interview Eli Greenbaum. March 2001
9   Interview Marvin Berman. June 2000
10   Interview Brian Gordon. March 2001
11   Interview Marc Kay. April 2001
12   Interview Amy Guggenheim. April 2001
13   Interview Jeff Metz. March 2001
14   Interview Rob and Debbie Bienstock. April 2001
15   Diane Klein. Interview by Dena Raminick. November, 2000
16   Interview Alan and Liz Warnick. April 2001
17   Interview Jeffrey Applebaum. April 2001.
18   Interview Jody and Howard Rankin. April 2001
19   Interview Joe and Stacey Lash. March 2001
20   Interview Erin Lowen. April 2001
21   Interview Ayanna Livney. April 2001
22   Kelby Shaw email correspondence. April 2001
23   Interview Clare Stephens. July 2000
24   Interview Beth Schwartz. April 2001.
25   Interview Julie Schaffer. February 2001.
26   Interview Jim and Ruth Grey. May 2000.
27   Interview Marshall Hersh. February 2001
28   Interview Lisa Zaks. May 2001
29   Interview Lillian and Oscar Genser. October 2000

INDEX

MEMORIES